T0207143

Quantitative Trading Strategies Using Python

Technical Analysis, Statistical Testing, and Machine Learning

Peng Liu

Apress®

Quantitative Trading Strategies Using Python: Technical Analysis, Statistical Testing, and Machine Learning

Peng Liu
Singapore, Singapore

ISBN-13 (pbk): 978-1-4842-9674-5 ISBN-13 (electronic): 978-1-4842-9675-2
https://doi.org/10.1007/978-1-4842-9675-2

Managing Director, Apress Media LLC: Welmoed Spahr
Acquisitions Editor: Celestin Suresh John
Development Editor: James Markham
Coordinating Editor: Mark Powers

Cover designed by eStudioCalamar

Cover image by Ahmad Ardity on Pixabay (www.pixabay.com)

Distributed to the book trade worldwide by Springer Science+Business Media New York, 1 New York Plaza, Suite 4600, New York, NY 10004-1562, USA. Phone 1-800-SPRINGER, fax (201) 348-4505, e-mail orders-ny@ springer-sbm.com, or visit www.springeronline.com. Apress Media, LLC is a California LLC and the sole member (owner) is Springer Science + Business Media Finance Inc (SSBM Finance Inc). SSBM Finance Inc is a Delaware corporation.

For information on translations, please e-mail booktranslations@springernature.com; for reprint, paperback, or audio rights, please e-mail bookpermissions@springernature.com.

Apress titles may be purchased in bulk for academic, corporate, or promotional use. eBook versions and licenses are also available for most titles. For more information, reference our Print and eBook Bulk Sales web page at http://www.apress.com/bulk-sales.

Any source code or other supplementary material referenced by the author in this book is available to readers on GitHub (github.com/apress). For more detailed information, please visit https://www.apress.com/gp/services/source-code.

Paper in this product is recyclable

Table of Contents

About the Author

Peng Liu is an assistant professor of quantitative finance (practice) at Singapore Management University and an adjunct researcher at the National University of Singapore. He holds a Ph.D. in statistics from the National University of Singapore and has ten years of working experience as a data scientist across the banking, technology, and hospitality industries. Peng is the author of *Bayesian Optimization* (Apress, 2023).

About the Technical Reviewer

 **Sonal Raj** is an engineer, mathematician, data scientist, and Python evangelist from India, who has carved a niche in the financial services domain. He is a Goldman Sachs and D. E. Shaw alumnus who currently serves as Vice President and Head of Data Management and Research for a leading high-frequency trading firm.

Sonal holds dual masters in computer science and business administration and is a former research fellow of the Indian Institute of Science. He is a doctoral candidate in data science at the Swiss School of Business Management, Geneva. His areas of research range from image processing and real-time graph computations to electronic trading algorithms. Sonal is the author of the titles *The Pythonic Way* (BPB, 2021) and *Neo4j High Performance* (Packt, 2015). During his career, Sonal has created low latency trading algorithms, trading strategies, market signal models, and components of electronic trading systems. He is also a community speaker and a Python and data science mentor to young minds in the field.

When not engrossed in reading fiction or playing symphonies, he spends far too much time watching rockets lift off.

He is a loving son and husband and a custodian of his personal library.

CHAPTER 1

Quantitative Trading: An Introduction

Quantitative trading, also called algorithmic trading, refers to automated trading activities that buy or sell particular instruments based on specific algorithms. Here, an algorithm can be considered a model that transforms an input into an output. In this case, the input includes sufficient data to make a proper trading decision, and the output is the action of buying or selling an instrument. The quality of a trading decision thus relies on the sufficiency of the input data and the suitability and robustness of the model.

Developing a successful quantitative trading strategy involves the collection and processing of vast amounts of input data, such as historical price data, financial news, and economic indicators. The data is passed as input to the model development process, where the goal is to accurately forecast market trends, identify trading opportunities, and manage potential risks, all of which are reflected in the resulting buy or sell signals.

A robust trading algorithm is often identified via the process of backtesting, which involves simulating the algorithm's performance using historical data. Simulating the performance of the algorithm under different scenarios allows us to assess the strategy's potential effectiveness better, identify its limitations, and fine-tune the parameters to optimize its results. However, one also needs to be aware of the potential risks of overfitting and survivorship bias, which can lead to inflated metrics and potentially poor test set performance.

In this chapter, we start by covering a few basic and important concepts related to quantitative trading. We then switch to hands-on examples of working with financial data using Python.

© Peng Liu 2023
P. Liu, *Quantitative Trading Strategies Using Python*, https://doi.org/10.1007/978-1-4842-9675-2_1

Overview of Quantitative Trading

Quantitative trading refers to the use of mathematical models and algorithms to analyze large datasets (structured or unstructured), identify consistent patterns, and generate robust trading signals. The key components of quantitative trading include data collection and preprocessing, feature engineering, model development, backtesting, optimization, and execution. Quantitative strategies can vary greatly in complexity, ranging from simple moving average crossovers to advanced machine learning techniques, all of which are covered in later chapters of the book.

A good trading strategy could be as simple as buying low and selling high (i.e., long a security) or selling high and buying low (i.e., short a security). The underlying trading model can consume different types of input data. For example, the input data could include structured features such as specific performance metrics of a particular stock or unstructured news contents pertinent to the company of the stock. When the input is financial news, the challenge is often concerned with converting unstructured textual information to structured features in a consistent and principled manner. The input data could also be raw financial ratios readily available from the balance sheet or derived features such as firm-specific technical indicators.

We can categorize the input data into the following four general groups:

- Market states: Security-specific price movements such as tick data that measures the minimum upward or downward movement in the price of a security, or market-specific factors such as bid-ask spread in limit-order books (LOB) in high-frequency trading. Besides the tick size, other resolution parameters of a LOB include the lot size, which specifies the smallest amount of a stock that can be traded.

- Financial news: Macroeconomic news, analyst reports, earnings conference call transcripts, etc.

- Fundamentals: Overall economic or sector-specific conditions and firm-specific metrics such as revenue, cash flow, earnings per share (EPS), etc.

- Technicals: Derived technical indicators based on the raw price series, including moving averages, stochastic indicators, etc.

More generally, quantitative trading can be defined as the process of order execution based on trading signals generated using computer programs and algorithms. The purpose is either to seek profits and achieve an abnormal rate of return that beats the market (called *alpha*) or manage different types of risk.

In a nutshell, quantitative trading refers to an algorithm (also called a function or a model) that digests any of these structured or unstructured data sources and outputs a trading decision. The automatic trading strategies could be in the form of experience-based rules based on technical analysis or data-driven machine learning models trained based on historical data. Upon receiving the output as a trading signal, we would either buy (also called long) an asset to open a position or sell (also called short) an asset to close a position, make a profit, or stop a loss. Trading signals could occur intraday in a high-frequency setting (also called *day trading*) or in a longer term (also called *position trading*). Figure 1-1 illustrates this process.

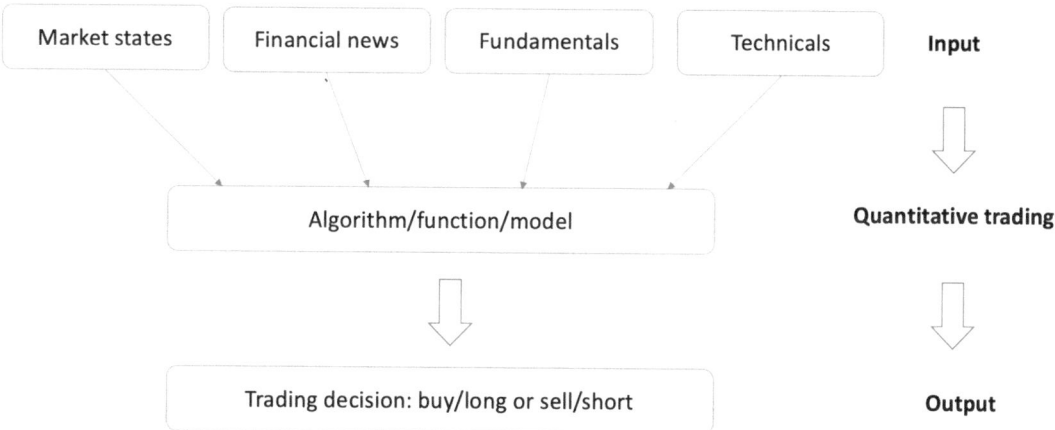

Figure 1-1. *Illustrating the overall quantitative trading process*

The model used to generate trading signals could be either rule-based or trained using data. The rule-based approach mainly relies on domain knowledge and requires explicitly writing out the logic flow from input to output, similar to following a cooking recipe. On the other hand, the data-driven approach involves training a model using machine learning techniques and using the model as a black box for prediction and inference. Let us review the overall model training process in a typical machine learning workflow.

Model Development Workflow

A typical model development workflow starts with some training data. The training data consists of input-output pairs in supervised learning tasks where both input and output data are given. Each input entry could contain multiple features that describe the same observation from different perspectives. The corresponding output has the true target, acting as the correct answer to guide the training process. Model training aims to generate a mapping function, a model, that correctly maps a given input to the corresponding output.

A trained model consists of two parts: parameters and architecture. Parameters are the integral components of a model, and the architecture specifies how these components interact with the input data to produce the final prediction output. This predicted value is then compared with the ground truth target to make an error metric jointly. Here, the error indicates the current cost on how close or far away it is between the prediction and the actual value. Following a particular optimization procedure, the training process adjusts the model parameters for a given architecture to reduce the training cost. After changing the weights, the new error is calculated again, forming a feedback loop. The whole model training process is depicted in Figure 1-2.

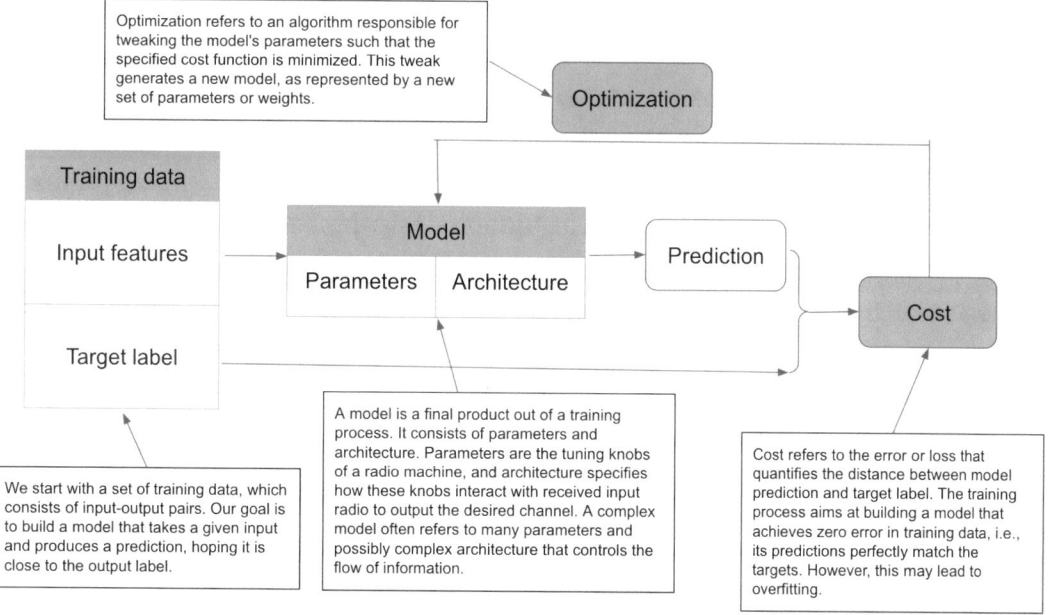

Figure 1-2. *Example of a typical model training process. The workflow starts with the available training data and gradually tunes a model. The tuning process requires matching the model prediction to the target output, where the gap is measured by a particular cost function and used as feedback for the next round of tuning. Each tuning produces a new model, and we want to look for one that minimizes the cost*

Now let us look at a specific type of algorithmic trading at large institutions: institutional algorithmic trading.

Institutional Algorithmic Trading

Since the underlying decision model could be a black box, algorithmic trading is also called automated trading, black-box trading, or robo-trading. It is used to generate and execute orders in markets with electronic access. In the context of large institutions, hedge funds, and trading desks, the trading volume is often quite large. In this case, institutional algorithmic trading often seeks to break up large orders into smaller ones to reduce the *execution risk*, which refers to the case when a large order cannot be fulfilled in the market.

Besides preserving anonymity in transactions, large institutions also use algorithmic trading to minimize the price impact of a trade. This is because even if a large order is executable, it is difficult to guarantee that the market price will not be impacted due to the execution of the large order. Thus, the main objective of institutional algorithmic trading is to control the market risk and the execution cost rather than gaining profits.

When executing a large order by an institutional investor, the demand for a large amount of liquidity will typically affect the cost of the trade negatively. This is called *slippage*, which refers to situations when a market participant receives a different execution price than initially intended. This could happen for many instruments, including stocks, bonds, currencies, and derivatives.

To execute these block trades anonymously without generating a noticeable impact in the market, large institutions often involve *dark pools* to carry out these trades. Dark pools are private exchanges that execute orders from institutional investors away from the central stock exchanges, thus exhibiting little transparency in the transactional process.

These large institutional orders, when split into small-sized orders, are also called *iceberg orders*. By partially exposing the tip of an iceberg, the majority of the orders could remain hidden and transition into visible orders afterward, thus minimizing the disruption to the trading market as opposed to a single large order. These smaller orders will then be executed electronically over minutes, hours, or days. To minimize the impact of these orders, institutional investors would trade more at the market opens and closes when the trading volume is relatively high and less during a slow period around lunchtime.

Let us look at a simple example of generating a small subset of iceberg orders from the original orders using Python. In Listing 1-1, we create a list of ten random integers saved in `total_order` to indicate all the orders to be executed by an institutional investor. We can randomly sample two indexes and use them to access the corresponding elements in `total_order` and save in `iceberg_order`, representing the iceberg orders to be exposed to the market.

Listing 1-1. Generating iceberg orders

```
# generate multiple random integers
total_order = [random.randint(0, 10) for p in range(0, 10)]
>>> total_order
[9, 6, 4, 3, 7, 6, 3, 0, 0, 6]
```

```
# randomly sample two indexes to identify iceberg orders
iceberg_order_idx = random.sample(total_order, 2)
>>> iceberg_order_idx
[0, 4]

# retrieve iceberg orders
iceberg_order = np.array(total_order)[iceberg_order_idx]
iceberg_order
array([9, 7])
```

The institutional algorithmic strategies generate optimal trading signals by analyzing daily quotes and prices. For example, an institutional algorithmic strategy may suggest entering a long position if the current stock price moves from below to above the *volume-weighted average price (VWAP)* over a day, a technical indicator often used by short-term traders. The institutional algorithmic strategies may also exploit *arbitrage* opportunities or price spreads between correlated securities. Here, arbitrage means making positive sure profits with zero investments. Arbitrage opportunities, if exist, would normally disappear very fast as many hedge funds and investors are constantly looking for such arbitrage opportunities.

The next section briefly introduces the role of a quant trader.

Being a Quant Trader

A quant trader is a specialized trader that uses mathematical models and quantitative analysis to evaluate different financial products and identify trading opportunities to buy or sell the best securities out of hundreds of thousands of candidates. Quant traders make use of data-driven methods to make model-based trading decisions, seeking to exploit temporary inefficiencies and underlying patterns in the market that may not be easily discernible through traditional qualitative analysis.

The first attribute of an aspiring quant trader is familiarity with numbers and mathematical models. As the majority of the time is spent on analyzing the data, proposing, backtesting, and implementing trading strategies to either buy, sell, or hold specific security, a quant trader needs to be comfortable with both mathematical models and programming, which often requires an advanced degree in financial modeling or related field. When a positive signal pops up, the quant trader needs to act swiftly using self-developed programs to capitalize on the current trading opportunities.

The second attribute lies in soft skills such as handling high pressure with a good temperament. This requires good emotional intelligence to neither assume too much risk nor be overly risk averse. Knowing when to exit a position and stop loss is a critical skill that requires discipline in daily trading activities.

The following section covers the major asset classes and various tradable instruments.

Major Asset Classes and Derivatives

Multiple tradable financial instruments are used to raise capital in public and private markets. Institutional and retail investors can enter into long or short positions involving different single or combinations of assets, profit-seeking, or risk management (i.e., hedging).

Let us first get a glimpse of the many tradable assets. In the following list, we provide a short definition of common assets used in the market:

- Stocks: Also called equity, a form of security representing proportionate ownership of the issuing company. A unit of stock is called a share, and the number of shares determines the proportionate ownership and, thus, profit sharing of the stock owner. The stock owner profits when the stock price increases or by receiving dividends.

- Bonds: Fixed-income debt instruments representing a fixed-duration loan from the investor/lender to the borrower (company or government). A bond provides the owner with fixed-rate coupon or variable interest payments, and the principal is paid to the owner at the end date. It is a fixed-income asset due to the regular and stable interest paid to the owner.

- Annuities: Insurance contracts from financial institutions that provide a fixed-income stream to the contract owner in the future. Investors mainly purchase annuities for retirement as they can receive a guaranteed stream of payments in the future for a specified period or the remainder of life.

- Cash and equivalents: Highly liquid short-term (less than 90 days) investment securities with low risk and low return (usually less than the inflation rate). The equivalents include bank accounts, near-term instruments such as US Treasury bills, and money market funds. These current assets can be easily accessed anytime and reflect the firm's ability to pay the short-term debt.

- Commodities: Basic goods used in commerce as raw inputs to produce other goods or services. Common commodities, such as gold, oil, and natural gas, can be traded in the spot (cash) market or via derivatives such as futures and options.

- Futures: Financial derivatives in the form of legal agreements that oblige the futures contract buyer to buy or sell the underlying asset at a prespecified price, amount, and time in the future. Futures are often used to hedge against price movements of the underlying asset and thus avoid losses due to unfavorable price changes in the future. The price of a futures contract is settled daily, that is, marked to market (MTM).

- Forward: Similar to the futures contract. The difference is that a forward contract is a private and customizable agreement traded over the counter (OTC), which is a decentralized marketplace where participants trade instruments directly without engaging a central exchange or a broker. The price of a forward contract is settled at the end of the agreement.

- Options: Financial derivatives that offer the buyer of the options contract the opportunity to buy (if it is a call option) or sell (if it is a put option) the underlying asset on or before a specific expiration (maturity) date and (strike) price. Options give the buyers the right, not the obligation, to long or short an underlying asset. They can be used for both hedging and speculation. Note that we focus on the European option by default.

- Currencies: International currencies and currency derivatives traded via the (largest and most liquid) global electronic marketplace, also called the foreign exchange market or forex. Forex allows investors to exchange one currency for the equivalent value in another currency at the current market rate. Traders also speculate on the direction of currency values to profit from a favorable price movement of a particular pair of currencies.

- ETFs: Exchange-traded funds that refer to a type of pooled investment security that are baskets of securities (stocks, bonds, commodities, etc.) and are traded intraday like regular stocks.

- REITs: Real estate investment trusts that refer to companies that own, operate, or finance income-generating real estate. Investors in REITs (liquid and publicly traded like stocks) can earn a steady income stream from real estate investments without purchasing, managing, or financing the actual properties themselves.

- Mutual funds: A type of financial vehicle that consists of a portfolio of stocks, bonds, or other securities. Mutual funds are managed by professional money managers and allow individual investors to access diversified and professionally managed portfolios at the expense of annual fees. Mutual funds only can be purchased at the end of each trading day based on a calculated price known as the net asset value.

- Hedge funds: Actively managed investment pools that aim at earning above-average returns for investors via a wide range of (often risky) trading strategies at the expense of higher fees than conventional investment funds.

These tradable asset types can be grouped into different classes based on a particular perspective. We introduce a few popular perspectives in the following section.

Grouping Tradable Assets

An asset class is a collection of investment instruments that exhibit similar fundamental characteristics in terms of risk and return. There are four major asset classes: equities, fixed-income instruments, cash and equivalents, and alternative investments, defined as financial assets that do not fall into prior investment categories. Figure 1-3 illustrates the four classes of investment securities.

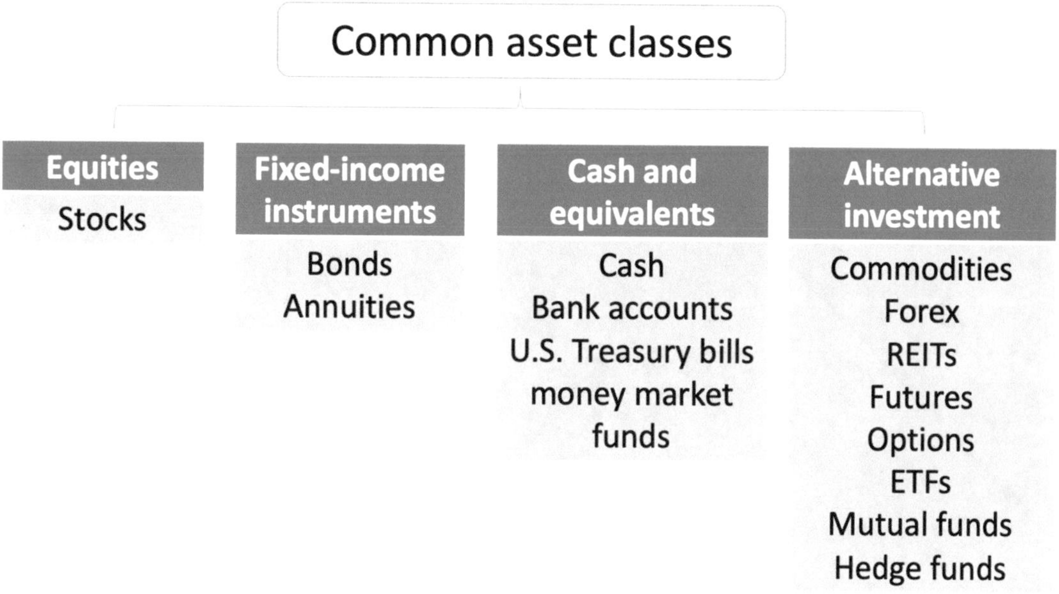

Common asset classes

Equities	Fixed-income instruments	Cash and equivalents	Alternative investment
Stocks	Bonds	Cash	Commodities
	Annuities	Bank accounts	Forex
		U.S. Treasury bills	REITs
		money market	Futures
		funds	Options
			ETFs
			Mutual funds
			Hedge funds

Figure 1-3. *Grouping common investment assets into four major classes*

Alternatively, we can group tradable assets based on the type of maturity. Stocks, currencies, and commodities are asset classes with no maturity, while fixed-income instruments and derivatives have maturities. For vanilla security with a maturity date, such as a futures contract, it is possible to compute its fair price based on the *no-arbitrage* argument, a topic we will discuss in Chapter 3.

We can also group assets based on the linearity of the payoff function at maturity for certain derivative instruments. For example, a futures contract allows the buyer/seller to buy/sell the underlying asset at an agreed price at maturity. Let us assume the underlying (stock) price at the maturity date is S_T and the agreed price is K. When a buyer enters/longs a futures contract to buy the stock at price K, the buyer would make a profit of $S_T - K$ if $S_T \geq K$ (purchase the stock at a lower price) or suffer a loss of $K - S_T$ if $S_T < K$ (purchase the stock at a higher price). A similar analysis applies to the case of entering a short position in a futures contract. Both functions are linear with respect to the underlying asset's price upon exercise. See Figure 1-4 for an illustration of linear payoff functions.

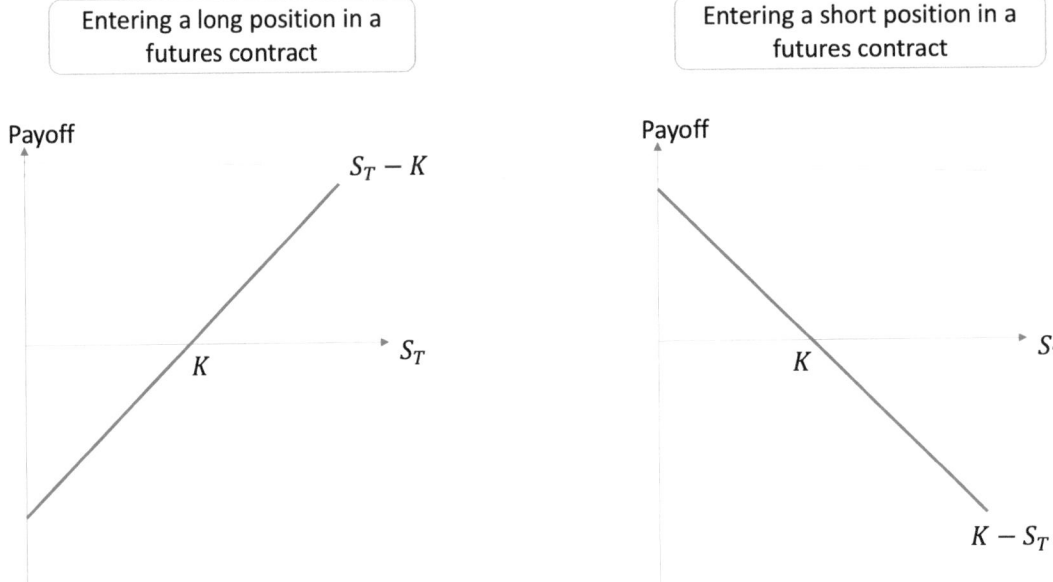

Figure 1-4. *Illustration of the linear payoff function of entering a long or short position in a futures contract*

Other derivative products with linear payoff functions include forwards and swaps. These are easy to price since their prices are linear functions of the underlying asset. We can price these instruments irrespective of the mathematical model for the underlying price. In other words, we only require the underlying asset's price, not the mathematical model around the asset. These assets are thus subject to model-independent pricing.

Let us look at the nonlinear payoff function from an options contract. A call option gives the buyer a choice to buy the underlying asset at the strike price K at the maturity date T when the underlying asset price is S_T, while a put option changes such choice to selling the underlying asset at the strike price K. Under both situations, the buyer can choose not to exercise the option and therefore gains no profit. Given that an investor can either long or short a call or put option, there are four combinations when participating in an options contract, as listed in the following:

- Long a call: Buy a call option to obtain the opportunity to buy the underlying asset at a prespecified strike price upon maturity.

- Short a call: Sell a call option to allow the buyer the opportunity to buy the underlying asset at a prespecified strike price upon maturity.

- Long a put: Buy a put option to obtain the opportunity to sell the underlying asset at a prespecified strike price upon maturity.

- Short a put: Sell a put option to allow the buyer the opportunity to sell the underlying asset at a prespecified strike price upon maturity.

Figure 1-5 contains the payoff functions for the four different combinations, all of which are nonlinear functions of the underlying asset price S_T.

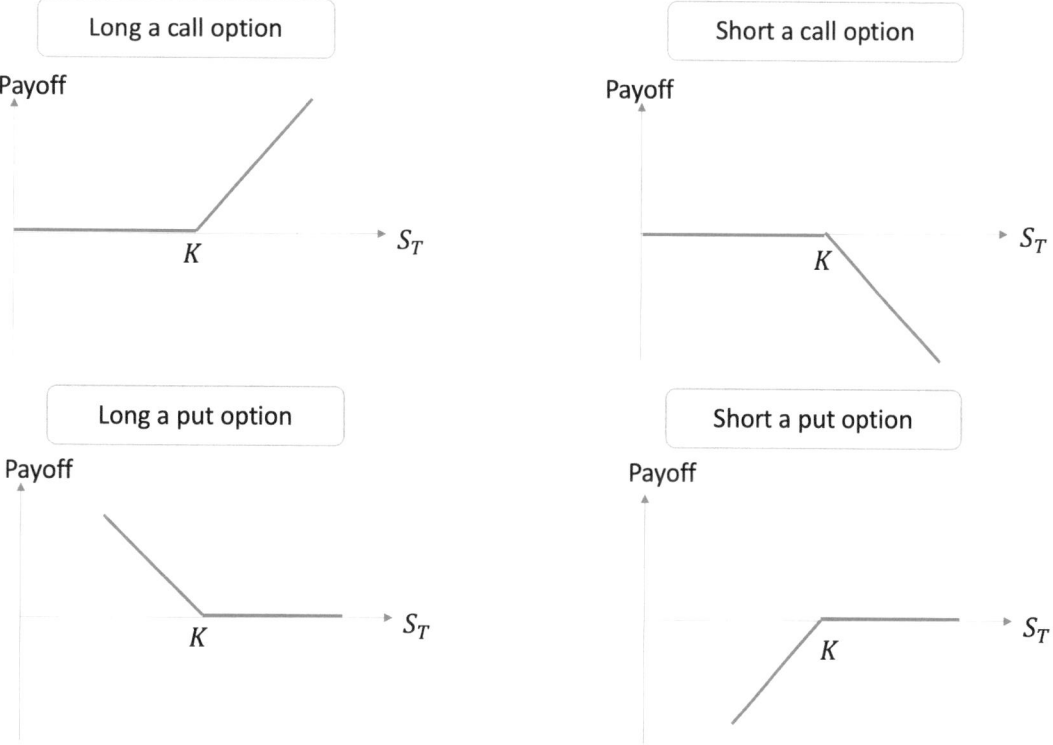

Figure 1-5. *Four types of nonlinear payoff functions in an options contract*

Note that tradable instruments within the same asset class exhibit similar characteristics but will differ from one another in some aspects. The market behavior will differ for tradable instruments that follow their respective price dynamics.

We can also group a tradable asset according to whether it belongs to the *cash market* or the *derivative market*. The cash market, also called the spot market, is a marketplace where trading instruments are exchanged at the point of sale, and purchasers take immediate possession of the trading products. For example, the stock exchange falls into the cash market since investors receive shares of stock almost immediately in exchange for cash, thus settling the transactions on the spot.

On the other hand, the derivative market completes a transaction only at a prespecified date in the future. Take the futures market, for example. A buyer who pays for the right to receive a good only gets to expect the delivery at a prespecified future date.

The next section introduces common trading avenues and steps.

Common Trading Avenues and Steps

As mentioned earlier, investors engage in trading activities for the purpose of profit-making or risk management. When the purpose is to invest and make profits, the next sequence of actions is to observe and analyze the market and act upon the trading signals. For example, if investors use predictive methods to predict when the market will go up or down, they can initiate trades to turn the market into profits and make short, instant wins. Such activity is referred to as *market timing*, where an investor enters or exits a position or *rebalances a portfolio* (moving money between assets) based on predicted market movement in the near future. This is opposite to the *buy-and-hold* strategy, where an investor purchases trading instruments and holds them for a long period, irrespective of the market's volatility (ups and downs).

When engaging in trading activity, it is important to understand the short-term and long-term seasonality effect for a particular tradable asset. Take stock trading, for example. Short-term swings in stock prices tend to occur when the market opens and closes, falling under the regular trading hours of major stock exchanges and forming the opening and closing prices of the particular day. In the longer term, trading activities at the end of the year tend to be quieter than other periods of the particular year.

Trading activities can happen at one of the following four avenues:

- Regulated exchanges, such as the New York Stock Exchange (NYSE) and NASDAQ

- Dark pools, private exchanges that are less regulated

- Brokered market, where transactions between the buyer and the seller are performed via middlemen called brokers (or agents, intermediaries)

- Over-the-counter (OTC) market, a decentralized market that allows direct transactions between buyers and sellers

Let us look at the anatomy of a trade. There are four usual steps involved when performing a trade:

- Acquisition of information and quotes: Before engaging in a trade, it is important to access quality information about the asset and gain transparency in many tangible and intangible factors such as supply and demand, the risk attitude of investors, and the overall economic and geopolitical environment. Information on the market structure, liquidity, and information flow eventually determine the price discovery of the tradable asset.

- Routing of order, such as selecting the broker(s) to handle the trade(s) or deciding which market(s) to transmit and execute the trade(s).

- Execution of order, matching and executing the trading orders between buyers and sellers according to the rules of the particular market.

- Confirmation, clearance, and settlement: This happens at the end of executing a trading order. Clearance is the recording and comparison of trade records, and settlement involves the actual delivery of the security and its payment.

In the next section, we will look at different market structures.

Market Structures

Before 2010, *open outcry* was a popular way to communicate trade orders in trading pits (floor). Traders would tap into temporary information asymmetry and use verbal communication and hand signals to perform trading activities at stock, option, and futures exchanges. Traders would arrange their trades face to face on the exchange's trading floor, cry out bids and offers to offer liquidity, and listen for bids and offers to take liquidity. The open outcry rule is that traders must announce their bids and offers so that other traders may react to them, avoiding whispering among a small group of traders. They must also publicly announce that they accept bids (assets sold) or offers (assets taken) of particular trades. The largest pit was the US long-term treasury bond futures market, with over 500 floor traders under the *Chicago Board of Trade (CBOT)*, a major market maker that later merged into the CMT Group.

As technology advanced, the trading markets moved from physical to electronic, shaping a fully automated exchange. First proposed by Fischer Black in 1971, the fully automated exchange was also called *program trading*, which encompasses a wide range of portfolio trading strategies.

The trading rules and systems together define a trading market's market structure. One type of market is called the *call market*, where trades are allowed only when the market is called. The other type of market is the *continuous market*, where trades are allowed anytime during regular trading hours. Big exchanges such as NYSE, LSE (London Stock Exchange), and SGX (Singapore Exchange) allow a hybrid mode of market structure.

The market structure can also be categorized based on the nature of pricing among the tradable assets. When the prices are determined based on the bid (buy) and ask (sell) quotations from market makers or dealers, it is called a *quote-driven* or *price-driven market*. The trades are determined by dealers and market makers who participate in every trade and match orders from their inventory. Typical assets in a quote-driven market include bonds, currencies, and commodities.

On the other hand, when the trades are based on the buyers' and sellers' requirements, it is called an *order-driven market* where the bid and ask prices, along with the number of shares desired, are put on display. Typical assets in an order-driven market include stock markets, futures exchanges, and electronic communications networks (ECNs). There are two basic types of orders: *market orders*, based on the asset's market price, and *limit orders*, where the assets are only traded based on the preset limit price.

Let us look at a few major types of buy-side stock investors.

Major Types of Buy-Side Stock Investors

Buy-side investors include institutional (account for the majority) and retail investors. Here, buy-side activities include purchasing stocks, bonds, or other financial securities based on the specific requirements and strategies of the institution's or client's portfolio. The buy side is a segment of financial markets made up of investing institutions and retail investors that purchase financial products for money-management purposes.

Typical buy-side institutional investors include

- Mutual fund

- Passive exchange-traded fund (ETF)

- Pension fund

- Sovereign wealth fund

- Hedge fund

- Insurance company

- Bank

- Corporate nominee

Typical buy-side retail investors include

- Start-up investor

- Family business

- Household/individual

The next section introduces the concept of market making.

Market Making

Market maker refers to a firm or an individual that actively quotes the two-sided markets (buy side and sell side) of a particular security. The market maker provides *bids*, meaning the particular price of the security along with the quantity it is willing to buy. It also provides *offers* (*asks*), meaning the price of the security and the quantity it is willing to sell. Naturally, the asking price is supposed to be higher than the bid price, so that the market maker can make a profit based on the *spread* of the two quote prices.

Market makers post quotes and stand ready to trade, thereby providing immediacy and *liquidity* to the market. By quoting bid and ask prices, market makers make the assets more liquid for potential buyers and short sellers.

A market maker also takes a significant risk of holding the assets because a security's value may decline between its purchase and sale to another buyer. They need capital to finance their inventories. The capital available to them thus limits their ability to offer liquidity. Because market making is very risky, investors generally dislike investing in market-making operations. Market-making firms with significant external financing typically have excellent risk management systems that prevent their dealers from generating large losses.

The next section introduces the concept of scalping.

Scalping

Scalping is a type of trading that makes small and fast profits by quickly (typically no more than a few minutes in large positions) and continuously acquiring and unwinding their positions. Traders that engage in scalping are referred to as scalpers.

When engaged in scalping, a trader requires a live feed of quotes in order to move fast. The trader, also called the *day trader*, must follow a strict exit strategy because one large loss could eliminate the many small gains the trader worked to accumulate.

Active traders such as day traders are strong believers in *market timing*, a key component of actively managed investment strategies. For example, if traders can predict when the market will go up and down, they can make trades to turn that market move into a profit. Obviously, this is a difficult and strenuous task as one needs to watch the market continuously, from daily to even hourly, as compared to long-term *position traders* that invest for the long run.

The next section introduces the concept of portfolio rebalancing.

Portfolio Rebalancing

As time goes on, a portfolio's current asset allocation will drift away from an investor's original target asset allocation. If left unadjusted, the portfolio will either become too risky or too conservative. Such rebalancing is completed by changing the position of one or more assets in the portfolio, either buying or selling, with the goal of maximizing the portfolio return or hedging another financial instrument.

Asset allocations in a portfolio can change as market performance alters the values of the assets due to price changes. Rebalancing involves periodically buying or selling the assets in a portfolio to regain and maintain that original, desired level of asset allocation defined by an investor's risk and reward profile.

There are several reasons why a portfolio may deviate from its target allocation over time, such as due to market fluctuations, additional cash injection or withdrawal, and changes in risk tolerance. We can perform portfolio rebalancing using either a time-based rebalancing approach (e.g., quarterly or annually) or a threshold-based rebalancing approach, which occurs when the allocation of an asset class deviates from the target by a predefined percentage.

In the world of quantitative trading, Python has emerged as a powerful tool for formulating and implementing trading algorithms. Part of the reason is its comprehensive open source libraries and strong community support. In the next section, we will discuss the practical aspect of financial data analysis and start by acquiring and summarizing the stock data using Python.

Getting Started with Financial Data Analysis

Financial data analysis is the process of processing and analyzing financial data to support decision-making in various financial applications, such as investing, trading, risk management, and corporate finance. It involves the use of advanced analytical techniques and models to identify the underlying patterns, trends, and relationships in the data, which will be used to support more informed financial decisions.

The interval of stock data can be different, such as by minute, hour, or day. Since time is continuous, we need a measure to summarize the profile of the stock price data within the interval. Let us start by introducing one of the most popular ways to summarize stock data.

Summarizing Stock Prices

The most common type of summary for stock data is the daily *OHLC* prices (open, high, low, close). An OHLC chart is a bar chart that shows open, high, low, and closing prices for each period, often daily. They present a day's four major data points, with the closing price considered the most important indicator by many traders.

The OHLC chart, similar to the candlestick chart shown in Figure 1-6, is useful because it can show increasing or decreasing momentum. When the open and closing prices have a big gap in between, it shows a strong momentum for an increase or decrease in the day. When the open and closing prices are close, it shows indecision or a weak momentum. The high and low prices show the full price range and can be used to assess the volatility.

Figure 1-6 shows two candlestick charts, both summarizing the price movements over a specified period, for example, daily. The color represents emotions for the stock price movement, with an up candle shaded green and a down candle shaded red, although these colors can be altered in the specific trading platform. A collection of candlestick charts can be used to determine the direction of the market movement. Each candlestick chart consists of four main points: open, high, low, and close, following the sequence of time in the period. The open and close points determine the real body of the candlestick. The green color represents a bullish candlestick, that is, the stock price closes above where it opens. Similarly, the red color represents a bearish candlestick, that is, the stock price closes below where it opens.

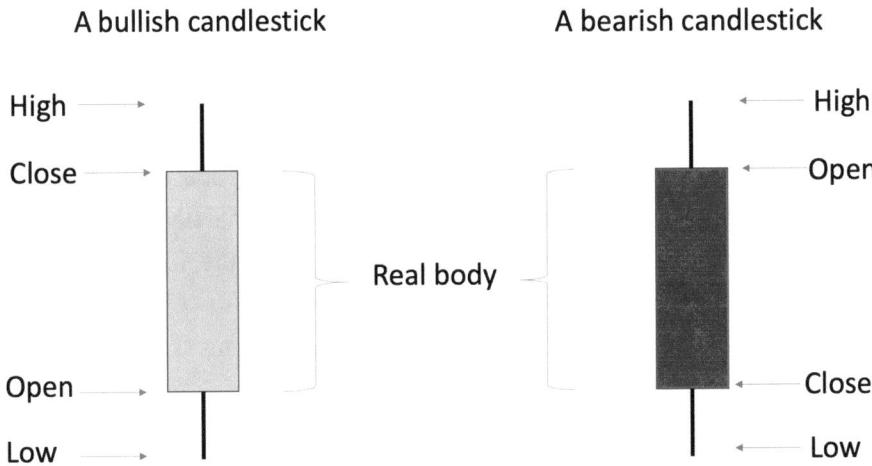

Figure 1-6. *Illustrating the bullish candlestick in green and bearish candlestick in red*

Let us examine the bullish candle in the green of a trading day. When the market starts, the stock assumes an opening price and starts to move. Across the day, the stock will experience the highest price point (high) and the lowest price point (low), where the gap in between indicates the momentum of the movement. We know for a fact that the high will always be higher than the low, as long as there is movement. When the market closes, the stock registers a close. Figure 1-7 depicts a sample movement path summarized by the green candlestick.

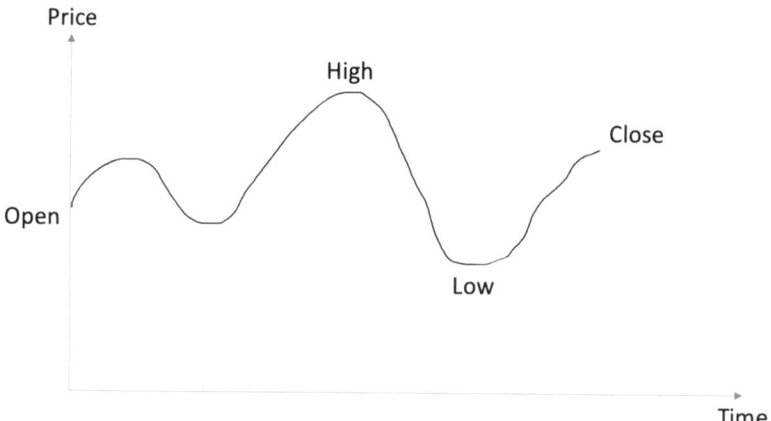

Figure 1-7. *A sample path of stock price movement represented by the green candlestick chart. When the market starts, the stock assumes an opening price and starts to move. It will experience the highest price point (high) and the lowest price point (low), where the gap in between indicates the momentum of the movement. When the market closes, the stock registers a close*

Next, we will switch gears and start working on the actual stock price data using Python. We will download the data from Yahoo! Finance and introduce different ways to graph the data.

Downloading Stock Price Data

Yahoo! Finance is a common source where we can get market data. To download the stock price data, we can use the yfinance library, a popular open source (and free) library, to access the financial data available on Yahoo! Finance. It is relatively quick to set up and offers a high level of granularity in the data (covering daily or even per-minute data).

To start with, we need to install the yfinance package via the pip command in the Jupyter notebook environment and import it:

```
!pip install yfinance
import yfinance as yf
```

Next, we can use the Ticker() module from the yfinance package to observe the profile information of a specific stock. The following code snippet obtains the ticker information on Microsoft and prints it out via the info attribute:

```python
# use the Ticker module to access ticker data
msft = yf.Ticker("MSFT")

# get stock info
>>> msft.info
{'zip': '98052-6399',
 'sector': 'Technology',
 'fullTimeEmployees': 221000,
 'longBusinessSummary': 'Microsoft Corporation develops, licenses, and
 supports software, services, devices, and solutions worldwide. The
 company operates in three segments: Productivity and Business Processes,
 Intelligent Cloud, and More Personal Computing. The Productivity and
 Business Processes segment offers Office, Exchange, SharePoint, Microsoft
 Teams, Office 365 Security and Compliance, Microsoft Viva, and Skype for
 Business; Skype, Outlook.com, OneDrive, and LinkedIn; and Dynamics 365, a
 set of cloud-based and on-premises business solutions for organizations and
 enterprise divisions. The Intelligent Cloud segment licenses SQL, Windows
 Servers, Visual Studio, System Center, and related Client Access Licenses;
 GitHub that provides a collaboration platform and code hosting service
 for developers; Nuance provides healthcare and enterprise AI solutions;
 and Azure, a cloud platform. It also offers enterprise support, Microsoft
 consulting, and nuance professional services to assist customers in
 developing, deploying, and managing Microsoft server and desktop solutions;
 and training and certification on Microsoft products. The More Personal
 Computing segment provides Windows original equipment manufacturer (OEM)
 licensing and other non-volume licensing of the Windows operating system;
 Windows Commercial, such as volume licensing of the Windows operating
 system, Windows cloud services, and other Windows commercial offerings;
 patent licensing; and Windows Internet of Things. It also offers Surface,
 PC accessories, PCs, tablets, gaming and entertainment consoles, and
 other devices; Gaming, including Xbox hardware, and Xbox content and
 services; video games and third-party video game royalties; and Search,
 including Bing and Microsoft advertising. The company sells its products
 through OEMs, distributors, and resellers; and directly through digital
 marketplaces, online stores, and retail stores. Microsoft Corporation was
 founded in 1975 and is headquartered in Redmond, Washington.',
```

```
'city': 'Redmond',
'phone': '425 882 8080',
'state': 'WA',
'country': 'United States',
'companyOfficers': [],
'website': 'https://www.microsoft.com',
'maxAge': 1,
'address1': 'One Microsoft Way',
'fax': '425 706 7329',
'industry': 'Software-Infrastructure',
'ebitdaMargins': 0.48672,
'profitMargins': 0.34366,
'grossMargins': 0.6826,
'operatingCashflow': 87693000704,
'revenueGrowth': 0.106,
'operatingMargins': 0.41691002,
'ebitda': 98841001984,
'targetLowPrice': 234,
'recommendationKey': 'buy',
'grossProfits': 135620000000,
'freeCashflow': 46155874304,
'targetMedianPrice': 290,
'currentPrice': 238.73,
'earningsGrowth': -0.133,
'currentRatio': 1.84,
'returnOnAssets': 0.15223,
'numberOfAnalystOpinions': 45,
'targetMeanPrice': 296.91,
'debtToEquity': 44.442,
'returnOnEquity': 0.42875,
'targetHighPrice': 411,
'totalCash': 107244003328,
'totalDebt': 77136003072,
'totalRevenue': 203074994176,
'totalCashPerShare': 14.387,
```

```
'financialCurrency': 'USD',
'revenuePerShare': 27.142,
'quickRatio': 1.585,
'recommendationMean': 1.8,
'exchange': 'NMS',
'shortName': 'Microsoft Corporation',
'longName': 'Microsoft Corporation',
'exchangeTimezoneName': 'America/New_York',
'exchangeTimezoneShortName': 'EST',
'isEsgPopulated': False,
'gmtOffSetMilliseconds': '-18000000',
'quoteType': 'EQUITY',
'symbol': 'MSFT',
'messageBoardId': 'finmb_21835',
'market': 'us_market',
'annualHoldingsTurnover': None,
'enterpriseToRevenue': 8.615,
'beta3Year': None,
'enterpriseToEbitda': 17.7,
'52WeekChange': -0.30287635,
'morningStarRiskRating': None,
'forwardEps': 11.18,
'revenueQuarterlyGrowth': None,
'sharesOutstanding': 7454470144,
'fundInceptionDate': None,
'annualReportExpenseRatio': None,
'totalAssets': None,
'bookValue': 23.276,
'sharesShort': 40445360,
'sharesPercentSharesOut': 0.0054,
'fundFamily': None,
'lastFiscalYearEnd': 1656547200,
'heldPercentInstitutions': 0.72300005,
'netIncomeToCommon': 69788999680,
'trailingEps': 9.29,
```

```
'lastDividendValue': 0.68,
'SandP52WeekChange': -0.19752294,
'priceToBook': 10.256488,
'heldPercentInsiders': 0.00059,
'nextFiscalYearEnd': 1719705600,
'yield': None,
'mostRecentQuarter': 1664496000,
'shortRatio': 1.38,
'sharesShortPreviousMonthDate': 1667174400,
'floatShares': 7447764118,
'beta': 0.933189,
'enterpriseValue': 1749498331136,
'priceHint': 2,
'threeYearAverageReturn': None,
'lastSplitDate': 1045526400,
'lastSplitFactor': '2:1',
'legalType': None,
'lastDividendDate': 1668556800,
'morningStarOverallRating': None,
'earningsQuarterlyGrowth': -0.144,
'priceToSalesTrailing12Months': 8.763292,
'dateShortInterest': 1669766400,
'pegRatio': 1.92,
'ytdReturn': None,
'forwardPE': 21.353308,
'lastCapGain': None,
'shortPercentOfFloat': 0.0054,
'sharesShortPriorMonth': 36909448,
'impliedSharesOutstanding': 0,
'category': None,
'fiveYearAverageReturn': None,
'previousClose': 238.19,
'regularMarketOpen': 236.11,
'twoHundredDayAverage': 261.927,
'trailingAnnualDividendYield': 0.010663755,
```

```
'payoutRatio': 0.26700002,
'volume24Hr': None,
'regularMarketDayHigh': 238.87,
'navPrice': None,
'averageDailyVolume10Day': 35831410,
'regularMarketPreviousClose': 238.19,
'fiftyDayAverage': 240.6454,
'trailingAnnualDividendRate': 2.54,
'open': 236.11,
'toCurrency': None,
'averageVolume10days': 35831410,
'expireDate': None,
'algorithm': None,
'dividendRate': 2.72,
'exDividendDate': 1676419200,
'circulatingSupply': None,
'startDate': None,
'regularMarketDayLow': 233.9428,
'currency': 'USD',
'trailingPE': 25.697523,
'regularMarketVolume': 21206982,
'lastMarket': None,
'maxSupply': None,
'openInterest': None,
'marketCap': 1779605569536,
'volumeAllCurrencies': None,
'strikePrice': None,
'averageVolume': 30495014,
'dayLow': 233.9428,
'ask': 238.45,
'askSize': 800,
'volume': 21206982,
'fiftyTwoWeekHigh': 344.3,
'fromCurrency': None,
'fiveYearAvgDividendYield': 1.17,
```

```
 'fiftyTwoWeekLow': 213.43,
 'bid': 238.2,
 'tradeable': False,
 'dividendYield': 0.0114,
 'bidSize': 1000,
 'dayHigh': 238.87,
 'coinMarketCapLink': None,
 'regularMarketPrice': 238.73,
 'preMarketPrice': None,
 'logo_url': 'https://logo.clearbit.com/microsoft.com',
 'trailingPegRatio': 2.1113}
```

The result shows a long list of information about Microsoft, useful for our initial analysis of a particular stock. Note that all this information is structured in the form of a dictionary, making it easy for us to access a specific piece of information. For example, the following code snippet prints the market cap of the stock:

```
# access a specific attribute from the dictionary
>>> msft.info["marketCap"]
1779605569536
```

Such structured information, also considered metadata in this context, comes in handy when we analyze multiple tickers together.

Now let us focus on the actual stock data of Microsoft. In Listing 1-2, we download the stock price data of Microsoft from the beginning of 2022 till the current date. Here, the current date is determined automatically by the today() function from the datetime package, which means we will obtain a different (bigger) result every time we run the code on a future date. We also specify the format of the date to be "YYYY-mm-dd," an important practice to unify the date format.

Listing 1-2. Downloading stock price data

```
# download daily stock price data by passing in specified ticker and
date range
from datetime import datetime
today_date = datetime.today().strftime('%Y-%m-%d')
print(today_date)
data = yf.download("MSFT", start="2022-01-01", end=today_date)
```

We can examine the first few rows by calling the head() function of the DataFrame. The resulting table contains price-related information such as open, high, low, close, and adjustment close prices, along with the daily trading volume:

```
# view the first few rows.
>>> data.head()
            Open        High        Low         Close       Adj Close  Volume
Date
2022-01-03  335.350006  338.000000  329.779999  334.750000  331.642456  28865100
2022-01-04  334.829987  335.200012  326.119995  329.010010  325.955750  32674300
2022-01-05  325.859985  326.070007  315.980011  316.380005  313.442993  40054300
2022-01-06  313.149994  318.700012  311.489990  313.880005  310.966217  39646100
2022-01-07  314.149994  316.500000  310.089996  314.040009  311.124725  32720000
```

We can also view the last few rows using the tail() function:

```
>>> data.tail()
            Open        High        Low         Close       Adj Close  Volume
Date
2022-12-30  238.210007  239.960007  236.660004  239.820007  239.820007  21930800
2023-01-03  243.080002  245.750000  237.399994  239.580002  239.580002  25740000
2023-01-04  232.279999  232.869995  225.960007  229.100006  229.100006  50623400
2023-01-05  227.199997  227.550003  221.759995  222.309998  222.309998  39585600
2023-01-06  223.000000  225.759995  219.350006  224.929993  224.929993  43597700
```

It is also a good habit to check the dimension of the DataFrame using the shape() function:

```
# check data dimension/size
>>> data.shape
(254, 6)
```

The following section will look at visualizing the time series data via interactive charts.

Visualizing Stock Price Data

The `plotly` package is an interactive graphing library that supports exploratory and expository visualizations. Let us demonstrate its use via a few examples, focusing on the stock's closing price for now.

First, let us visualize the closing price as a time series plot. As the name suggests, a time series is a sequence of data with a timestamp in each data point. Thus, when plotted on a graph, the horizontal axis indicates the time that flows from left to right, and the vertical axis represents the quantity of interest, that is, the daily closing price. Also, since each timestamp corresponds to one stand-alone point on the graph, we will connect all neighboring points via straight lines to form the final time series plot and show the trending patterns.

Listing 1-3 completes this task. Here, we pass the index of the DataFrame to indicate the dates on the x-axis (passed to the x argument) and the closing pricing on the y-axis (passed to the y argument) and specify the presentation mode to be in lines.

Listing 1-3. Plotting the daily closing price

```
# plot closing price as a time series chart
import plotly.graph_objects as go

fig = go.Figure(data=go.Scatter(x=data.index,y=data['Close'],
mode='lines'))
fig.show()
```

Running the code produces Figure 1-8. Note that the graph is interactive; by hovering over each point, the corresponding date and closing price come forward.

Figure 1-8. *Interactive time series plot of the daily closing price of Microsoft*

We can also enrich the graph by overlaying the trading volume information, as shown in Listing 1-4.

Listing 1-4. Overlaying trading volume in the daily closing price chart

```
# overlay the trading volume
from plotly.subplots import make_subplots

fig2 = make_subplots(specs=[[{"secondary_y": True}]])
fig2.add_trace(go.Scatter(x=data.index,y=data['Close'],name='Price'),
secondary_y=False)
fig2.add_trace(go.Bar(x=data.index,y=data['Volume'],name='Volume'),
secondary_y=True)
fig2.show()
```

Running the code generates Figure 1-9. Note that the trading volume assumes a secondary y-axis on the right, by setting secondary_y=True.

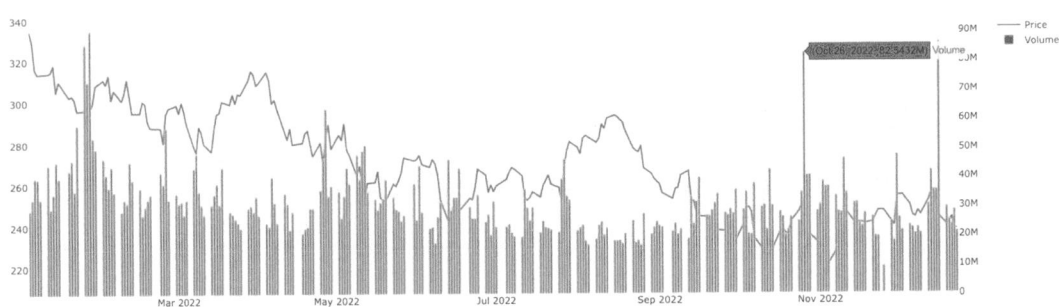

Figure 1-9. *Visualizing the daily closing price and trading volume of Microsoft*

Based on this graph, a few bars stand out, making it difficult to see the line chart. Let us change it by controlling the magnitude of the secondary y-axis. Specifically, we can enlarge the total magnitude of the right y-axis to make these bars appear shorter, as shown in Listing 1-5.

Listing 1-5. Rescaling the y-axis

```
# rescale volume
fig2.update_yaxes(range=[0,500000000],secondary_y=True)
fig2.update_yaxes(visible=True, secondary_y=True)
fig2
```

Running the code generates Figure 1-10. Now the bars appear shorter given a bigger range (0 to 500M) of the y-axis on the right.

Figure 1-10. *Controlling the magnitude of the daily trading volume as bars*

Lastly, let us plot all the price points via candlestick charts. This requires us to pass in all the price-related information in the DataFrame. The `Candlestick()` function can help us achieve this, as shown in Listing 1-6.

Listing 1-6. Plotting the candlestick chart

```
# switch to candlestick chart
fig3 = make_subplots(specs=[[{"secondary_y": True}]])
fig3.add_trace(go.Candlestick(x=data.index,
                              open=data['Open'],
                              high=data['High'],
                              low=data['Low'],
                              close=data['Close'],
                              ))
fig3
```

Running the code generates Figure 1-11. Each bar represents one day's summary points (open, high, low, and close), with the green color indicating an increase in price and red indicating a decrease in price at the end of the trading day.

Figure 1-11. *Visualizing all daily price points of Microsoft as candlestick charts*

Notice the sliding window at the bottom. We can use it to zoom in a specific range, as shown in Figure 1-12. The dates along the x-axis are automatically adjusted as we zoom in. Also, note that these bars come in groups of five. This is no incidence—there are five trading days in a week.

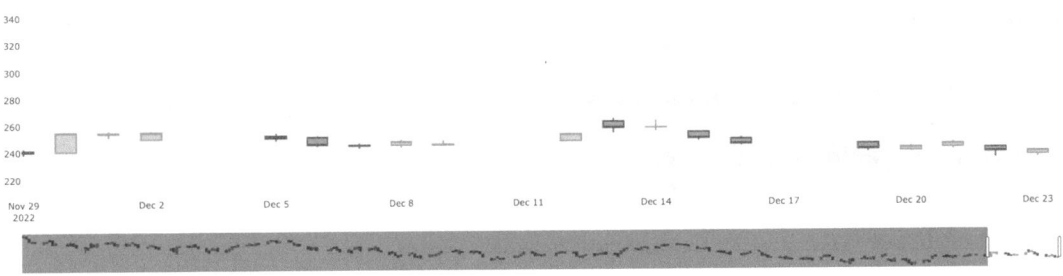

Figure 1-12. *Zooming in a specific range*

Summary

In this chapter, we covered the basics of quantitative trading, covering topics such as institutional algorithmic trading, major asset classes, derivatives such as options, market structures, buy-side investors, market making, scalping, and portfolio rebalancing. We then delved into exploratory data analysis of the stock data, starting with summarizing the periodic data points using candlestick charts. We also reviewed the practical side of things, covering data retrieval, analysis, and visualization via interactive charts. These will serve as the building blocks as we develop different trading strategies later on.

Exercises

- List a few financial instruments and describe the risk and reward profile.

- Can a model get exposed to the test set data during training?

- A model is considered better if it does better than another model on the training set, correct?

- For daily stock price data, can we aggregate it as weekly data? How about hourly?

- What is the payoff function for the issuer of a European call option? Put option? How is it connected to the payoff function of the buyer?

- Suppose you purchase a futures contract that requires you to sell a particular commodity one month later for a price of $10,000. What is your payoff when the price of the commodity grows to $12,000? Drops to $7000?

- What about the payoff for the buyer in both cases?

- How do the results change if we switch to an options contract with the same strike price and delivery date?

- Draw a sample stock price curve of a red candlestick.

- Download the stock price data of Apple, plot it as both a line and a candlestick chart, and analyze its trend.

- Calculate the YTD (year-to-date) average stock price of Apple.

CHAPTER 2

Electronic Market

In this chapter, we delve into the world of electronic markets, which have revolutionized the way financial instruments are traded. With the rapid advancements in technology and the widespread adoption of the Internet, electronic markets have largely replaced traditional, floor-based trading venues, ushering in an era of speed, efficiency, and accessibility for market participants around the globe.

Electronic markets facilitate the buying and selling of financial instruments, such as stocks, bonds, currencies, and commodities (covered in Chapter 1), through computerized systems and networks. They have played a critical role in democratizing access to financial markets, enabling a broader range of participants, including retail investors, institutional investors, and high-frequency traders, to engage in trading activities with ease and transparency. At the heart of electronic markets lies the trading mechanism, which governs how buy and sell orders are matched, executed, and settled.

Furthermore, electronic markets offer a variety of order types that cater to the diverse needs and objectives of traders. These order types can be used to achieve specific goals, such as minimizing market impact, ensuring a desired level of execution, or managing risk. In this chapter, we will examine the most common types of orders, including market orders, limit orders, stop orders, and their various iterations.

As we progress through this chapter, readers will gain a comprehensive understanding of the inner workings of electronic markets, the trading mechanisms that drive them, and the wide array of order types available to market participants.

Introducing Electronic Market

The electronic market operates on the basis of a discrete price grid where prices are arranged linearly according to the price magnitude. Every market has a minimum tick size. One tick is the minimum price difference between any two adjacent prices on the price grid of a trading instrument in a market. The price movements of different

P. Liu, *Quantitative Trading Strategies Using Python*, https://doi.org/10.1007/978-1-4842-9675-2_2

trading instruments could vary a lot, and we use their respective tick sizes to represent the minimum amount they can move up or down on an exchange. Stocks generally trade in one-cent tick size increments, currencies in pips (percentage in point or price interest point), and rates in basis points (bps). When the price grid is such that prices are arranged from the smallest price to the largest price, it is called the price ladder.

The price ladder plays a crucial role in electronic markets by providing a visual representation of the order book, which contains a list of all pending buy and sell orders for a specific trading instrument. The order book is continuously updated in real time, reflecting the dynamic nature of the market as new orders are placed, modified, or canceled. Each rung of the price ladder corresponds to a specific price level, with buy orders (or bids) listed on one side and sell orders (or asks) on the other. The highest bid and the lowest ask are referred to as the best bid and best ask, respectively, and the gap between them is known as the bid-ask spread.

Market participants can use the information provided by the price ladder and order book to gain valuable insights into a particular trading instrument's supply and demand dynamics. This data can help traders identify potential trading opportunities, assess liquidity, and gauge the depth of the market at various price levels. For instance, large clusters of orders at specific price points may indicate significant support or resistance levels, while a thinning order book might suggest a lack of liquidity and increased price volatility. By carefully analyzing the price ladder and order book, traders can make more informed decisions and develop strategies that take advantage of the prevailing market conditions. Additionally, understanding the role of tick sizes in the price grid is crucial for traders when placing orders, managing risk, and executing trades, as even small changes in tick sizes can have a substantial impact on the potential profit or loss of a trade.

Electronic Order

The rise of electronic trading has brought about significant improvements in the efficiency, speed, and accessibility of financial markets. Transactions that once took minutes or hours to complete can now be executed in milliseconds or even microseconds, thanks to the power of high-speed networks and advanced computer algorithms. As a result, market participants can take advantage of fleeting trading opportunities, react more swiftly to market news, and benefit from tighter bid-ask spreads, which translate into lower transaction costs.

Moreover, electronic trading has democratized access to global financial markets, allowing individual investors to trade alongside institutional players such as hedge funds, banks, and proprietary trading firms. Through user-friendly online trading platforms, retail investors can access a vast array of financial instruments, from stocks and bonds to currencies and derivatives, and participate in various markets around the world. These platforms provide a wealth of market data, research tools, and risk management features, empowering investors to make more informed decisions and execute their trading strategies with precision and ease. At the same time, the increased transparency and availability of market data have fostered a more competitive landscape, driving innovation in trading strategies, algorithms, and financial products.

Orders are short messages to the exchange through the broker. An order is a set of instructions the trader gives to the exchange. It must contain at least the following instructions:

- Contract/security (or contracts/securities) to trade

- Buy or sell or cancel or modify

- Size: How many shares or contracts to trade

From an investor's perspective, making a trade via a computer system is simple and easy. However, the complex process behind the scenes sits on top of an impressive array of technology. What was once associated with shouting traders and wild hand gestures in open outcry markets has now become more closely associated with computerized trading strategies.

When you place an order to trade a financial instrument, the complex technology enables your brokerage to interact with all the securities exchanges looking to execute the trade. Those exchanges simultaneously interact with all the brokerages to facilitate trading activities.

For example, the Singapore Exchange (SGX), a Singaporean investment holding company, acts through its central depository (CDP) as a central counterparty to all matched trades (mainly securities) executed on the SGX ST Trading Engine, as well as privately negotiated married trades that are reported to the clearing house for clearing on the trade date. Being a central counterparty (CCP), CDP assumes the role of the seller to the buying clearing member and buyer to the selling clearing member. CDP, therefore, takes the buyer's credit risks and assumes the seller's delivery risks. This interposing of CDP as the CCP eliminates settlement uncertainty for market participants. SGX provides a centralized order-driven market with automated order routing, supported by decentralized computer networks. There are no designated market makers (liquidity providers), and member firms act as brokers or principals for clearing and settlement.

Proprietary and Agency Trading

In the world of finance, the distinction between proprietary and agency trading plays a crucial role in determining the objectives and motivations behind trading activities. While both types of trading involve the execution of orders in financial markets, they serve different purposes and are subject to different regulations and risk profiles.

Proprietary trading allows financial institutions to generate profits by leveraging their own capital and expertise in market analysis, risk management, and trading strategies. Prop traders often engage in various strategies such as arbitrage, market making, and statistical arbitrage, seeking opportunities to capitalize on market inefficiencies and price discrepancies. However, proprietary trading carries a higher degree of risk due to the full responsibility for potential losses. As a result, proprietary trading desks are often subject to strict risk management controls and regulatory oversight, particularly in the wake of the 2008 financial crisis.

On the other hand, agency trading focuses on providing execution services for clients, prioritizing the best execution of client orders, and ensuring that clients' interests are aligned with the broker's actions. The primary goal of agency trading is to achieve the most favorable terms for the client while minimizing the impact of the trade on the market. Brokers engaged in agency trading earn income through commissions and fees, rather than by taking positions in the market. Since agency traders do not assume market risk on behalf of their clients, they are subject to different regulatory and compliance requirements than proprietary traders.

A broker or trading agency can execute trading orders for their clients or their own agency. The main difference between agency and proprietary trading is the trading client, that is, for whom the trade is executed, and whose investment portfolio is changed as a result of trading. Agency trading is any type of trade that a broker executes for their clients/investors who are charged a brokerage fee. Proprietary trading, also known as prop trading, refers to when an agency or broker executes trades for the benefit of its own institution. The orders submitted by traders for their own accounts/institutions are called proprietary orders. Since most traders cannot access the markets directly, most orders are agency orders, which a broker presents to the market.

Agency orders can be held or not held. Held orders are those when the broker has an obligation to a client to fill the order. Market-not-held orders are institutional orders where the trader hires a broker-dealer to execute the order. Working on an order means a broker-dealer takes some time to fill the order.

Understanding the differences between proprietary and agency trading is essential for market participants to navigate the complex world of financial markets. While proprietary trading focuses on generating profits through active market participation, agency trading emphasizes the execution of client orders in the best possible manner, ensuring that the interests of clients are at the forefront of the broker's actions.

Order Matching Systems

A securities exchange needs to pair one or more unsolicited buy orders to one or more sell orders to make trades. This process is called matching the trading orders. When an investor wants to purchase a specific amount of stock, and another wants to sell the same quantity at the same price, the orders from both sides match, and a transaction takes place. The process of pairing these orders is called order matching, whereby exchanges identify buy orders, or bids, with corresponding sell orders, or asks, to pair and execute both orders.

This order matching process has become almost entirely automated, using rule-based systems to execute the pair of trades if certain conditions are satisfied. Most exchanges, some brokerages, and almost all electronic communication networks use rule-based order matching systems. These trading rules arrange trades from the orders of specific sizes that traders submit to them, not requiring face-to-face negotiation. Note that these systems follow particular order precedence rules.

Order precedence rules are a set of guidelines that dictate the priority in which orders are matched and executed in the market. These rules aim to ensure a fair and efficient order matching process by determining which orders take precedence over others in the queue. There are three primary order precedence rules followed by most trading systems: price, time, and size.

- Price precedence: Orders with better prices are given priority over orders with worse prices. In the case of buy orders, higher bids have precedence, while for sell orders, lower asks are prioritized. This rule ensures that market participants who are willing to buy at higher prices or sell at lower prices get their orders executed first.

- Time precedence: If two or more orders have the same price, the order that was placed earlier takes precedence. This rule, also known as the "first-come, first-served" principle, rewards traders who submit their orders earlier, ensuring that they are not disadvantaged by others submitting orders at the same price later.

- Size precedence: In some markets, when multiple orders have the same price and time priority, the order with the larger size may be given precedence. This rule encourages market participants to place larger orders, which can contribute to enhanced liquidity in the market.

There are three common types of orders that an electronic exchange sees: limit orders, market orders, and cancelation orders. Limit orders must include information such as the limit price, order size, and trade direction (buy or sell). Market orders must include the order size and trade direction. A cancelation order cancels a standing limit order entirely or reduces its order size.

Note that some exchanges, such as the London Stock Exchange and the NYSE Group, support functionality to allow traders to specify whether their limit orders are to be displayed or not on the limit order book (LOB). This is called lit (displayed) or unlit (not displayed). In that case, the limit order must have at least the following:

- Limit price

- Order size

- Trade direction

- Display or non-display

- If displayed, the size to be displayed

Several common order precedence rules are considered for execution. For the order type precedence, market orders always rank above limit orders. For the price precedence, a more competitive price rule is. The display precedence takes the form of lit or unlit preference, and the time precedence observes the time of arrival for the orders.

The rule used by most exchanges is the price/display/time precedence rule to determine the priority of execution. Specifically, the highest bids and lowest offers always execute before lower bids and higher offers. Among equally priced orders, displayed orders always get executed before non-displayed orders. Among displayed and non-displayed orders at the same price level, the time of arrival determines an order's priority.

The price/display/time precedence rule ensures a fair and efficient trading environment by prioritizing orders based on their competitiveness, visibility, and time of submission. By adhering to this rule, electronic exchanges can maintain a transparent and orderly market, encouraging market participants to submit competitive orders and enhancing liquidity.

In addition to the common order types and precedence rules discussed earlier, many electronic exchanges also offer a variety of advanced order types and conditional orders designed to cater to the diverse needs of traders. These may include

- Stop orders: These are orders that are triggered once a specific price level is reached. Stop orders can be used to limit losses, protect profits, or enter a position once a particular price level is breached. They can be further classified into stop-market and stop-limit orders.

- Iceberg orders: These are large orders that are divided into smaller parts, with only a portion of the order visible on the order book at any given time. Once the visible portion is executed, the next portion is revealed. This helps to minimize the market impact of large orders and can prevent information leakage.

- Trailing stop orders: These orders allow traders to set a stop price that trails the market price by a specific distance. As the market price moves in a favorable direction, the stop price adjusts accordingly, helping to protect gains while giving the position room to run.

By offering a diverse range of order types and adhering to well-defined precedence rules, electronic exchanges can provide market participants with a flexible and efficient trading environment. This enables traders to effectively manage risk, optimize execution, and tailor their trading strategies to the unique characteristics of the financial instruments they trade.

Market Order

The market order is the most common transaction type in the stock markets. It is an instruction by an investor to a broker to buy or sell stock shares, bonds, or other assets at the best available price in the current financial market. This means a market order instructs the broker to buy or sell a security immediately at the current price. Since there will be plenty of willing buyers and sellers for large-cap stocks, futures, or ETFs, market orders are best used for buying or selling these financial instruments with high liquidity.

Since the market order is an instruction to trade a given quantity at the best price possible, the priority of the market-order trader is to execute the order immediately with no specific price limit. Thus, the main risk is the uncertainty of the ultimate execution price. Once submitted, the market order cannot be canceled since it has already been executed.

Note that the electronic market orders don't wait. Upon receipt of a market order, the exchange will match it against the standing limit orders immediately until it is completely filled. Such immediacy characterizes market orders compared to limit orders (introduced in the following section). This means that when filling a market order, the order matching system will buy at the (ideally) lowest ask price or sell at the highest bid price, thus ending up paying the bid/ask spread.

Given the nature of market orders, they are particularly suitable for situations where the primary goal is to execute a trade quickly, rather than achieving a specific target price. This makes market orders especially useful in fast-moving or volatile market conditions, where getting in or out of a position promptly is crucial. However, the urgency of market orders also exposes investors to the risk of price slippage, which occurs when the actual execution price differs from the expected price due to rapid market fluctuations.

It is important for investors to understand that market orders offer no price protection, meaning that the execution price may be significantly different from the current market price, especially for illiquid or thinly traded instruments. In such cases, limit orders may be a more appropriate choice, as they allow investors to specify a maximum purchase price or a minimum sale price for their orders, providing some level of price control. However, limit orders come with the trade-off of potentially not being executed if the specified price is not met.

Limit Order

A limit order, which instructs the broker to buy or sell at the best price available only if the price is no worse than the price limit specified by the investor, is the main alternative to the market order for most individual investors. It is preferable when buying or selling a less frequently traded or highly volatile asset.

During regular hours, limit orders are arranged according to the exchange's limit price and time of receipt. When a buy market order arrives, first in the queue limit order selling at the lowest ask price gets matched first. When a sell market order arrives, first in the queue limit orders bidding at the highest bid price gets executed first. If the order is not executable, the order will be a standing offer and placed in a file called a limit order book.

A buy limit order is an order to purchase a financial instrument at or below a specified price, allowing traders to control how much they would pay for the instrument. In other words, the investor is guaranteed to pay that price or less by using a limit order to make a purchase.

Although the price is guaranteed, the order being filled is not guaranteed to be executed in time. After all, a buy limit order will only be executed if the asking price is at or below the specified limit price. If the asset does not reach the specified price or moves too quickly through the price, the order is not filled and will be stacked into the limit order book, causing the investor to miss out on the trading opportunity. That is, by using a buy limit order, the investor is guaranteed to pay the buy limit order price or better but is not guaranteed to have the order filled.

The same reasoning applies to the sell limit order, where the investor will sell the financial instrument at or above a specified selling price. A sell limit order allows traders to set a minimum selling price for their financial instruments. In this case, the investor is guaranteed to receive the specified price or a better price for the sale, but there is no guarantee that the order will be executed. A sell limit order will only be filled if the bid price is at or above the specified limit price. If the asset does not reach the specified price or moves too quickly through the price, the order is not filled and will be stored in the limit order book, potentially causing the investor to miss out on the trading opportunity.

Limit orders offer more control over the execution price than market orders and can be particularly useful when trading illiquid or volatile assets, where price slippage is more likely. However, they also come with the risk that the order may not be executed if the specified price is not reached, potentially resulting in missed trading opportunities.

To maximize the chances of a limit order being executed, traders should carefully monitor market conditions and adjust their limit prices accordingly. They may also consider using other advanced order types, such as stop-limit orders or trailing stop-limit orders, which combine the features of limit orders with additional conditions, providing even greater control over the execution price and risk management.

Limit Order Book

Note that a limit order book likely contains multiple bids and asks for the same instrument. These two types of trading directions, that is, bid and ask, represent the demand and supply side of the market. These limit orders are shelved on the book because they are not executable at the moment, for a reason. That reason is the bid/ask spread, defined as the price difference between the best bid and the best offer/ask of a LOB for a given instrument.

The best bid represents the limit order with the highest price the underlying investor from the demand side is willing to pay for the specific asset, and the best offer/ask is the lowest price some other investor from the supply side is willing to sell out the specific asset. When this gap is negative, the bordering trades will be automatically filled, creating a new spread based on the new best bid and offer. Popular large-cap stocks will have little or no spread, as you can almost always find another party who is willing to make the trade. The spread becomes wider for those less popular instruments. This means you should be careful when entering a position for these less frequently traded assets, as it will be challenging to exit the position later on.

The bid/ask spread plays a critical role in trading as it directly relates to the cost of trading and the liquidity of the trading market for the specific asset. A small spread indicates a highly liquid market where multiple buyers and sellers are involved. This leads to lower transaction costs and faster order execution. On the other hand, a big spread suggests a less liquid market. In this case, fewer market participants are interested in trading the asset, leading to potentially higher transaction costs and slower order execution.

Market makers provide liquidity by continuously quoting both bid and ask prices for a particular asset, thus playing an essential role in maintaining a healthy bid/ask spread and providing sufficient liquidity to the market. These market participants stand ready to buy or sell the asset at their quoted prices, ensuring that there is always a counterparty available for traders looking to execute their orders. As a result, the presence of active market makers can, and are incentivized to, help reduce the bid/ask spread and improve overall market efficiency.

Figure 2-1 illustrates the limit order book for a particular asset. There are multiple price points (along with their sizes/volumes) for the demand from the buy side and the supply from the sell side. We take the lowest ask price of the upper box as the best offer and the highest bid price of the lower box as the best bid. The difference between the two gives the bid/ask spread. A bigger gap corresponds to lower liquidity. A market maker would be incentivized to reduce the gap by providing more liquidity to the market, making the trades of this asset more executable.

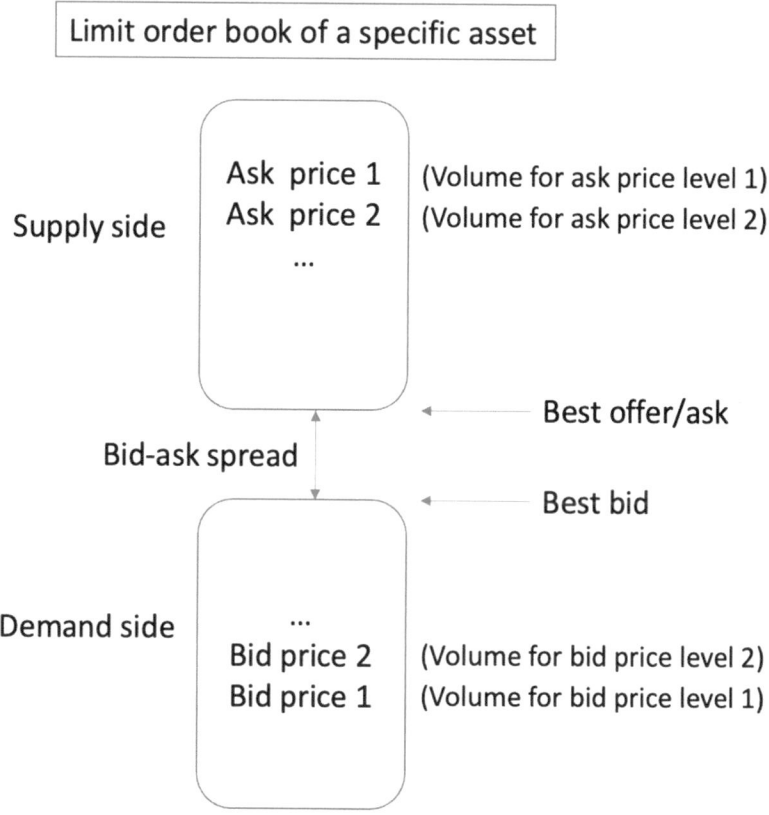

Figure 2-1. *Illustrating the limit order book that consolidates all standing limit orders (prices and quantities) from the buy side and the sell side. A market maker is incentivized to reduce the gap by providing more liquidity to the market, serving as the liquidity provider, and making the trades of this asset more executable*

We can also look at the marketability of buy and sell orders at different ranges. As shown in Figure 2-2, we divide the limit order book into five different regions: above the best offer, at the best offer, between the best bid and best offer, at the best bid, and below the best bid. For a buy order, it will be (easily) marketable if the price is at regions 1 and 2, since those eager to sell the asset (at the bottom part of the top box) would love to see a buyer with an expected or even higher bid. We call the buy order in the market if it lives within region 3, a situation in flux. Region 4 is borderline and is called at the market, representing the best bid of all the buyers in the limit order book. When the price of the buy order drops to region 5, there is no marginal competitiveness, and the order will simply be buried among the rest of the buy orders, leaving it behind the market. The same reasoning applies to the marketability of sell orders as well.

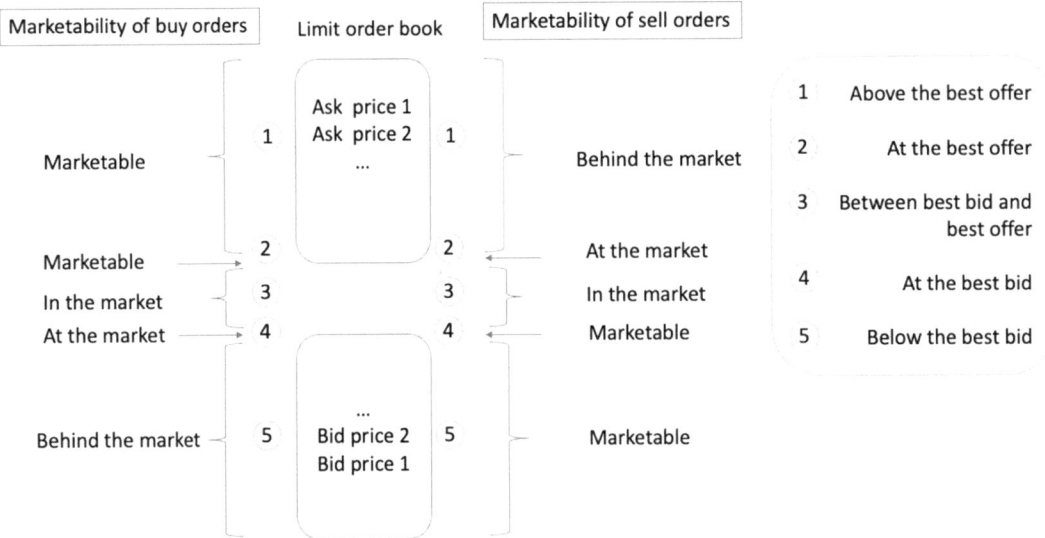

Figure 2-2. *Analyzing the marketability of buy and sell orders within different regions of the limit order book*

It is important for traders and investors to understand the marketability of buy and sell orders in these different regions so as to optimize their order execution strategies. By strategically placing orders in the appropriate regions, traders can increase the likelihood of their orders being executed at the desired price levels, thus minimizing transaction costs and better managing trading risks. Furthermore, by monitoring the market dynamics and the depth of the limit order book (the number of levels of buy and sell limit orders available in the order book at a given point in time), traders can gain valuable insights into the market dynamics of the asset.

Display vs. Non-display Orders

A display order is a visible order, and a non-display order is a hidden one that is not displayed on the limit order book. The former is much more heavily regulated than the latter.

A visible order is prohibited from crossing the market. For example, if an offer is already on one exchange, another exchange cannot post a bid for the same price or higher, thus creating a locked market. These regulations ensure a stable bid/ask spread for a particular asset. On the other hand, hidden orders have no such regulation.

Hidden, or non-display, orders offer traders a degree of anonymity by concealing their intentions and visibility from other market participants. This is particularly useful for large institutional investors who want to avoid revealing their large positions and prevent other traders from front-running or anticipating their trades. While hidden orders provide anonymity, they usually have lower execution priority compared to visible orders at the same price level. This means that when equally priced orders are matched, visible orders are executed first, followed by hidden orders based on their time of arrival.

The choice between using display and non-display orders depends on specific trading objectives and market conditions. Display orders are suitable for traders who prioritize execution speed and are willing to reveal their intentions to the market. Non-display orders, on the other hand, are more appropriate for traders who prioritize discretion and want to minimize the resulting market impact. However, they may have to accept the trade-off of lower execution priority and increased time to fill the order.

Stop Order

By default, a stop order is a market order conditioned on a preset stop price. A stop order becomes a market order as soon as the current market price reaches or crosses the preset stop price.

A stop order is always executed in the direction that the asset price is moving, assuming that such movement will continue in its original direction. For instance, if the market for a particular asset is moving downward, the stop order will be to sell at a preset price below the current market price. This is called a stop-loss order, which is placed to limit potential losses when the investor is in an open position of the asset. The stop-loss order will take the investor out of the open position at a preset level if the market moves against the existing position.

Stop-loss orders are essential, especially when one cannot actively keep an eye on the market. It's thus recommended to always have a stop-loss order in place for any existing position in order to gain protection from a sudden drop in price due to adverse market news. We can also call it a sell-stop order, which is always placed below the current market price and is typically used to limit a loss or protect a profit on a long stock position.

Alternatively, if the price is moving upward, the stop order will be to buy once the security reaches a preset price above the current market price. This is called a stop-entry order, or buy-stop order, which can be used to enter the market in the direction the market is moving. A buy-stop order is always placed above the current market price.

Therefore, before entering a position, we can use a stop-entry (buy-stop) order to long an asset if the market price exceeds the preset stop price, and use a sell-stop order to short an asset if the market price drops below the preset stop price. If we are already in a long (or short) position, we can use a sell-stop (or buy-stop) order to limit the loss of the position in case the market price drops (or rises).

Also, note that stop orders can be subject to slippage, that is, the difference between the expected execution price and the actual execution price. Since stop orders are triggered and converted into market orders once the preset stop price is reached, there is a possibility that the order may be executed at a worse price than initially anticipated, especially in fast-moving or illiquid markets. As a result, slippage can lead to a larger loss or a smaller profit than originally expected.

Let us look at one example. Say you observe that a particular stock has been moving in a sideways range (a fairly stable range without forming any distinct trends over some period of time) between $20 and $30, and you believe it will ultimately break out the upper limit and move higher. You would like to employ breakout trading, which means you will take a position within the early stage of an upward-moving trend. In this case, you could place a stop-entry order above the current upper limit of $30. The price of the stop-entry order can be set as $30.25 to allow for a margin of error. Placing the stop-entry order gets you into the market once the sideways range is broken to the upside. Also, now that you're long in the position, if you're a disciplined trader, you'll want to immediately establish a regular stop-loss sell order to limit your losses in case the upward trend is false.

When placing a stop order, we have (unknowingly) entered into the world of algorithmic trading. Here, the logic of algorithmic trading is simple: if the market price reaches or crosses the stop price, issue a market order; else, keep checking the market price.

Stop-Limit Order

A stop-limit order is similar to a stop order in that a stop price will activate the order. However, unlike the stop order, which is submitted as a market order when elected, the stop-limit order is submitted as a limit order. A stop-limit order combines the features of a stop order and a limit order, providing more control over the execution price while still allowing for the possibility of protecting against significant losses or locking in profits. Specifically, when the market price reaches the preset stop price, the stop-limit order becomes a limit order that will be executed at the specified limit price or better. This ensures that the order will not be executed at a price worse than the limit price, thus mitigating the risk associated with market orders.

A stop-limit order is a conditional trade that combines the features of a stop order with those of a limit order and is used to mitigate risk. So a stop-limit order is a limit order contingent on a preset stop price and a limit price. A stop-limit order eliminates the price risk associated with a stop order where the execution price cannot be guaranteed. However, it exposes the investor to the risk that the order may never fill even if the stop price is reached. A stop-limit order gives traders precise control over when the order should be filled, but the order is not guaranteed to be executed. Traders often use stop-limit orders to lock in profits or limit downside losses, although they could "miss the market" altogether, resulting in missed opportunities if the asset's price moves in the desired direction but doesn't satisfy the limit price condition.

In summary, stop-limit orders offer a balance between limiting the execution price and stopping potential loss due to significant adverse market movements. However, they come with the risk of not being executed if the limit price is not met, potentially causing traders to miss out on potential profits or fail to limit their losses effectively.

Let us look at an example algorithm behind the stop-limit order. Suppose research shows that the slippage is usually three ticks. Regarding the algorithmic rule for a buy-stop-limit order, if the market price reaches or crosses the stop price, the system would issue a limit order of a limit price three ticks above the stop price. Otherwise, it will keep checking the market price. Regarding the algorithmic rule for a sell-stop-limit order, if the market price reaches or crosses the stop price, the system would issue a limit order of a limit price three ticks below the stop price. Otherwise, it will keep checking the market price.

Pegged Order

A pegged order is a type of order that allows the limit price to be dynamic, adjusting automatically based on a reference price. This can be particularly useful in spread trading or other trading strategies that require staying in sync with the market's best bid, best offer, or mid-price.

The price in a limit order is fixed and static; we can only issue a new order to have a new limit price. However, there are situations when we would like the limit price to be dynamic. For example, suppose a trading strategy must trade at an offset of the best bid or best ask. But these two quotes fluctuate, and you want your limit order prices to change in sync with them. Pegged orders allow you to do just that.

Placing a pegged order requires specifying the reference price to track, along with an optional differential offset. The differential offset can be a positive or negative multiple of the tick size that represents the minimum price movement for the particular asset. The trading system will then manage the pegged order by automatically modifying its price on the order book as the reference price moves, maintaining the desired price relationship.

A pegged order is a limit order with a dynamic limit price. It allows traders to keep their orders in line with the changing market conditions without having to monitor and adjust their orders manually and constantly. This can be particularly beneficial in fast-moving markets or when trading strategies require maintaining specific price relationships with the best bid, best offer, or mid-price. However, it's essential to understand that pegged orders still carry the risk of not being executed if the market moves unfavorably, and the dynamic limit price never reaches a level at which the order can be filled.

The pegged order is often used in spread trading, which involves the simultaneous buying and selling of related securities as a unit, designed to profit from a change in the spread (price difference) between the two securities. Here, spread trading is a strategy that takes advantage of the price difference, or spread, between two related securities. In this strategy, a trader simultaneously buys one security and sells another security to profit from changes in the spread between the two. The objective is to capitalize on the temporary mispricing or changing price relationship between the securities rather than betting on the direction of the individual securities themselves.

So how does a pegged order work? When entering a pegged order, you must specify a reference price they wish to track, which could be the best bid, best offer, or mid-price. Best bid and best offer pegs may track at a differential offset, which is specified as a multiple of the whole tick size. This means that the trading system will manage the pegged order by automatically modifying the pegged order's price on the order book as the reference price moves.

Let us look at an example of pegged order. Suppose your strategy requires you to buy a limit order to be filled at three ticks lower than the current best bid and a sell limit order to be filled at two ticks higher than the current best offer. When the bid price changes, the pegged order becomes a composite order comprising

- A cancelation order of total order size (one buy limit order and one sell limit order)

- A new buy limit order with a limit price pegged at the new best bid less an offset of three ticks, and a new sell limit order with a limit price pegged at the new best ask plus an offset of two ticks

Let's say the current best bid is $100, and the best offer is $101. According to this strategy, we will place a buy limit order at $100 – (3 ticks) and a sell limit order at $101 + (2 ticks). Assuming each tick is $0.01, the buy limit order will be placed at $99.97, and the sell limit order will be placed at $101.02.

Now, if the best bid changes to $100.50 and the best offer changes to $101.50, the pegged orders will automatically adjust to the new reference prices. Specifically, the buy limit order will now be placed at $100.50 – (3 ticks) = $100.47, and the sell limit order will be placed at $101.50 + (2 ticks) = $101.52.

The pseudocode for the algorithm behind a pegged buy order with an offset of x is as follows:

1. If the bid price increases to B_+

   a. Cancel the current limit order

   b. Submit a buy limit order at a price of $B_+ - x$

2. Else

   a. If the bid price decreases to B_-

      i. If the current limit order is not filled

         1. Cancel the current limit order

         2. Submit a buy limit order at a price of $B_- - x$

      ii. Else

         1. Keep checking whether the bid price has changed

When the bid price changes, the algorithm checks if the change is an increase or a decrease. If the bid price increases, the current limit order is canceled, and a new buy limit order is submitted at the new bid price minus the offset x. If the bid price decreases, the algorithm first checks if the current limit order has been filled or not. If the current limit order is not filled, the order is canceled, and a new buy limit order is submitted at the new bid price minus the offset x. If the order is filled, no further action is needed. The algorithm will continue monitoring the bid price for changes and adjust the buy limit order accordingly.

Pay attention to the inner if condition in the else statement. Here, we check if the current limit order is filled. Since there is a price drop, we would execute the limit order if it drops to the limit price of the buy limit order.

We can similarly write out the pseudocode for the algorithm behind a pegged sell order with an offset of x as follows:

1. If the ask price decreases to A_-

    a. Cancel the current limit order

    b. Submit a sell limit order at a price of $A_- + x$

2. Else

    a. If the ask price increases to A_+

        i. If the current limit order is not filled

            1. Cancel the current limit order

            2. Submit a sell limit order at a price of $A_- + x$

        ii. Else

            1. Keep checking whether the bid price has changed

Trailing Stop Order

Suppose you have a winning position and want to make it run. And you want to protect your gain. This can be achieved with a stop order. But stop order is static. If the run continues, you want to raise the stop order automatically in tandem.

So trailing stop order is invented for this purpose. A trailing (sell) stop order sets the initial stop price at a fixed amount below the market price. As the market price rises, the stop price rises by the trailing amount. But if the stock price falls, the stop price remains unchanged. When the stop price is hit, a market order is submitted. Reverse this for a buy trailing stop order. This strategy may allow a trader to limit the maximum possible loss without limiting possible gain.

A trailing stop order is a useful tool for managing positions in a dynamic market. It allows investors to secure gains and limit losses by automatically adjusting the stop price as the market moves in a favorable direction. This flexibility is particularly beneficial when a position is experiencing significant price fluctuations, as it helps protect profits without limiting potential upside.

Therefore, a trailing stop is a modification of a typical stop order that can be set at a defined percentage or dollar amount away from a security's current market price. An investor places a trailing stop loss below the current market price for a long position and a trailing stop above the current market price for a short position. It is designed to lock in profits or limit losses as a trade moves favorably.

Note that the trailing stops only move if the price moves favorably. Once it moves to lock in a profit or reduce a loss, it does not move back in the other direction. The trailing stop order is thus a dynamically changing stop order.

Market If Touched Order

A market if touched (MIT) is an order to buy (sell) below (above) the market. This order is held in the system until the trigger price is touched and is then submitted as a market order if and when a specified price level is reached. It is a conditional order that becomes a market order when a security reaches a specified price. When using a buy MIT order, a broker will wait until the security reaches the specified level before purchasing the asset. Correspondingly, a sell MIT order will trigger a market sell order when the security reaches a specified sell price.

Note that MIT orders are typically used to buy when the price falls or sell when the price rises. This is in contrast to stop orders and limit orders. For example, a buy MIT order looks for the price of an asset to fall, while a buy-stop order activates when the market value of the security increases past a specified level. On the other hand, the buy limit order only activates when the market value of the security reaches the limit price.

Take an asset whose current price is $288.7, for example. There is a large buy limit order size of $287.9. You want to buy at $288.0 and be among the first to buy. With an MIT, you can send a market order to buy when touched.

Summarizing Major Types of Orders

Table 2-1 summarizes the major types of orders, including market order, limit order, stop order, stop-limit order, pegged order, trailing stop order, and market if touched order.

Table 2-1. *Major types of orders*

Order Type	Attributes	Note
Market order	Trading direction and volume	Buy or sell immediately at the current best price by matching against standing limit orders; no price limit; uncertainty in the execution price; pay for the bid-ask spread
Limit order	Limit price, trading direction, and volume	Guaranteed to buy/sell an asset at the specified limit price or better for a buy/sell limit order; execution not guaranteed; order is shelved into the LOB if not executable; different marketability
Stop order	Stop price, trading direction, and volume	Market order with a stop price; executed in the direction of asset price movement; applicable for both entering a position and already in a position
Stop-limit order	Stop price, limit price, trading direction, and volume	A limit order is contingent on a preset stop price and a limit price; execution is not guaranteed
Pegged order	Reference price, offset, trading direction, and volume	A limit order with a dynamic limit price; consists of a cancelation order and a new limit order when reference price changes
Trailing stop order	Trailing amount, trading direction, and volume	Dynamic stop order; trailing stops only move if the price moves favorably
Market if touched order	Trigger price, trading direction, and volume	A market order to buy (sell) below (above) the market; buy when the price falls or sell when the price rises

More Order Types: Limit and Cancelation

There exist some other order types. For example, fill or kill (FOK) is a conditional type of order used in securities trading that instructs a brokerage to execute a transaction immediately and completely (the fill part) or not at all (the kill part). With FOK, the limit order is either completely filled at a specified or better price or completely canceled. It combines an all-or-none (AON) specification indicating it must be filled entirely; if not, it will be canceled. FOK orders are often used when a trader wants to ensure that a large order is executed quickly and fully without partial fills. This type of order is more suitable for large orders or illiquid markets, where a trader wants to avoid the risk of moving the market price.

Similarly, fill and kill (FAK) is a limit order that is executed against any existing orders at the stated limit price or better, up to the volume of the order. Any residual volume from this order is then immediately canceled. FAK orders are useful when a trader wants to take advantage of short-term market opportunities without leaving an open order on the books. FAK orders provide a balance between getting an immediate fill for the desired quantity, but without the all-or-none restriction of an FOK order.

Both FOK and FAK orders can be useful in specific trading scenarios, depending on the trader's objectives and market conditions. These conditional order types offer greater control over trade executions and can help traders manage risk and capture market opportunities more effectively.

In addition, in high-frequency trading (HFT), an "immediate or cancel" (IOC) order is a type of order that must be executed as soon as it is placed in the market. The unfilled portion is immediately canceled when the order cannot be fully executed.

Price Impact

It is important to note the potential price impact of large market orders, which tend to move prices. And the reason is the lack of sufficient liquidity for large orders to fill at the best price. Large market orders can have a significant impact on prices, especially when there is insufficient liquidity at the best price level. This phenomenon is known as price slippage, which occurs when the actual execution price of an order differs from the expected price due to insufficient liquidity.

For example, suppose that a 10K-share market buy order arrives, and the best offer is $100 for 5K shares. Half the order will fill at $100, but the next 5K shares will have to fill at the next price in the book, say at $100.02 (where we assume there are also 5K shares offered). The volume-weighted average price for the order will be $100.01, which is larger than $100.00. Thus, the price might move further following the trade.

To mitigate the impact of large market orders on prices, traders can consider using alternative order types or strategies, such as using limit orders to control the price at which their orders get executed or iceberg orders that divide large orders into smaller parts, thus reducing the visibility of the order's total size.

Order Flow

In trading, order flow is an important concept. It is the overall trade direction at any given period of time. Ex post, order flow can be inferred from the trade direction. For example, a trade is said to be buyer initiated if the trade took place at the ask price or higher. In this case, the buyer is willing to absorb the bid/ask spread and pay a higher price. The trade sign is +1.

Conversely, a trade is seller initiated if the trade occurred at the bid price or lower. In this case, the seller is willing to absorb the bid/ask spread and sell for a low price. The trade sign is –1.

In essence, the order flow suggests the net direction of the market. When there were more buy (sell) market orders (MO) than sell (buy) MO, the market direction would typically be up (down). Many papers in the literature have provided ample evidence of this intuitive observation. It is also well known among traders. By analyzing the order flow, traders can identify buying and selling pressure and anticipate potential price movements. The concept of order flow is based on the premise that the net direction of market orders can provide insights into market trends and potential price changes.

A positive net order flow, where there are more buy market orders than sell market orders, generally indicates a bullish market with upward price movement. Conversely, a negative net order flow, where there are more sell market orders than buy market orders, signals a bearish market with a downward price movement. This correlation between order flow and market direction is well documented in academic literature and widely recognized by traders.

So how do we measure the direction of market order flows? One way is to use the net trade sign: the total number of buyer-initiated trades less the total number of seller-initiated trades. We can also use the net trade volume sign: the aggregate size of buyer-initiated trades less the aggregate size of seller-initiated trades.

That being said, if we can forecast the direction of order flow ex ante, the trade direction in the future can be anticipated. In other words, a positive order flow suggests the market is likely to go up, while a negative order flow suggests the market is likely to go down.

Therefore, we can use some models to forecast the order flow on the fly. A simple model is to generate a trading signal if the forecasted order flow for the next period exceeds some threshold. This threshold can be determined via backtesting (to be covered in a later chapter).

In the following section, we will look at a sample limit order book data and develop familiarity with both concepts and implementation.

Working with LOB Data

The LOB data mainly consists of limit prices and associated trading volume at each price level. Due to the vast disparity in different trading platforms, compiling all LOB data for a specific asset is difficult. Fortunately, we begin to see a coordinated effort in the research community in compiling and sharing such data with open access.

One example is a recent paper in 2020 titled "Benchmark Dataset for Mid-Price Forecasting of Limit Order Book Data with Machine Learning Methods," where the authors share the first publicly available benchmark dataset of high-frequency limit order markets for mid-price prediction. The paper extracted normalized data representations of time series data for five stocks from the NASDAQ Nordic stock market for a time period of ten consecutive days, leading to a dataset of around four million time series samples in total and covering a complete market-wide history of ten trading days.

The dataset shared by the paper is available at `https://etsin.fairdata.fi/dataset/73eb48d7-4dbc-4a10-a52a-da745b47a649`. We have downloaded a sample file named "`Train_Dst_NoAuction_DecPre_CF_7.txt`" and placed it in the `data` folder. Listing 2-1 imports a few packages for data processing and visualization, followed by loading the dataset into `df`.

Listing 2-1. Loading the LOB dataset

```
import numpy as np
import pandas as pd
import plotly.express as px
from plotly.subplots import make_subplots
import plotly.graph_objects as go

df = np.loadtxt('data/Train_Dst_NoAuction_DecPre_CF_7.txt')
```

We can access the dimensions of the sample dataset via the shape attribute:

```
>>> df.shape
(149, 254750)
```

In this dataset, the rows indicate features such as asset price and volume, and the columns indicate timestamps. Typically, we would use the rows to indicate observation-level data per timestamp and use the columns to represent features or attributes. We would need to transpose the dataset.

Also, based on the documentation on the dataset, the first 40 rows carry 10 levels of bid and ask from the order book, along with the volume of each particular price point. We have a total of 40 entries per timestamp since each side (buy and sell) contains 10 price levels, and each level includes two points: price and volume. In other words, the limit order book in a single time snapshot shows up as an array of 40 elements.

The following code prints out price-volume data of ten price levels for the sell and the buy sides at the first timestamp:

```
>>> df[:40,0]
array([0.2615 , 0.00353, 0.2606 , 0.00326, 0.2618 , 0.002   , 0.2604 ,
       0.00682, 0.2619 , 0.00164, 0.2602 , 0.00786, 0.262   , 0.00532,
       0.26    , 0.00893, 0.2621 , 0.00151, 0.2599 , 0.00159, 0.2623 ,
       0.00837, 0.2595 , 0.001   , 0.2625 , 0.0015 , 0.2593 , 0.00143,
       0.2626 , 0.00787, 0.2591 , 0.00134, 0.2629 , 0.00146, 0.2588 ,
       0.00123, 0.2633 , 0.00311, 0.2579 , 0.00128])
```

Since each level consists of a price-volume pair for both sides (buy and sell), we know that for the first four entries, 0.2615 indicates the ask price, 0.00353 as the volume at that ask price level, 0.2606 as the buy price, and 0.00326 as the volume at that buy price level. Every two entries constitute a price-volume pair, and every price level corresponds to two consecutive pairs. We have a total of 10 price levels, corresponding to 20 price-volume pairs, including 10 for the buy side and 10 for the sell side. Also, we know that price levels on the sell side should always be higher than on the buy side, and a quick check verifies this.

Let us extract the price-volume pairs across all timestamps. Remember to transpose the dataset, which is achieved by accessing the .T attribute. The final result is then converted into a Pandas DataFrame format for better processing later. Remember to print a few rows of the transformed dataset in df2 for a sanity check:

```
df2 = pd.DataFrame(df[:40, :].T)
```

Understanding Label Distribution

The dataset comes with target labels that assume one of the following three values: up, down, or stationary movements. This label is used to describe the direction of movement of the mid-price for the limit order book. This label is further differentiated by different windows of lookahead in order to analyze the lagging effect further. Specifically, we would look at the direction of movement after 10, 20, 30, 50, and 100 events (timestamps).

Information on the target labels is contained between rows 145 and 149 of the original DataFrame. In Listing 2-2, we define a function to plot the distribution of the three movements as bar plots (histograms) for each lookahead window, repeated across all five windows. These five subplots are arranged together in one row and five columns via the make_subplots() function.

Listing 2-2. Plotting the label distribution of the mid-point movement

```
labels = ["Up", "Stationary", "Down"]

def printdistribution(dataset):
    fig = make_subplots(rows=1, cols=5,
                        subplot_titles=("k=10", "k=20", "k=30", "k=50",
                        "k=100"))

    fig.add_trace(
        go.Histogram(x=dataset[144,:], histnorm='percent'),
        row=1, col=1
    )
```

```
fig.add_trace(
    go.Histogram(x=dataset[145,:], histnorm='percent'),
    row=1, col=2
)

fig.add_trace(
    go.Histogram(x=dataset[146,:], histnorm='percent'),
    row=1, col=3
)

fig.add_trace(
    go.Histogram(x=dataset[147,:], histnorm='percent'),
    row=1, col=4
)

fig.add_trace(
    go.Histogram(x=dataset[148,:], histnorm='percent'),
    row=1, col=5,
)

fig.update_layout(
    title="Label distribution of mid-point movement",
    width=700,
    height=300,
    showlegend=False
)
fig.update_xaxes(ticktext=labels, tickvals=[1, 2, 3], tickangle = -45)
fig.update_yaxes(visible=False, showticklabels=False)
fig.layout.yaxis.title.text = 'percent'
fig.show()
```

```
>>> printdistribution(df)
```

Running the code generates Figure 2-3. The plot suggests an increasingly obvious trend for upward and downward movements as the lookahead window gets large.

Label distribution of mid-point movement

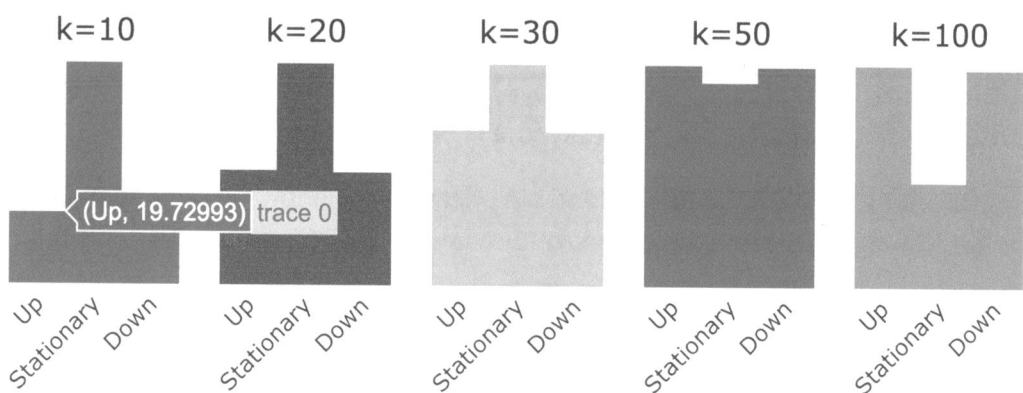

Figure 2-3. *Histogram of three types of movement across different lookahead windows in the limit order book*

Understanding Price-Volume Data

We stored the price-volume data in the df2 variable earlier. This DataFrame has 40 columns, corresponding to 10 price levels for each side, with a unique price-volume pair at each price level. For example, the first four columns belong to the level 1 price. Within the first four columns, the first is the level 1 ask price, the second is the level 1 ask volume, the third is the level 1 bid price, and the fourth is the level 1 bid volume. This pattern repeats across all 10 price levels, thus forming a total of 40 columns. Each row is a snapshot at a particular timestamp, and together these 40 columns form that snapshot.

Let us get the dimension of df2:

```
>>> df2.shape
(254750, 40)
```

Now we would like to dissect this DataFrame and allocate each component to a separate DataFrame. In Listing 2-3, we subset the DataFrame based on the sequence of columns for each component, resulting in four DataFrames: dfAskPrices, dfAskVolumes, dfBidPrices, and dfBidVolumes. Subsetting the DataFrame is completed by calling the loc() function and supplying the corresponding row and column indexes.

Listing 2-3. Extracting the bid/ask prices and volumes

```
dfAskPrices = df2.loc[:, range(0,40,4)]
dfAskVolumes = df2.loc[:, range(1,40,4)]
dfBidPrices = df2.loc[:, range(2,40,4)]
dfBidVolumes = df2.loc[:, range(3,40,4)]
```

One thing to note is that the ask and bid prices do not follow the same sequence order. Printing out the first row of dfAskPrices and dfBidPrices helps us verify this:

```
>>> dfAskPrices.loc[0,:]
0      0.2615
4      0.2618
8      0.2619
12     0.2620
16     0.2621
20     0.2623
24     0.2625
28     0.2626
32     0.2629
36     0.2633
Name: 0, dtype: float64

>>> dfBidPrices.loc[0,:]
2      0.2606
6      0.2604
10     0.2602
14     0.2600
18     0.2599
22     0.2595
26     0.2593
30     0.2591
34     0.2588
38     0.2579
Name: 0, dtype: float64
```

The results show that the ask prices follow an increasing sequence, while the bid prices follow a decreasing sequence. Since we often work with price data that follow an increasing sequence in analyses such as plotting, we need to reverse the order of the bid prices. The order could be reversed by rearranging the sequence of columns in the DataFrame. The current sequence of the columns is

```
>>> dfBidPrices.columns
Int64Index([2, 6, 10, 14, 18, 22, 26, 30, 34, 38], dtype='int64')
```

We can reverse the ordering by the [::-1] command:

```
>>> dfBidPrices.columns[::-1]
Int64Index([38, 34, 30, 26, 22, 18, 14, 10, 6, 2], dtype='int64')
```

Now let us reverse both bid prices and volumes, where we passed the reversed column names to the respective DataFrames based on column selection:

```
dfBidPrices = dfBidPrices[dfBidPrices.columns[::-1]]
dfBidVolumes = dfBidVolumes[dfBidVolumes.columns[::-1]]
```

Examining the first row of dfBidPrices shows an increasing price trend now:

```
>>> dfBidPrices.loc[0,:]
38      0.2579
34      0.2588
30      0.2591
26      0.2593
22      0.2595
18      0.2599
14      0.2600
10      0.2602
6       0.2604
2       0.2606
Name: 0, dtype: float64
```

Note that the index for each entry still stays the same. We may need to reset the index depending on the specific follow-up process.

Since the price increases from the bottom (buy side) to the top (sell side) in a limit order book, we can join the price tables from both sides to show the continuum. There are multiple ways to join two tables, and we choose outer join to avoid missing any entry. Listing 2-4 joins the price and volume tables from both sides, followed by renaming the columns.

Listing 2-4. Concatenating bid and ask tables

```
# Concatenate Bid and Ask together to form complete orderbook picture
dfPrices = dfBidPrices.join(dfAskPrices, how='outer')
dfVolumnes = dfBidVolumes.join(dfAskVolumes, how='outer')

#Rename columns starting from 1->20
dfPrices.columns = range(1, 21)
dfVolumnes.columns = range(1, 21)
```

We can print out the first row of dfPrices to check the prices across all levels at the first timestamp:

```
>>> dfPrices.loc[0,:]
1       0.2579
2       0.2588
3       0.2591
4       0.2593
5       0.2595
6       0.2599
7       0.2600
8       0.2602
9       0.2604
10      0.2606
11      0.2615
12      0.2618
13      0.2619
14      0.2620
15      0.2621
16      0.2623
17      0.2625
18      0.2626
```

```
19    0.2629
20    0.2633
Name: 0, dtype: float64
```

The result shows that all prices are in increasing order. Since the first ten columns show the buy-side prices and the last ten columns belong to the sell-side prices, the best bid price would be the highest price at the buy side, that is, 0.2606, while the best ask price (best offer) would be the lowest price at the sell side, that is, 0.2615. The difference between the two price points gives us the bid/ask spread for the current snapshot, and its movement across different snapshots indicates market dynamics.

We can plot these prices as time series, where each price curve represents the evolution of price for the specific particular of a buy or sell trading side. As a matter of fact, these curves should not intersect with each other; otherwise, they would have been transacted and jointly removed from that price level. Listing 2-5 plots the 20 price curves for the first 50 timestamps.

Listing 2-5. Visualizing sample price curves

```
fig = go.Figure()

for i in dfPrices.columns:
    fig.add_trace(go.Scatter(y=dfPrices[:50][i]))

fig.update_layout(
    title='10 price levels of each side of the orderbook',
    xaxis_title="Time snapshot index",
    yaxis_title="Price levels",
    height=500,
    showlegend=False,
)

>>> fig.show()
```

Running the code generates Figure 2-4. Note the big gap in the middle; this is the bid/ask spread of the limit order book. The figure also tells us something about market dynamics. For example, at time step 20, we observe a sudden jump in ask prices, which may be caused by a certain event in the market, causing the sellers to raise the prices as a whole.

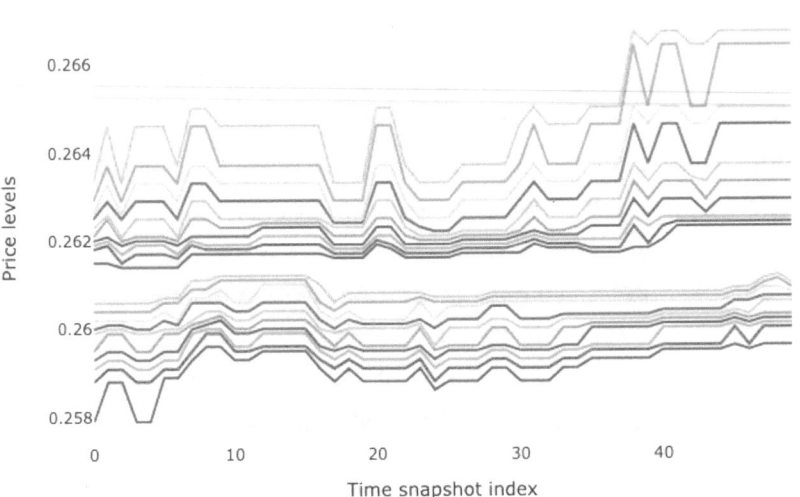

10 price levels of each side of the orderbook

Figure 2-4. *Visualizing the 10 price curves for both sides for the first 50 time snapshots. Each curve represents the price evolution at a particular price level and will not intersect with each other. The big gap in the middle presents the bid/ask spread of the limit order book*

Note that the graph is interactive, offering the usual set of flexible controls (such as zooming, highlighting via selection, and additional data upon hovering) based on the `plotly` library.

We can also plot the volume data as stacked bar charts. The following code snippet retrieves the first 5 snapshots of volume data and plots the 20 levels of volumes as stack bars:

```
px.bar(dfVolumnes.head(5).transpose(), orientation='h')
```

Running this code generates Figure 2-5.

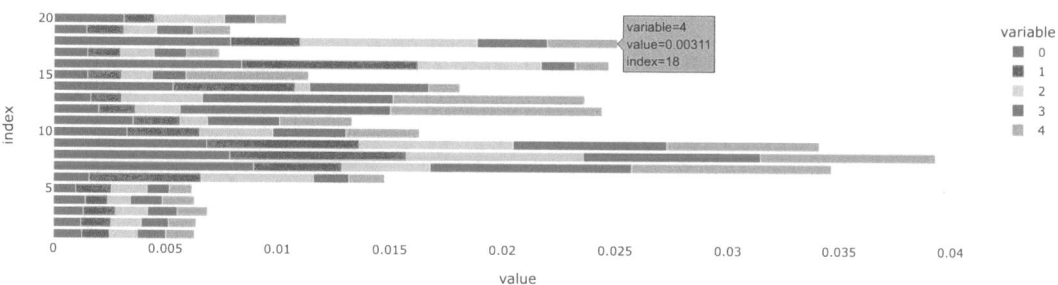

Figure 2-5. *Plotting the first 5 snapshots of volume as bar charts across all 20 price levels*

Let us plot the volume at each price level for a particular time snapshot. We can use the `iloc()` function to access a particular portion based on the positional index. For example, the following code prints out the first row of `dfPrices`:

```
>>> dfPrices.iloc[0]
1       0.2579
2       0.2588
3       0.2591
4       0.2593
5       0.2595
6       0.2599
7       0.2600
8       0.2602
9       0.2604
10      0.2606
11      0.2615
12      0.2618
13      0.2619
14      0.2620
15      0.2621
16      0.2623
17      0.2625
18      0.2626
19      0.2629
20      0.2633
Name: 0, dtype: float64
```

We can plot the volume data of a particular timestamp as bars. As shown in Listing 2-6, we use list comprehension to format the prices to four decimal places before passing them to the y argument in the go.Bar() function.

Listing 2-6. Visualizing the volume data

```
colors = ['lightslategrey',] * 10
colors = colors + ['crimson',] * 10

fig = go.Figure()
timestamp = 0

fig.add_trace(go.Bar(
    y= ['price-'+'{:.4f}'.format(x) for x in dfPrices.iloc[timestamp].
    tolist()],
    x=dfVolumnes.iloc[timestamp].tolist(),
    orientation='h',
    marker_color=colors
))

fig.update_layout(
    title='Volume of 10 price levels of each side of the orderbook',
    xaxis_title="Volume",
    yaxis_title="Price levels",
#     template='plotly_dark'
)

fig.show()
```

Running the code generates Figure 2-6.

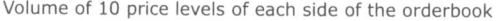
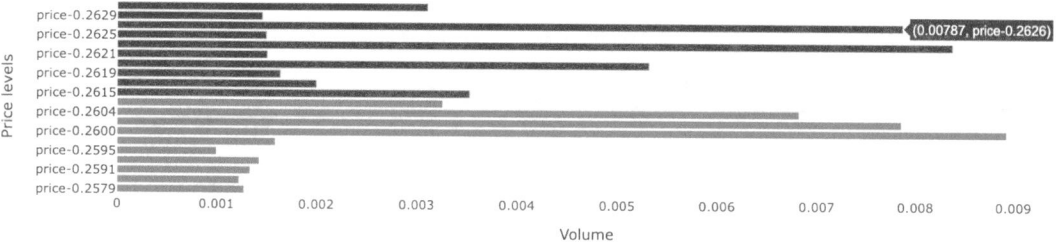

Figure 2-6. *Volume data of 20 price levels (10 for the sell side and 10 for the buy side) for a particular snapshot in time*

We can also combine the previous two charts together, as shown in Listing 2-7.

Listing 2-7. Combining multiple charts together

```
fig = make_subplots(rows=1, cols=2)

for i in dfPrices.columns:
    fig.add_trace(go.Scatter(y=dfPrices.head(20)[i]), row=1, col=1)

timestamp = 0

fig.add_trace(go.Bar(
    y= ['price-'+'{:.4f}'.format(x) for x in dfPrices.iloc[timestamp].
    tolist()],
    x= dfVolumnes.iloc[timestamp].tolist(),
    orientation='h',
    marker_color=colors
), row=1, col=2)

fig.update_layout(
    title='10 price levels of each side of the orderbook for multiple time
    points, bar size represents volume',
    xaxis_title="Time snapshot",
    yaxis_title="Price levels",
    template='plotly_dark'
)

fig.show()
```

Running the code generates Figure 2-7.

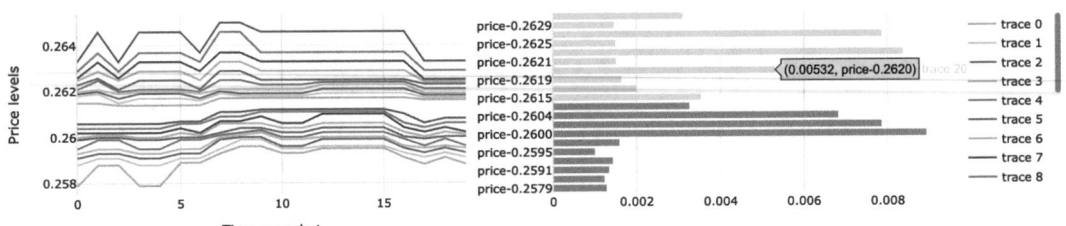

10 price levels of each side of the orderbook for multiple time points, bar size represents volume

Figure 2-7. *Combining the price and volume data for each price level*

Visualizing Price Movement

The price at each price level may move across different timestamps as a reflection of market dynamics. Visualizing the whole times series of the price index may be too granular at first glance, since there are too many observations, given the nature of the ultra high-frequency data. Instead, we can pick a fixed-size window to plot the price at a particular period within the window and then move the window forward in time to show the change in price. The rolling window can then be used to generate an animation of prices moving up and down.

Listing 2-8 achieves the desired plotting effect. Here, we set the window length to 100 and choose the second price level for visualization. The animation is essentially a collection of frames changing from one to another. Thus, we supply the corresponding sequence of data for each frame in the animation.

Listing 2-8. Animating the price movement

```
widthOfTime = 100
priceLevel = 1

fig = go.Figure(
    data=[go.Scatter(x=dfPrices.index[:widthOfTime].tolist(),
    y=dfPrices[:widthOfTime][priceLevel].tolist(),
                    name="frame",
                    mode="lines",
                    line=dict(width=2, color="blue")),
        ],
```

```
      layout=go.Layout(width=1000, height=400,
#                      xaxis=dict(range=[0, 100], autorange=False,
                       zeroline=False),
#                      yaxis=dict(range=[0, 1], autorange=False,
                       zeroline=False),
                   title="10 price levels of each side of the orderbook",
                   xaxis_title="Time snapshot index",
                   yaxis_title="Price levels",
                   template='plotly_dark',
                   hovermode="closest",
                   updatemenus=[dict(type="buttons",
                                     showactive=True,
                                     x=0.01,
                                     xanchor="left",
                                     y=1.15,
                                     yanchor="top",
                                     font={"color":'blue'},
                                     buttons=[dict(label="Play",
                                                   method="animate",
                                                   args=[None])])]),
   frames=[go.Frame(
       data=[go.Scatter(
          x=dfPrices.iloc[k:k+widthOfTime].index.tolist(),
          y=dfPrices.iloc[k:k+widthOfTime][priceLevel].tolist(),
          mode="lines",
          line=dict(color="blue", width=2))
       ]) for k in range(widthOfTime, 1000)]
)

fig.show()
```

Running the code generates Figure 2-8. We can click the Play button to start animating the line chart, which will change shape as we move forward.

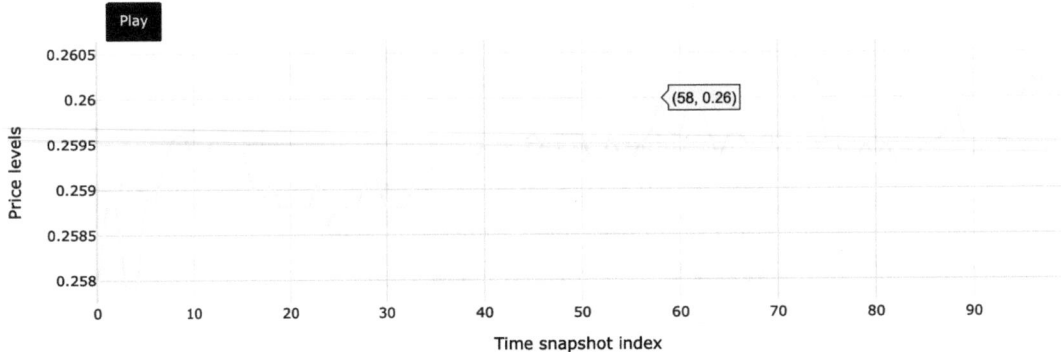

Figure 2-8. *Animating the price changes of a selected price level via a rolling window of 100 timestamps*

In addition, we can also plot the animation of change in the volume across all the price levels, as shown in Listing 2-9. The change in volume also indicates the market dynamics in terms of supply and demand, although less so direct than the price itself.

Listing 2-9. Animating the volume movement

```
timeStampStart = 100

fig = go.Figure(
    data=[go.Bar(y= ['price-'+'{:.4f}'.format(x) for x in
    dfPrices[:timeStampStart].values[0].tolist()],
                x=dfVolumnes[:timeStampStart].values[0].tolist(),
                orientation='h',
                name="priceBar",
                marker_color=colors),
        ],
    layout=go.Layout(width=800, height=450,
                title="Volume of 10 buy, sell price levels of an
                orderbook",
                xaxis_title="Volume",
                yaxis_title="Price levels",
                template='plotly_dark',
                hovermode="closest",
                updatemenus=[dict(type="buttons",
```

```
                         showactive=True,
                         x=0.01,
                         xanchor="left",
                         y=1.15,
                         yanchor="top",
                         font={"color":'blue'},
                         buttons=[dict(label="Play",
                                        method="animate",
                                        args=[None])])]),
    frames=[go.Frame(
        data=[go.Bar(y= ['price-'+'{:.4f}'.format(x) for x in dfPrices.
        iloc[k].values.tolist()],
                    x=dfVolumnes.iloc[k].values.tolist(),
                    orientation='h',
                    marker_color=colors)],
        layout=go.Layout(width=800, height=450,
                    title="Volume of 10 buy, sell price levels of an
                    orderbook [Snapshot=" + str(k) +"]",
                    xaxis_title="Volume",
                    yaxis_title="Price levels",
                    template='plotly_dark',
                    hovermode="closest")) for k in
range(timeStampStart, 500)]
)

fig.show()
```

Running the code generates Figure 2-9.

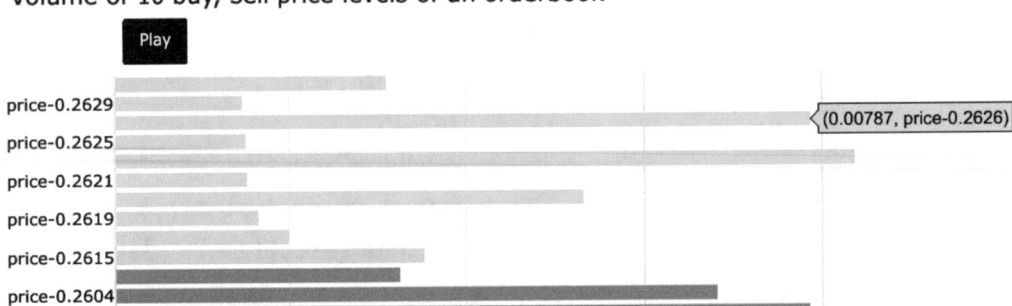

Figure 2-9. *Visualizing the change in the volume across all the price levels*

Summary

In this chapter, we covered the basics of the electronic market and the different types of electronic orders, including market order, stop order, limit order, and other forms of dynamic order (e.g., pegging, trailing stop, market if touched, limit, and cancelation). We discussed the mechanism of the order matching system and order flow.

In the second section, we looked at real LOB data and discussed different ways to visualize the price and volume data, such as their movement across time. Working with the actual data by first plotting them out and performing some initial analysis is a common and important first step in the whole pipeline of devising and implementing trading strategies.

Exercises

- Write a function in Python to illustrate the algorithm of a pegged buy order and sell order. (Hint: Start by defining your own input and output.)

- What's the difference between the market if touched order (MIT) and the stop order?

- How to calculate mid-price in a limit order book? Implement the logic in code. (Hint: Start by defining your own input and output.)

- Describe how a buy trailing stop order works.

- Should the trailing stop-loss order be placed above or below the current market price for an investor in a long position? A short position?

## CHAPTER 3

Forward and Futures Contracts

In financial markets, forward and futures contracts serve as popular financial instruments for hedging risk (preventing or reducing potential loss) and speculation (seeking abnormal and risky profits). These contracts offer market participants the opportunity to mitigate or enlarge the impact of price fluctuations on their positions. The use of forward and futures contracts has grown exponentially over the years, as market participants increasingly recognize their potential benefits in risk management and portfolio diversification. As such, understanding the mechanics, advantages, and limitations of these contracts is essential in the dynamic financial markets.

Forward and futures contracts find their roots in the age-old practice of producers and consumers entering into agreements to exchange goods at a future date for a predetermined price. Today, these contracts become popular financial vehicles traded on a much larger scale, encompassing a wide variety of underlying assets, including commodities, currencies, interest rates, and equity indices. Forwards are typically traded over the counter (OTC) and customized to the specific needs of the counterparties on both sides. Futures contracts are standardized products traded on regulated exchanges, just like stocks. Futures and forward contracts differ in liquidity, counterparty risk, and transparency.

In this chapter, we delve deeper into the world of forward and futures contracts, exploring their unique characteristics, similarities, and differences. We will discuss the process of entering and settling these contracts, their role in managing risk, and the strategies employed by market participants to capitalize on anticipated price movements.

P. Liu, *Quantitative Trading Strategies Using Python*, https://doi.org/10.1007/978-1-4842-9675-2_3

Introducing Forward and Futures Contracts

Forward and futures contracts are very similar in nature. Both obligate the buyer (or seller) to buy (or sell) a predetermined quantity of an underlying asset at a predetermined delivery date and price. Since the price is fixed in advance, market participants can rely on this investment vehicle to better manage their operational activities. For example, a farmer produces wheat and sells the wheat to a food manufacturing company. The wheat price changes every year, causing unexpected fluctuations on both sides of the trade. By entering a forward contract, both sides lock in the trading price and quantity, thus eliminating future uncertainty in the wheat price.

Let us look at the buy side and the sell side when entering a given forward/futures contract. On the buy side, the buyer of the forward/futures contract takes on the obligation to purchase and receive the underlying asset at the time point when the forward/futures contract expires. On the sell side, the seller of the forward/futures contract is obliged to provide and deliver the underlying asset to the buyer at the expiration date.

Both are derivative products because they depend on another underlying asset: grain, livestock, energy, currencies, or even securities. It obliges the buyer to purchase the underlying asset (or the seller to sell that asset) at a predetermined future price and date.

Note that counterparty risk often constitutes the biggest risk in a forward contract. A forward contract can only be rolled forward based on the consent of both parties. Without such consent, the forward contract cannot be exercised afterward; it can only be settled between the two parties at the prespecified date.

Futures contracts are more standardized products when compared to forward contracts. Forwards, which are similar agreements that lock in a future price at the current time, are traded OTC and have customizable terms between the counterparties. On the other hand, futures contracts come with the same terms for all counterparties, thus making futures contracts highly standardized and tradable products. In other words, we can choose to use the contract even before its expiry. For example, we can further buy or sell the contract at any time point before the expiry date, which essentially transfers the contract to another counterparty in the futures market.

Specifically, while forward contracts are tailor-made for the specific needs of the counterparties, a futures contract is a standardized and regulated financial product (in small increments) that allows the investor to buy or sell a particular commodity asset or financial security at a predetermined price and at a specified time in the future over an exchange. It is a fixed-price deal in the future. Futures contracts have standardized features such as contract size, expiration dates, and settlement procedures. This standardization makes futures contracts more accessible and liquid, as they can be easily traded on exchanges. Since the future price for the commodity or security of interest is fixed, there is no risk due to potential fluctuations in the future price. Investors thus often use futures to hedge the risk of big changes in price.

Futures contracts are traded through centralized futures exchanges, which serve as the middleman and eliminate the counterparty risk, that is, one party does not fulfill the obligation required by the futures contract. The counterparty risk exists in the forward contract, which is considered a customized OTC trading instrument and is traded directly between two parties.

In addition, another key difference between forward and futures contracts is the manner in which they are settled. Forward contracts are typically settled through physical delivery of the underlying asset upon expiry, whereas futures contracts can be settled either through physical delivery or cash settlement (more on this later).

Moreover, the role of margin accounts in futures trading is another distinguishing factor between forward and futures contracts. Futures exchanges require both parties to maintain a margin account to cover potential price fluctuations in the underlying asset. This ensures that the parties have sufficient funds to cover their obligations, thereby mitigating the risk of default. In contrast, forward contracts do not involve margin accounts, leaving the parties more exposed to counterparty risk.

In summary, forward and futures contracts are financial instruments that enable market participants to manage risk and speculate on the future prices of underlying assets. Although both instruments share some similarities, they also have key differences in terms of standardization, trading venues, settlement procedures, and risk management. The futures exchange profits by maintaining a spread between the quoted prices from the buyer and the seller of the futures contract. Since the futures contracts are standardized, the futures exchange can add a small margin to them before exposing them to potential buyers while maintaining a lower price for those who short the futures contract. Again, as a measure of protection, the futures exchange also requires both sides of the trade to open and maintain a margin account in case the price of the underlying asset moves against the exchange, such as a drop in price.

Parameters of a Futures Contract

A standardized futures contract features the following four parameters:

- Lot size

- Contract value

- Margin

- Expiration date

Let us look at these parameters in detail. The lot size of a futures contract specifies the quantity of the underlying asset that an investor will have to trade upon entering a futures position. The quantity to be traded in the futures contract must be a predetermined multiple of the minimum quantity. The lot size determines the predefined quantity of the underlying asset to form a single futures contract. This lot size ensures that futures contracts are standardized and easily tradable on exchanges. Take the futures contract of Apple's shares, for example. Say the lot size for Apple's future is 100. Therefore, any futures contract would come in a multiple of 100 shares.

The contract value specifies the total monetary value of the futures contract in terms of the underlying asset, calculated by multiplying the lot size by the current market price of the underlying asset. This value represents the notional exposure of the investor's position in the contract. Suppose Apple stock is trading at $125 per share. Thus, the total contractual value of Apple's futures contract will be equal to $12,500 ($125 × 100), assuming the futures contract obligates the investor to purchase one lot (100 shares) of Apple's stock. The contract value is the product of the lot size and the asset price.

Margin is the amount of deposit from the investor to enter a futures contract position, consisting of an initial margin and a maintenance margin. The initial margin is the initial amount of deposit to open the margin account, and the maintenance margin is the minimum amount required by the futures exchange in order to maintain the futures position and keep it open. Therefore, we do not need the entire contract value to get into a futures position. All we need to do is to deposit the required initial margin of the contract value with the broker to sign the futures contract. The margin is blocked upon entering a futures contract and released upon exiting it. These margins thus help to mitigate counterparty risk and ensure that both parties can fulfill their obligations under the contract.

The expiration date is the date of delivery/settlement for the futures contract, via either physical delivery or cash settlement. Each futures contract is time-bound and ceases to exist after the expiration date. A futures investor needs to close or roll over the futures position on or before the expiration date to avoid settlement.

Understanding these parameters is crucial for investors who wish to trade futures contracts, as they determine the contract's structure, risk profile, and potential return on investment. By carefully considering the lot size, contract value, margin requirements, and expiration date, investors can tailor their futures positions to align with their specific financial goals and risk tolerance.

Hedging and Speculation

There are two purposes when engaging in a futures contract. The first purpose is speculation, as a futures contract allows the investor to speculate on the direction of movement for the underlying asset. The second purpose is hedging, so as to help prevent losses from unfavorable price changes. This constitutes the two types of participants in the market: hedgers and speculators.

Hedging is a common practice for producers and manufacturers who wish to ensure a stable production process by locking the price of products or raw materials in the future. By entering a futures contract to guarantee the price at which the commodity is sold or purchased, hedgers ensure that they transact the commodity at a satisfactory price, thus hedging against any changes in the market.

Hedgers are typically involved in the production, processing, or consumption of the underlying asset, and they use futures contracts to manage their exposure to fluctuations in the asset's price. By locking in a predetermined price for the asset, they can reduce the risk of unexpected price changes impacting their operations or profitability. For example, an airline company might hedge against rising fuel prices by entering into a futures contract to buy oil at a specific price in the future. This ensures that the company's fuel costs remain predictable, regardless of market volatility.

Speculators, in contrast, are primarily interested in profiting from price fluctuations in the underlying asset. Since many commodity prices tend to move in predictable ways, many speculators (traders and fund managers) aim to make a profit by trading futures, even if they do not have a direct interest in the underlying commodity. They do not typically have a direct stake in the production, processing, or consumption of the asset. Instead, they trade futures contracts to capitalize on their market predictions and generate profits. Speculators use futures to bet on the price movement of the underlying asset. This provides liquidity to the futures market, as their trading activity helps to create a market for hedgers to enter and exit positions. By taking on the risk of price changes, speculators can earn a return on their investment if their predictions are accurate.

Obligations at Maturity

There are two types of settlement upon expiration of a futures (and options) contract: physical delivery and cash settlement. Such derivative contracts will either be physically delivered or cash-settled.

The first type is the physical delivery of the underlying asset. A deliverable futures contract stipulates that the buyer in the long position of the futures contract will pay the agreed-upon price to the seller, who in turn will deliver the underlying asset to the buyer on the predetermined date (settlement date of the futures contract). This process is called delivery, where the actual underlying asset needs to be delivered upon the specified delivery date, rather than being traded out with offsetting contracts.

For example, a buyer enters a one-year crude oil futures contract with an opposing seller at a price of $60. We know that one futures contract corresponds to 1000 barrels of crude oil. This means the buyer is obligated to purchase 1000 barrels of crude oil from the seller, regardless of the commodity's spot price on the settlement date. If the spot price of the crude oil on the agreed settlement date one year later is below $58, the long contract holder loses a total of ($60 – $58) × $1000 = $2000, and the short position holder gains $2000. Conversely, if the spot price rises to $65 per barrel, the long position holder gains ($65 – $60) × $1000 = $5000, and the short position holder loses $5000.

The second type is cash settlement. When a futures contract is cash-settled, the net cash position of the contract on the expiry date is transferred between the buyer and the seller. It permits the buyer and seller to pay the net cash value of the position on the delivery date.

Take the previous case, for example. When the spot price of the crude oil drops to $58, the long position holder will lose $2000, which happens by debiting $2000 from the buyer's account and crediting this amount to the seller's account. On the other hand, when the spot price rises to $65, the account of the long position holder will be credited $5000, which comes from debiting the account of the short position holder.

It is important to understand that the majority of futures contracts are not held until maturity, and most participants in the futures market do not actually take or make delivery of the underlying asset. Instead, they are traded out before the settlement date. Traders and investors often choose to close their positions before the contract's expiration date to avoid the obligations associated with physical delivery or cash settlement. This can be achieved by entering into an offsetting transaction that effectively cancels out the original position. For example, a trader with a long position in a futures contract can sell an identical contract to offset the position, while a trader with a short position can buy an identical contract to close the position.

The process of closing out a futures position before maturity is a common practice in the market, as it allows participants to lock in gains or limit losses without having to deal with the actual delivery or cash settlement of the underlying asset. This flexibility is one of the key features of futures trading, as it enables market participants to manage their risk exposure and capitalize on market opportunities efficiently.

In conclusion, while futures contracts carry obligations at maturity in the form of physical delivery or cash settlement, most participants in the futures market choose to close their positions before the expiration date. By engaging in offsetting transactions, traders and investors can effectively manage their risk exposure and profit from price movements in the underlying asset without having to deal with the logistics of taking or making the delivery.

Leverage in a Futures Contract

As we already know, we only need to deposit a certain margin in the margin account to enter a futures contract. This means that high leverage can be used in the futures market. The higher the leverage, the higher the risk, and the higher the potential profit.

Let us continue with the previous example. Say we enter a futures contract on Apple's stock that allows us to buy 100 shares at $125 per share, with an initial margin of $1000. The total contract value is $125 \times 100 = \$12,500$. If the stock price goes up to $140, the contract value becomes $140 \times 100 = \$14,000$, with the additional $1,500 amount credited to our margin account due to daily settlement. We made a profit of $1,000 by blocking an initial deposit of $1,000.

Suppose now the price of Apple's stock goes down to $110. The total contract value becomes $110 \times 100 = \$11,000$, registering a loss of $1500. We would get a margin call to deposit another ($1000 – $1500 + $1500) = $1000 to bring it back to the amount required by the initial margin.

Leverage is a double-edged sword in the futures market, as it can amplify both gains and losses. It allows investors and traders to control a larger contract value with a smaller amount of capital through the use of margin. While leverage can significantly increase potential profits, it can also lead to substantial losses if the market moves against the trader's position.

When utilizing leverage, it is crucial for market participants to employ proper risk management strategies to protect their capital. This may involve using stop-loss orders to limit potential losses or closely monitoring the position to ensure the margin requirements are met. Clearly, this is a zero-sum game. Money moves from the losers to the winners on a daily basis. The profit made by the buyer is equivalent to the loss made by the seller and vice versa.

Clearing House

Farmers who sell futures contracts do not sell directly to the buyers. Rather, they sell to the clearing house of the futures exchange. As a designated intermediary between a buyer and seller in the financial market, the clearing house validates and finalizes each transaction, ensuring that both the buyer and the seller honor their contractual obligations. The clearing house thus guarantees that all of the traders in the futures market will honor their obligations, thus avoiding potential counterparty risk.

The clearing house serves this role by adopting the buyer's position to every seller and the seller's position to every buyer. Every trader in the futures market has obligations only to the clearing house. The clearing house takes no active position in the market, but interposes itself between all parties to every transaction. As the middleman, the clearing house provides the security and efficiency integral to financial market stability. So as far as the farmers are concerned, they can sell their goods to the clearing house at the price of the futures contract when the contract expires.

The clearing house will then match and confirm the details of the trades executed on the exchange, including the contract size, price, and expiration date, ensuring that all parties have accurate and consistent information. Order matching and confirmation is thus one of the main roles of a clearing house.

The clearing house of the futures market also has a margin requirement, which is a sum of the deposit that serves as the minimum maintenance margin for the (clearing) member of the exchange. All members of an exchange are required to clear their trades through the clearing house at the end of each trading session and satisfy the margin requirement to cover the corresponding minimum balance requirement. Otherwise, the member will receive a margin call to top up the remaining balance when the margin account runs low due to fluctuation in asset price. Clearing houses thus collect and monitor margin requirements from their members, ensuring that all participants have sufficient collateral to cover potential losses. This helps to maintain the financial stability of the market and reduces the likelihood of default.

Figure 3-1 illustrates the clearing house as a middle party between the buyer and the seller.

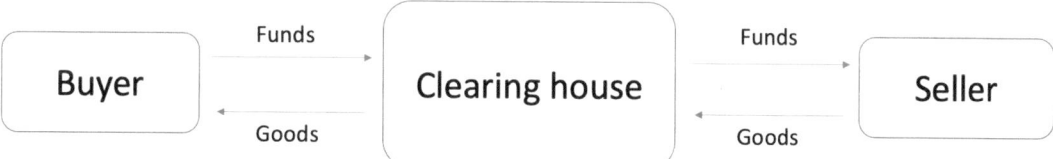

Figure 3-1. *Illustrating the role of the clearing house as an intermediary between buyers and sellers in a futures market*

Mark-to-Market

Mark-to-market involves updating the price of a futures contract to reflect its current market value rather than the book value, so as to ensure that margin requirements are being met. If the current market value of the futures contract causes the margin account to fall below its required level, the trader will receive a margin call from the exchange to top up the remaining balance.

Mark-to-market is a process of pricing futures contracts at the end of every trading day. Made to accounts with open futures positions, the cash adjustment in mark-to-market reflects the day's profit or loss, based on the settlement price of the product, and is determined by the exchange. Since mark-to-market adjustments affect the cash balance in a futures account, the margin requirement for the account is being assessed on a daily basis to continue holding an open position.

Let us look at a mark-to-market example and understand the daily change in the price of the futures contract due to fluctuating prices in the underlying asset. First, note the two counterparties on either side of a futures contract, that is, a long position trader and a short position trader. The long trader goes bullish as the underlying asset is expected to increase in price, while the trader shorting the contract is considered bearish due to the expected drop in the price of the underlying asset.

The futures contract may go up or down in value at the end of the trading day. When its price goes up, the long margin account increases in value due to mark-to-market, with the daily gain credit to the margin account of the long position trader. Correspondingly, the short position trader on the opposing side will suffer a loss of an equal amount, which is debited from the margin account.

Similarly, when the price of the futures contract goes down, the long margin account decreases in value due to mark-to-market, with the daily loss debited from the margin account of the long position trader. This amount will be credited to the margin account of the short position trader, who will realize a gain of an equal amount.

By updating the price of a futures contract to reflect its current market value, the exchange can monitor the risk exposure of traders in real time. This helps to ensure that margin requirements are being met and that traders have enough funds to cover their positions, which essentially reduces risk exposure to the traders. This also allows traders to accurately assess their profit or loss and make informed decisions about their positions.

Figure 3-2 illustrates the two types of traders with an open position in the same futures contract and their respective profit and loss due to mark-to-market.

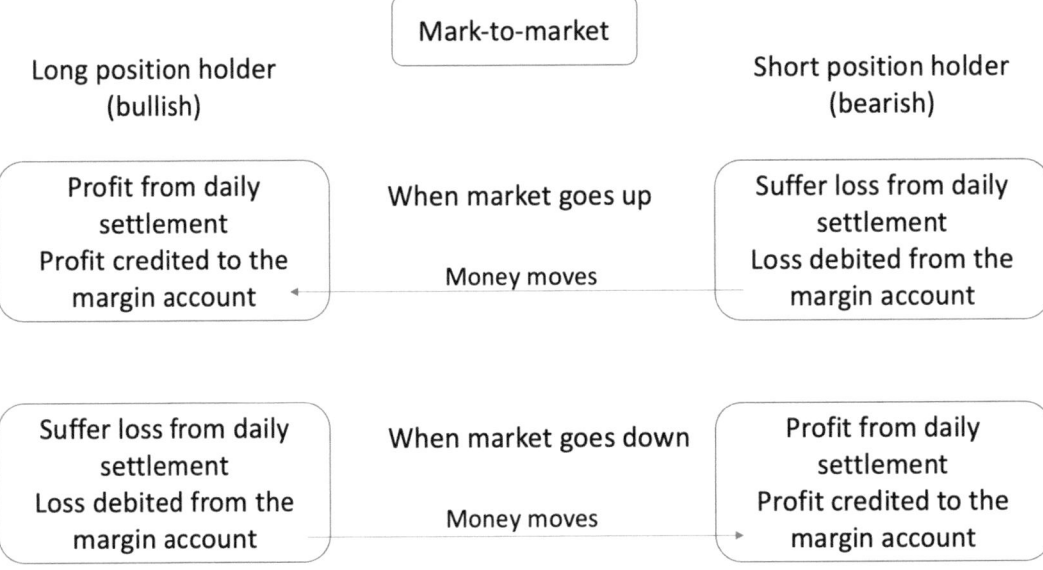

Figure 3-2. *Illustrating the mark-to-market process and the resulting effect on the margin account of long and short position traders for the same futures contract*

To better understand the daily dynamics for traders of different positions as a result of the daily mark-to-market exercise by the exchange, let us look at a concrete example. As shown in Figure 3-3, we plot the daily amount of the margin account for both the long and short position holders. The initial amount in the margin account is $100 for both traders. Given the increase in asset value on day 1, a $5 increase in the margin account of the long position holder is realized ($100 + $5 = $105), while a $5 decrease for the short position holder enters ($100 − $5 = $95). On day 2, the net change is −$20 for the long position margin account, bringing it from $105 to $85, lower than the minimum requirement (called maintenance margin) of $90. The long position trader then gets a margin call from the exchange and tops up $15 to increase their margin account to $100, based on the required initial amount. The short position trader benefits a total of $20, ending with an end-of-day amount of $115 in their margin account.

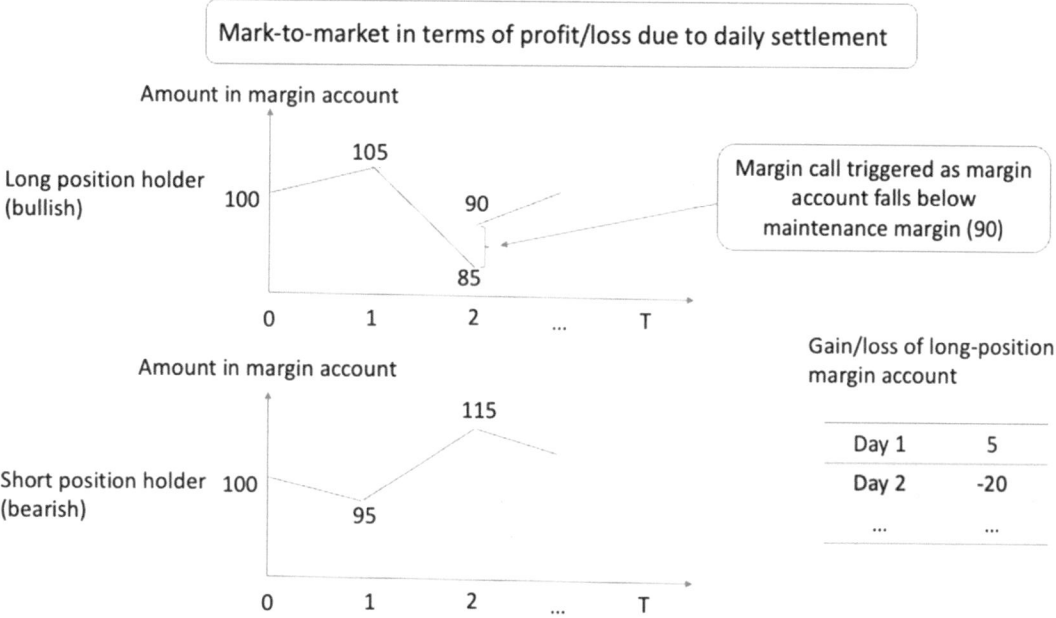

Figure 3-3. *An example of daily changes in the margin account of long and short position traders due to mark-to-market*

Note that the margin account changes the balance daily due to gain/loss from mark-to-market exercise. Although the final settlement price at the delivery date could be different from the intended price upon entering the futures position, the traders on both sides would still end up transacting at an effective price equal to the initially intended price, thus hedging the risk of price fluctuations.

Now let us look at how to price this derivative product, starting with its similar twin: forward contract.

Pricing Forward Contract

A forward contract is a customizable contract between two parties to buy or sell an asset at a specified price on a future date. Different from the futures contract, whose price is settled on a daily basis until the end of the contract, a forward contract is only settled at the end of the agreement and is traded over the counter. Therefore, it is easier to price.

The price of a forward contract is the predetermined delivery price for the underlying asset decided by the buyer and the seller. This is the price to be paid at a predetermined date in the future and is determined by the following formula:

$$F_0 = S_0 e^{rT}$$

where F_0 is the price of the forward contract at the current time point $t = 0$, and S_0 is the price of the underlying asset at $t = 0$. r is the risk-free bond interest rate, the theoretical rate of return of an investment with zero risk. T is the duration from the current time point $t = 0$ to the expiration date $t = T$. More generally, we can write the price of the forward contract as follows:

$$F_t = S_t e^{r(T-t)}$$

Here, multiplying the exponential constant simply means increasing the price of the forward contract, depending on the baseline interest rate r and the duration $T - t$ in a continuously compounding scheme. In other words, suppose we deposit $1000 in a bank, which promises a continuously compounded interest rate of r. We can thus expect to see the total value of the deposit grow to $1000e^r$ at the end of year 1, $1000e^{2r}$ at the end of year 2, etc. This is a common way of compounding in finance and accounting.

Now let us look at how this formula comes into shape. The reasoning follows the no-arbitrage argument, which says there is no arbitrage opportunity to make any riskless profit, no matter how the price of the underlying asset changes. Suppose we enter into a long forward contract that obligates us to buy the asset S at time T for a price of F_T. We are living at the current time point t, where the spot price of the asset is S_t, and the future price of the asset will be S_T. The nature of the agreement fixes the action for us at the delivery date; thus, we need to pay an amount of F_T to purchase the asset valued at S_T. In other words, our net profit/loss (P&L) at time T is $-F_T + S_T$, where the negative sign means cash outflow. Note that this happens in the future at time T and not yet for now at time t.

However, there is a risk involved upon entering this contract. Since the asset price fluctuates in the future, the asset price may drop a lot due to unforeseen circumstances in the future, leading to a very negative P&L upon delivery. Although the opposite could also be true and the final P&L could be very positive, this still poses a potential risk, especially for market participants such as farmers and manufacturers mentioned earlier.

To hedge this risk, we could short one unit of this asset at time t, since we know that a short position makes a profit if the asset price drops. A short position in the underlying asset profits us from losses in the future due to a decrease in the future asset price. It is one unit of the underlying asset because we can use the exact one unit of the asset bought based on the forward agreement to close the initial short position in the underlying asset, that is, return the asset back to where we borrowed it from.

Now we look at the process in more detail. Upon entering the short position of one unit of the underlying asset at time t, we obtain a cash inflow of S_t, as shorting means selling an asset and buying it back later. This means that we will have a cash outflow of S_T at the delivery date to pay back the asset and close the short position.

Note that the cash S_t at time t will not sit idle. Instead, we will invest the cash, such as depositing t in the bank to enjoy a risk-free interest rate. The money will grow to $S_t e^{r(T-t)}$ upon reaching the delivery date, with an investment period of $T - t$. This investment will be used to cover the short position in the underlying asset.

Figure 3-4 summarizes the positions in different products and the total portfolio value with the evolution of time. Here, we have three different products in our portfolio: a forward contract, an asset (e.g., one share of stock), and cash. These three constitute our portfolio, and we start with zero value in the portfolio at time t. To see this, we observe that the forward position is zero at time t since we only make the transaction upon reaching the delivery date. The stock position gives $-S_t$ since we are shorting the stock, and the cash position gives S_t, the income generated by shorting the stock. Adding up the value of these three positions gives zero value for the portfolio at time t. The net cash flow at time t is zero.

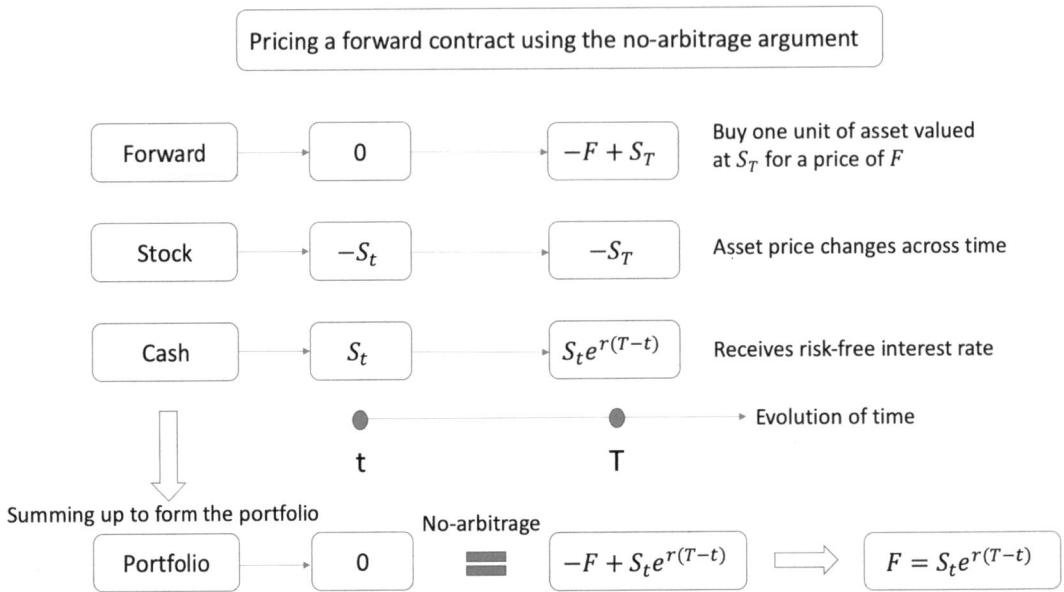

Figure 3-4. *Pricing the forward contract in a long position using the no-arbitrage argument. The stock and cash positions also constitute a replicating portfolio that offsets the randomness in the payoff function of the forward contract at the delivery date*

As time passes by, the value of each position will evolve. Specifically, the forward position becomes $-F + S_T$ since we would buy one asset valued at S_T for a price of F. Our stock position becomes $-S_T$ due to change in the stock price, and cash position becomes $S_t e^{r(T-t)}$.

Now, using the no-arbitrage argument, we would end up with zero value in our portfolio since we started with zero value. Adding the value of the three positions at time T gives the total portfolio value of $-F + S_t e^{r(T-t)}$. And by equating it to zero, we have $F = S_t e^{r(T-t)}$, thus completing the pricing of the forward contract using the no-arbitrage argument.

This is the formula for the price of a forward contract. It demonstrates that the forward price is determined by the current price of the underlying asset, the risk-free interest rate, and the time until the contract expires. By using this formula, both parties in a forward contract can agree on a fair price that eliminates arbitrage opportunities and reflects the true value of the underlying asset.

It is interesting to note that the stock and cash positions jointly constitute a replicating portfolio that offsets the randomness in the payoff function of the forward contract at the delivery date. This means that no matter what the price of the forward contract will be in the future, we will always be able to use another replicating portfolio to deliver the same payoff, *as if* we were in a position of the forward contract. This is called pricing by replication.

Let us see what happens if the price of the forward is not equal to the stock price with a continuously compounded interest rate. We can argue about arbitrage opportunities based on the riskless profit from the buy-low-sell-high principle. When $F > S_t e^{r(T-t)}$, we can borrow an amount of S_t and use the money to short a forward contract that allows us to sell one unit of the underlying asset at price F. Upon reaching the delivery date, we receive a total of F by selling the asset, pay back the borrowed money with interest $S_t e^{r(T-t)}$, and earn a net profit of $F - S_t e^{r(T-t)}$. This is arbitrage, where we made a riskless profit by taking advantage of the price difference at the future time T.

Similarly, when $F < S_t e^{r(T-t)}$, the forward contract is cheaper, and the asset is more expensive. In that case, we again exercise the buy-low-sell-high principle by longing a forward contract at time t that allows us to buy one unit of the underlying asset at price F and time T. We will also short one unit of the underlying asset at time t to gain a total amount of S_t, which further grows to $S_t e^{r(T-t)}$ upon reaching the delivery date. When the contract expires, we will close the short position in the underlying asset by purchasing one unit of the asset for a price of F. We get to keep the remaining balance $S_t e^{r(T-t)} - F$, thus also establishing the arbitrage argument and ensuring a riskless profit.

Note that the futures price is equal to the spot price of the underlying asset at the current time t. To see this, simply set $T = t$ and we have $F = S_t e^{r(t-t)} = S_t$.

In a nutshell, the future net cash flow predetermined or fixed in advance (today) must equal today's net cash flow to annihilate arbitrage opportunities. The no-arbitrage argument gives a fair price for the forward contract.

Pricing Futures Contract

The futures contract is priced in a similar way as the forward contract but involves a few more factors. Ultimately, the futures contract price is set by the supply and demand in the market. When a seller and a buyer agree on an equilibrium price for transacting a futures contract, that price is the futures contract price.

Say we would like to price the futures contract at the next month (front month). Also, assume that we enter a short position in the futures contract, obliged to sell one unit of the underlying asset at the expiration date. The extra factors to consider here are the cost and benefit of holding the asset until expiration.

For the cost of carrying the asset until the delivery date, we need to add it to the price of the futures contract since it poses an actual cost we need to factor in from entering the position all the way to the delivery date. For example, if we short a futures contract to sell 1000 barrels of oil at time T, we would borrow money to purchase 1000 barrels of oil from the spot market at time t so that we can fulfill the obligation at time T. Doing so requires storing these 1000 barrels of oil, which incurs a storage cost to be added to the price of the futures contract.

For the benefit of carrying the asset until the delivery date, we need to minus it from the futures contract price. This is called the convenience yield, where the party holding the underlying asset gains benefits through the course until the delivery date. Such a situation usually happens when holding the actual asset is preferred. For example, holding stocks may generate dividends payment, holding currencies may generate profits due to differences in the interest rate, and holding commodities is preferred when the market is in short supply of such commodities.

Building on top of the spot price with interest compounding, the fair price of the futures contract can be calculated via the following formula:

Fair price = spot price with compounded interest + cost of storage – convenience yield due to holding the asset

When the interest, cost, and convenience yield are all annually compounded, the fair price of the forward contract can be calculated via the following formula:

$$F = S_t \left(1 + r + s - c\right)^{T-t}$$

where S_t is the spot price of the underlying asset, r is the risk-free bond interest rate, s is the storage cost in percentage and compounded annually, and c is the convenience yield also in percentage and compounded annually. We raise it to the power of the duration $T - t$ to show the compounding effect in this period.

This formula shows that the futures contract price considers several factors: the spot price of the underlying asset, the risk-free interest rate, the storage cost, and the convenience yield. These components help market participants to determine a fair price for the futures contract, reflecting the true value of the underlying asset while accounting for the costs and benefits of holding the asset until the delivery date.

The futures contract price is essential for both buyers and sellers, as it determines their potential profits or losses when they enter into a futures contract. By understanding how the futures contract price is calculated, market participants can make informed decisions about whether to enter into a futures contract and at what price.

It's also important to note that the fair price of the futures contract is a theoretical value. In reality, the actual futures contract price in the market is influenced by supply and demand dynamics, which can cause the market price to deviate from the fair price. Market participants need to continuously monitor the futures market, paying attention to the changes in the underlying asset's spot price, interest rates, storage costs, and convenience yields, in order to adapt the strategies and make informed decisions about the futures contract positions.

Let us look at an example. Suppose the current spot price is $S_t = \$80$, the interest rate is $r = 2\%$, the storage cost is $s = 1\%$, the convenience yield is $c = 0.5\%$, and the position in the futures contract is three months. Since the compounding is done on an annual basis, we need to convert the duration to a yearly term, making $T - t = \dfrac{3}{12} = 0.25$. Therefore, the fair price of the futures contract can be calculated as

$$F = 80\left(1 + 0.02 + 0.01 - 0.005\right)^{0.25} = \$80.5$$

Figure 3-5 summarizes the process of calculating the fair price of a futures contract.

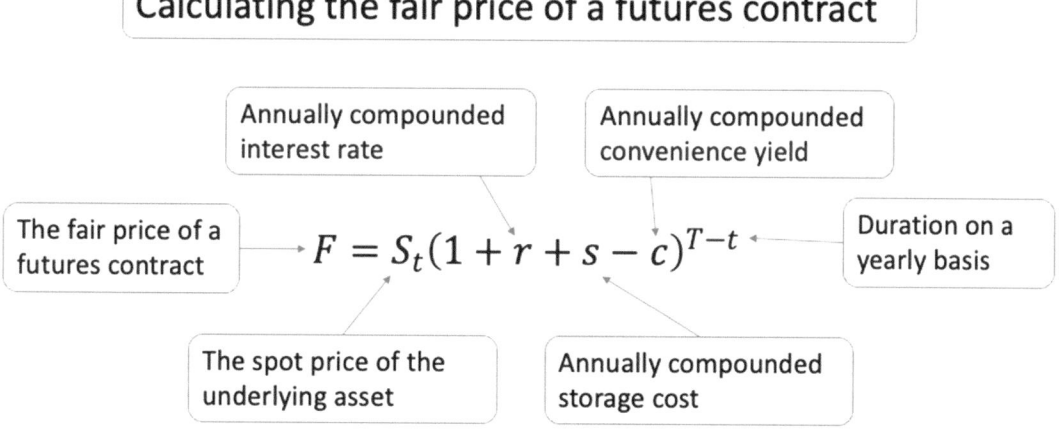

Calculating the fair price of a futures contract

$$F = S_t(1 + r + s - c)^{T-t}$$

- Annually compounded interest rate
- Annually compounded convenience yield
- The fair price of a futures contract
- Duration on a yearly basis
- The spot price of the underlying asset
- Annually compounded storage cost

Figure 3-5. *Calculating the fair price of a futures contract with an annually compounded interest rate, storage cost, and convenience yield*

Contango and Backwardation

There are a few extra terms often used in the futures world. These terms are listed as follows, where the contango is sort of the opposite of backwardation:

- Contango: The futures contract price is higher than the current spot price of the underlying asset.

- Normal contango: The futures contract price is higher than the expected spot price of the underlying asset.

- Backwardation: The futures contract price is lower than the current spot price of the underlying asset.

- Normal backwardation: The futures contract price is lower than the expected spot price of the underlying asset.

A close look into these terms helps us better understand the price dynamics of the futures contract. Let us start with contango. When we say the market for a specific futures contract is in contango, what this means is that we have an upward-sloping futures price curve. Here, the futures price curve specifies the (increasing) price of a futures contract with different delivery dates, at the current time snapshot. A futures contract with a longer duration is more expensive than another with a shorter duration. In addition, when we say the market is in normal contango, this means that the futures price is higher than the (theoretical) expected spot price. Different price points along the futures price curve correspond to different paths of price movements across time, with the final settlement price of the futures contract converging with the spot price at the same (future) delivery date.

The existence of contango or backwardation can have various underlying reasons. For instance, storage costs, seasonality, market expectations, and macroeconomic factors can all contribute to the formation of these pricing patterns in the futures market.

Contango is commonly observed in commodities markets where there are costs associated with holding and storing the underlying assets, such as oil or grain. These costs are factored into the futures contract price, causing it to be higher than the current spot price. Contango can also arise when market participants expect the underlying asset's price to rise in the future, causing them to bid up the price of longer-dated futures contracts.

Backwardation, on the other hand, can occur when market participants believe that the underlying asset's price will decline in the future. This could be due to a forecasted decrease in demand or an anticipated increase in supply. In such cases, market participants might be more willing to sell futures contracts at a lower price than the current spot price, as they expect the spot price to drop in the future.

Figure 3-6 provides an example to help put these statements in perspective. Here, we have two futures contracts with one and two months before the delivery date, respectively. A market in contango means an upward-trending price curve for the futures contracts as the duration gets longer, as shown on the left panel of the figure. As the asset price starts to move across time, as shown by the curve starting with the orange dot, the futures contract price will gradually approach the spot price. Eventually, the futures price will be equal to the spot price when the delivery date is the current date.

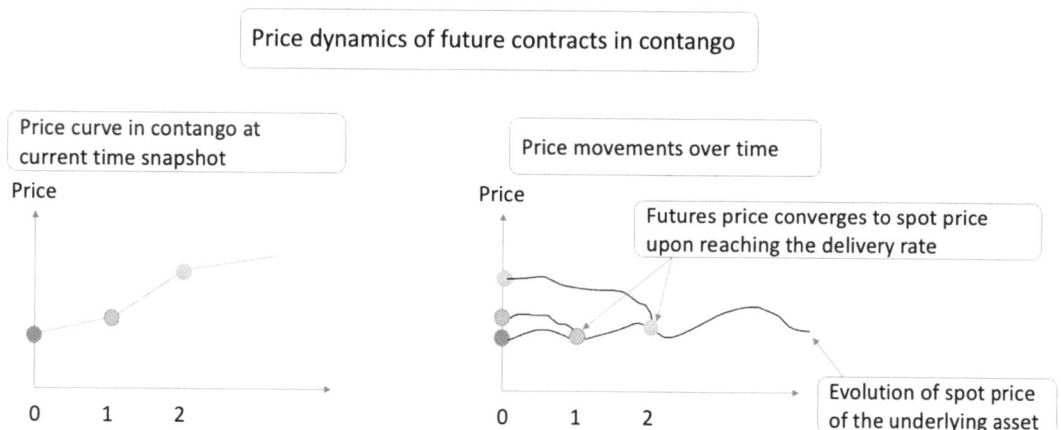

Figure 3-6. *Illustrating the price dynamics of the futures contract in contango. The left panel shows the price curve at the current time point, where a futures contract with a longer delivery date is more expensive. The right panel shows the price evolution of the asset and futures contract with different delivery dates, each converging to the spot price upon reaching the respective delivery date*

Correspondingly, a market in backwardation displays the opposite behavior, as shown in Figure 3-7.

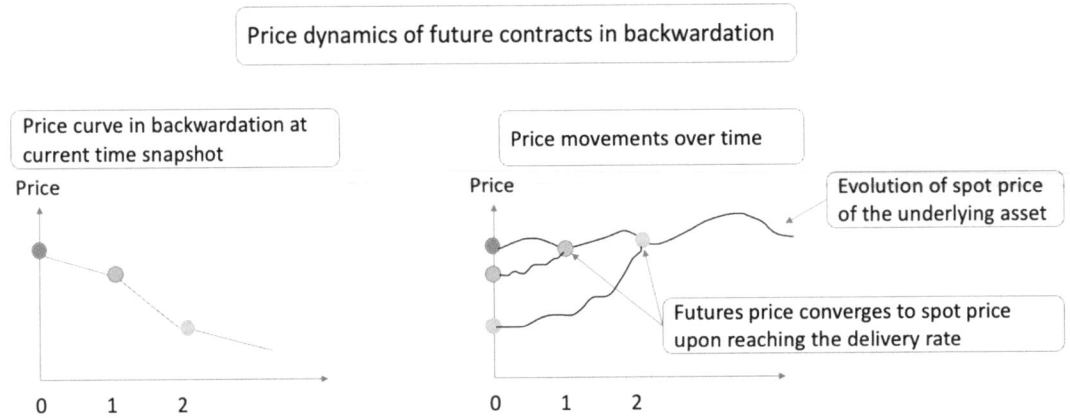

Figure 3-7. *Illustrating the price dynamics of the futures contract in backwardation*

Working with Futures Data

We can retrieve futures data using the yfinance package. In Listing 3-1, we download futures data on platinum for the year 2022. Note that the symbol is "PL=F". After downloading the dataset, we rewrite the index to the datetime format so that it facilitates plotting, as shown in Listing 3-1.

Listing 3-1. Downloading futures data

```
# For data manipulation
import pandas as pd

# To fetch financial data
import yfinance as yf

# For visualisation
import matplotlib.pyplot as plt
plt.style.use('seaborn-darkgrid')
%matplotlib inline

# Download the platinum prices
futures_data = yf.download("PL=F", start="2022-01-01", end="2022-12-31")

# Set the index to a datetime type
futures_data.index = pd.to_datetime(futures_data.index)
```

Let us plot the closing price via Listing 3-2. Note the use of the `fontsize` argument in adjusting the font size in the figure.

Listing 3-2. Visualizing the futures data

```
# Plot the close price
plt.figure(figsize=(15, 7))
futures_data['Adj Close'].plot()

# Set labels and sizes of the title and axis
plt.title('Platinum Futures Data', fontsize=16)
plt.xlabel('Year', fontsize=15)
plt.ylabel('Price ($)', fontsize=15)
plt.xticks(fontsize=15)
plt.yticks(fontsize=15)
plt.legend(['Close'], prop={'size': 15})

# Show the plot
plt.show()
```

Running this command generates Figure 3-8.

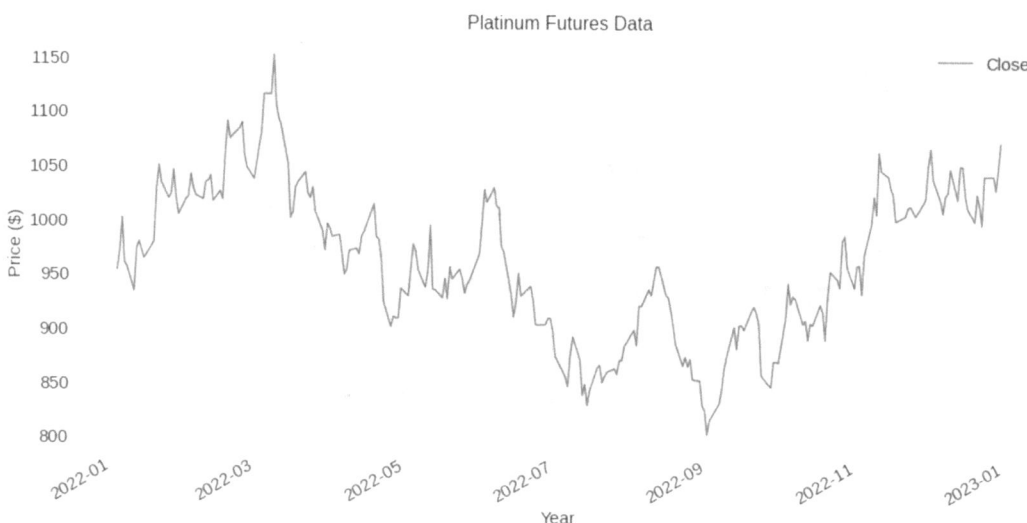

Figure 3-8. *Visualizing the closing price of platinum futures data in 2022*

We can also download multiple futures contracts in one shot. In Listing 3-3, we download the futures data for gold and copper, using the "GC=F" and "HG=F" symbols, respectively, followed by formatting the index and printing the last five rows.

Listing 3-3. Downloading multiple futures

```
# Fetch gold and copper futures prices
futures_data = yf.download(["GC=F","HG=F"], start="2022-01-01",
end="2022-12-31", group_by= 'tickers')

# Set the index to a datetime type
futures_data.index = pd.to_datetime(futures_data.index)

# Display the last five rows
futures_data.tail()
```

Note that the DataFrame has two levels of columns, with the first level specifying the symbol name and the second one showing the different price points.

Similarly, we can plot the closing price of the two sets of futures data, as shown in Listing 3-4.

Listing 3-4. Visualizing multiple futures time series

```
# Set the figure size
ax = plt.figure(figsize=(15, 7))

# Plot both futures close prices
ax = futures_data['GC=F']['Close'].plot(label='Gold Futures')
ax2 = futures_data['HG=F']['Close'].plot(secondary_y=True,
color='g',  ax=ax, label='Copper Futures')

# Set the title and axis labels and sizes
plt.title('Gold and Copper Futures Data', fontsize=16)
ax.set_xlabel('Year-Month', fontsize=15)
ax.set_ylabel('Gold Price ($)', fontsize=15)
ax2.set_ylabel('Copper Price ($)', fontsize=15)
ax.tick_params(axis='both', labelsize=15)
ax2.tick_params(axis='y', labelsize=15)
h1, l1 = ax.get_legend_handles_labels()
```

```
h2, l2 = ax2.get_legend_handles_labels()
ax.legend(h1+h2, l1+l2, loc=2, prop={'size': 15})

# Show the plot
plt.show()
```

Running this command generates Figure 3-9.

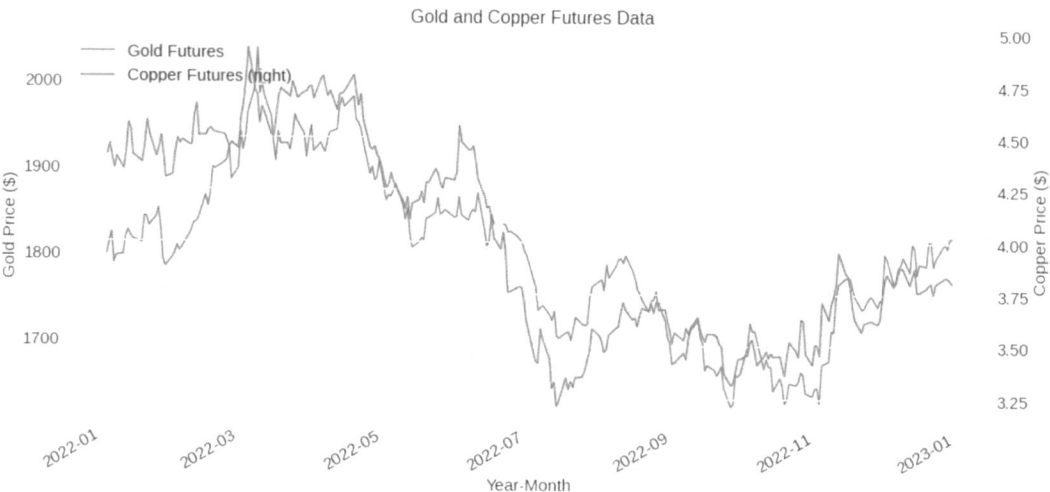

Figure 3-9. *Visualizing the closing price of gold and copper futures data in 2022*

Adding Technical Indicators

In this section, we will look at the popular S&P 500 E-Mini futures contract and discuss how to add common technical indicators to aid technical analysis. The S&P 500 E-Mini futures contract is a financial derivative product that tracks the performance of the S&P 500 index, which represents the 500 largest publicly traded companies in the United States. The E-Mini futures contract is a smaller version of the standard S&P 500 futures contract, making it more accessible and affordable for individual traders and investors.

Let us fetch the daily futures data for this specific contract using the symbol "ES=F" for the full year of 2022, as shown in Listing 3-5.

Listing 3-5. Downloading S&P 500 E-Mini futures data

```
futures_symbol = "ES=F"
futures_data = yf.download(futures_symbol, start="2022-01-01",
end="2022-04-01", interval="1d")
```

Now let us calculate a few technical indicators using the ta library. In this example, we will calculate the Relative Strength Index (RSI), Bollinger Bands, and MACD (Moving Average Convergence Divergence). The following list briefly describes these popular technical indicators:

> Relative Strength Index (RSI): RSI is a momentum oscillator that measures the speed and change of price movements. The RSI oscillates between 0 and 100, and traders often consider an asset overbought when the RSI is above 70 and oversold when it's below 30.

> Bollinger Bands: Bollinger Bands are a volatility indicator that measures the standard deviation of price changes. The indicator consists of three lines: the middle line (a simple moving average) and two outer lines (upper and lower bands) plotted at a specified number of standard deviations away from the moving average. When the bands widen, it indicates increased volatility, and when they narrow, it signifies decreased volatility. Prices often move between the upper and lower bands.

> Moving Average Convergence Divergence (MACD): MACD is a momentum indicator that shows the relationship between two moving averages of an asset's price. It consists of two lines: the MACD line (difference between short-term and long-term moving averages) and the signal line (a moving average of the MACD line). When the MACD line crosses above the signal line, it may suggest a bullish signal (buy), and when it crosses below the signal line, it may indicate a bearish signal (sell). Additionally, when the MACD line is above zero, it suggests an upward momentum, while below zero indicates a downward momentum.

Listing 3-6 calculates these technical indicators and concatenates them to the DataFrame.

Listing 3-6. Calculating common technical indicators

```
# Calculate RSI
futures_data["RSI"] = ta.momentum.RSIIndicator(futures_data["Close"]).rsi()

# Calculate Bollinger Bands
bbands = ta.volatility.BollingerBands(futures_data["Close"])
futures_data["BB_upper"] = bbands.bollinger_hband()
futures_data["BB_lower"] = bbands.bollinger_lband()

# Calculate MACD
macd = ta.trend.MACD(futures_data["Close"])
futures_data["MACD"] = macd.macd()
futures_data["MACD_signal"] = macd.macd_signal()
```

Now we can plot the raw futures time series data together with the technical indicators to facilitate analysis, as shown in Listing 3-7.

Listing 3-7. Visualizing futures data and technical indicators

```
# Create subplots for each indicator
fig, axes = plt.subplots(4, 1, figsize=(10, 15), sharex=True)

# Plot closing price
axes[0].plot(futures_data.index, futures_data["Close"], label="Close")
axes[0].set_title("S&P 500 E-Mini Futures - Closing Price")
axes[0].grid()

# Plot RSI
axes[1].plot(futures_data.index, futures_data["RSI"], label="RSI",
color="g")
axes[1].axhline(30, linestyle="--", color="r", alpha=0.5)
axes[1].axhline(70, linestyle="--", color="r", alpha=0.5)
axes[1].set_title("Relative Strength Index (RSI)")
axes[1].grid()
```

```
# Plot Bollinger Bands
axes[2].plot(futures_data.index, futures_data["Close"], label="Close")
axes[2].plot(futures_data.index, futures_data["BB_upper"], label="Upper
Bollinger Band", linestyle="--", color="r")
axes[2].plot(futures_data.index, futures_data["BB_lower"], label="Lower
Bollinger Band", linestyle="--", color="r")
axes[2].set_title("Bollinger Bands")
axes[2].grid()

# Plot MACD
axes[3].plot(futures_data.index, futures_data["MACD"], label="MACD",
color="b")
axes[3].plot(futures_data.index, futures_data["MACD_signal"], label="Signal
Line", linestyle="--", color="r")
axes[3].axhline(0, linestyle="--", color="k", alpha=0.5)
axes[3].set_title("Moving Average Convergence Divergence (MACD)")
axes[3].grid()
```

Running the code generates Figure 3-10.

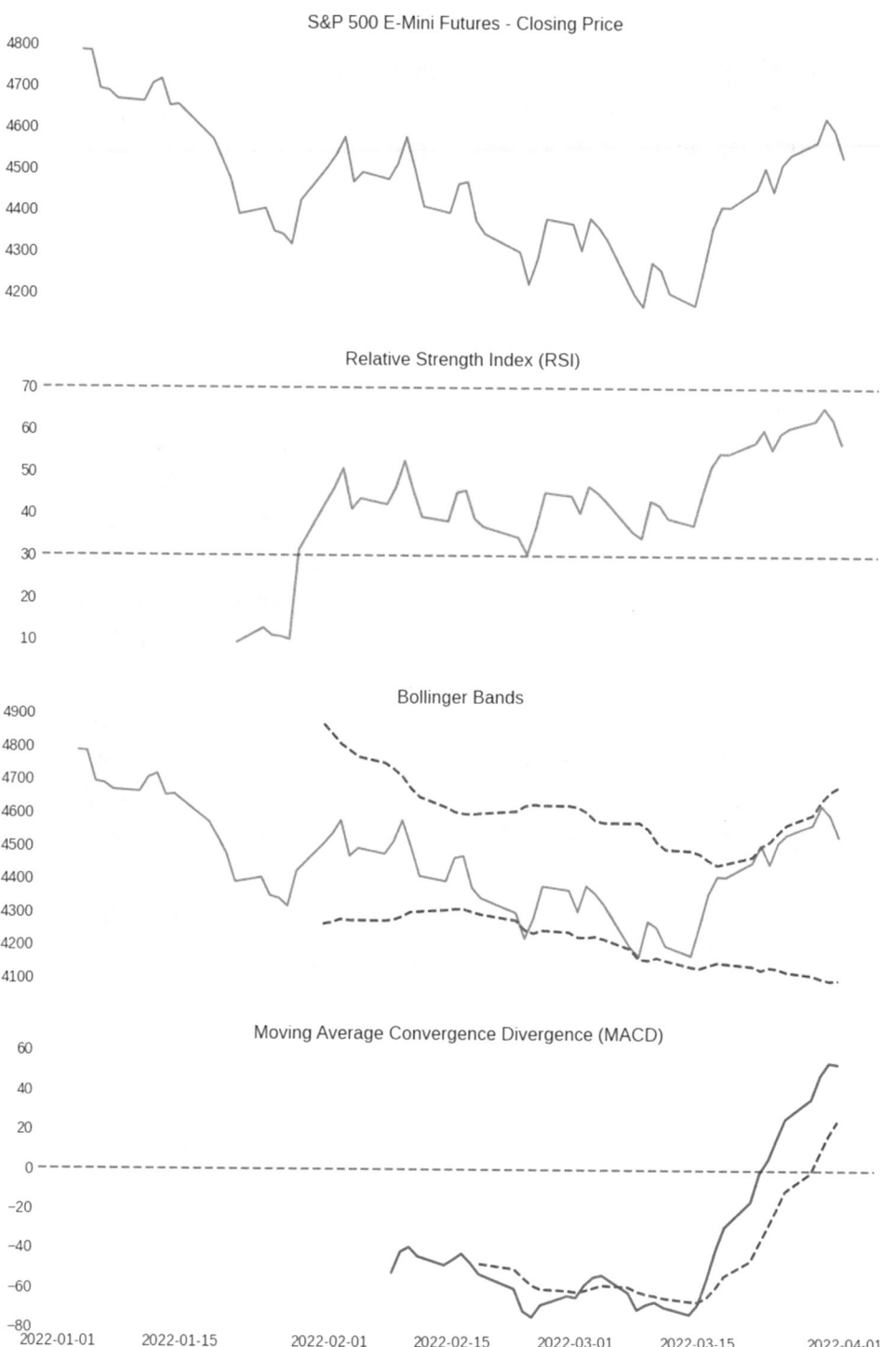

Figure 3-10. *Visualizing futures data and technical indicators*

We can plot a few things here. In the plotted RSI chart, we can observe periods when the RSI crossed below 30, which might signal potentially oversold conditions. Traders may use these signals to consider entering or exiting positions. In the plotted chart on Bollinger Bands, we can see periods when the price touched or crossed the bands, which may indicate potential trend reversals or support and resistance levels. In the MACD chart, we can observe periods when the MACD line crossed the signal line, which may signal potential entry or exit points for traders.

Summary

In this chapter, we delved into the world of options and futures contracts.

Forward contracts are customized, private agreements between two parties and are traded over the counter (OTC). They are only settled at the end of the agreement and are priced based on the spot price of the underlying asset, the risk-free interest rate, and the time to expiration. However, forward contracts come with potential counterparty risk as there is no clearing house to guarantee the fulfillment of the contractual obligations.

Futures contracts, on the other hand, are standardized contracts traded on regulated exchanges. They are marked to market daily, meaning that the price of the contract is adjusted to reflect its current market value, ensuring that margin requirements are met. The clearing house of the futures exchange serves as an intermediary between buyers and sellers, mitigating counterparty risk and ensuring the stability of the market.

We also covered the pricing of both types of contracts. For example, the pricing of futures contracts is influenced by factors such as the spot price of the underlying asset, the risk-free interest rate, storage costs, and convenience yield. In addition, futures markets can exhibit contango, where futures prices are higher than the spot price, or backwardation, where futures prices are lower than the spot price.

Exercises

- A farmer sells agricultural products, and a manufacturer purchases raw materials for production. In both cases, what position should they take in a futures contract in order to hedge against adverse price changes in the future?

- A wheat farmer takes a short position in ten wheat futures contracts on day 1, each valued at $4.5 and representing 5000 bushels. If the price of the futures contracts increases to $4.55 on day 2, what is the change in the farmer's margin account?

- Suppose we enter into a short forward position. What is the risk due to the fluctuating asset price in the future? How can we hedge the risk?

- Assume we could buy a barrel of oil for $80 today, and the current futures price is $85 for delivery three months from today. One futures contract can buy 1000 barrels of oil. How can you arbitrage in this situation? What is the profit? Assume a zero risk-free interest rate.

- Apply the same no-arbitrage argument to value a forward contract in a short position.

- Write a function to calculate the fair price of a futures contract given the spot price of the asset, risk-free interest rate, rate of storage cost, convenience yield, and delivery date. Allow for both annual compounding and continuous compounding.

- Explain the source of riskless profit when a forward contract is overpriced or underpriced than its theoretical no-arbitrage value.

## CHAPTER 4

Understanding Risk and Return

Any financial asset is characterized by its risk and return. Return means the financial reward it brings, such as the percentage increase in the asset value. We hope to maximize the percentage return of the asset as much as possible. However, a higher reward often comes with higher risk, where risk refers to the volatility of such return. That is, an asset displays high oscillations in its historical returns, making its future outlook more uncertain than, say, a stable product with little deviation from the expected gain, such as the bond. As an investor, the goal of making profits boils down to maximizing the return and, at the same time, minimizing the risk.

Return is a measure of the financial gain or loss of an investment over a specific period. It can be calculated as a percentage of the initial investment, taking into account factors such as capital appreciation, dividends, and interest payments. Returns can be either realized (already received) or unrealized (expected to be received in the future). There are various ways to measure returns, including absolute return, annualized return, and risk-adjusted return.

Risk is the variability or uncertainty in the returns of an investment. It represents the potential for losses due to factors such as market fluctuations, economic conditions, and company-specific events. There are several types of risk, including market risk, credit risk, liquidity risk, and operational risk, among others. In general, investments with higher risk tend to offer higher potential returns to compensate for the increased uncertainty.

© Peng Liu 2023
P. Liu, *Quantitative Trading Strategies Using Python*, https://doi.org/10.1007/978-1-4842-9675-2_4

Risk and Return Trade-Off

With the risk and return trade-off, a low-return asset is associated with low risk, and a high-return asset comes with a high risk. This is true for most financial instruments in the market. For example, the bond, as a fixed-income asset, is often considered a riskless asset that delivers a low return and comes with virtually no risk. The stock market offers a higher return but often displays higher volatility due to the uncertain and unpredictable future. Under such a trade-off, an investor can only gain a higher return and make more profits if they are willing to accept more risk, that is, a higher probability of losses.

The appropriate risk-return trade-off depends on various factors, including an investor's risk tolerance profile, years to retirement, and the potential to replace lost funds. The trade-off also depends on the time horizon for a given position. For example, position traders typically hold onto a position for a long period of time, which provides the trader with the potential to recover from the risks of bear markets and participate in bull markets, hoping for an increase in the asset value over the long term. On the other hand, swing traders or even day traders enter a position for a short time, seeking profits by speculating on the movement of the asset's price changes. The same equities (e.g., stocks) have a higher risk proposition when an investor can only invest in a short time frame.

It is important to note that each individual asset has its own risk and return profile, and a group of assets can form a portfolio with new risk and return characteristics. At the portfolio level, the risk-return trade-off assesses the concentration or diversity of holdings and whether the portfolio mix presents an excessive risk or a lower-than-desired potential for returns. Therefore, the risk-return trade-off applies to both individual assets and a portfolio of assets.

However, a diversified portfolio generally reduces the risks presented by individual investment positions. Diversification across various asset classes, industries, and geographies can help mitigate the impact of poor-performing assets on overall returns, providing a more balanced approach to risk management. A better understanding of the risk-return trade-off, along with different diversification strategies, allows us to tailor the portfolios to achieve the desired financial objectives and, at the same time, effectively manage the inherent risks associated with investing.

Let us draw a two-dimensional coordinate system to characterize the risk and return. We would often put risk on the horizontal axis and return on the vertical axis. As shown in Figure 4-1, the lower-left quadrant has low risk and low return. Representative products include fixed-income instruments such as bonds and treasury bills. Moving to the upper-right quadrant, we have products associated with high risk and return. Examples include stocks and derivative products. The other two quadrants are less frequent. For example, it is not so often to see financial instruments with a low risk and high return. Companies could experience an urgent need for funds and thus issue bonds with a higher return, but getting into such a situation itself implies an increased default risk already. On the other hand, it is very unlikely to see products with a low return but high risk, since this goes against the profit maximization nature of trading.

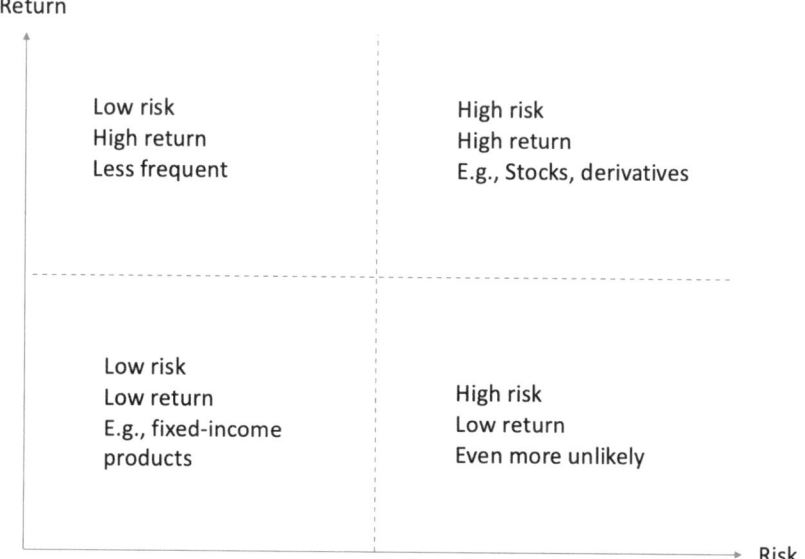

Figure 4-1. *Illustrating the four quadrants of risk and return profile*

In the following section, we will start by understanding the fundamentals of returns as a performance measure of financial assets. Understanding returns is crucial for us to evaluate the success of different investments and make informed decisions in managing portfolios.

Analyzing Returns

The return is the first and foremost metric most investors would look at for a specific investment vehicle. It represents the change in value of a financial asset over a specified period. It can be expressed in absolute terms (e.g., the dollar amount gained or lost) or as a percentage of the initial investment value. As a crucial metric on the performance of an asset or portfolio, the return allows us to compare across different investments.

When measured in percentage terms, the range could range from (theoretically) negative infinity to positive infinity. Suppose the asset price changes from S_{t-1} to S_t. The change in price is $S_t - S_{t-1}$, which could be positive or negative. Considering the price of an asset changes across different time points, and also the fact that multiple assets have multiple price levels, it is difficult to assess whether the price change $S_t - S_{t-1}$ is big or small. To standardize the price changes and make it easier for comparison, a more widely used measure is percentage return R_t, defined as

$$R_t = \frac{S_t - S_{t-1}}{S_{t-1}}$$

This equation essentially measures the change in asset price in proportion to the previous-period asset price, that is, the baseline. It allows us to transition from prices to returns. This percentage change in asset price thus allows us to assess and compare different assets. By calculating the percentage return R_t, we can effectively transition from focusing on the raw price changes to the proportional changes in asset prices. This transition allows us to evaluate the performance of different investments relative to a baseline, which is the previous-period asset price. This standardization is particularly useful when evaluating investments with different price levels or those that experience different magnitudes of price fluctuations.

Note that we may also write the return as $R_{t-1,t}$ to emphasize the fact that the return measures the relative change in prices between period $t-1$ and t:

$$R_{t-1,t} = \frac{S_t - S_{t-1}}{S_{t-1}}$$

Let us analyze some dummy return data to make these calculations tangible.

Working with Dummy Returns

In Listing 4-1, we first create two five-element (or five-period) lists representing the returns of two different assets, stored in `asset_return1` and `asset_return2`, respectively. The returns are constructed such that their mean returns are the same. We can verify the equality using the `==` operator.

Listing 4-1. Simulating two asset returns

```
asset_return1 = [0.05, 0.3, -0.1, 0.35, 0.2]
asset_return2 = [0.5, -0.2, 0.3, 0.5, -0.3]
>>> print(np.mean(asset_return1))
>>> print(np.mean(asset_return2))
>>> print(np.mean(asset_return1) == np.mean(asset_return2))
0.16
0.16
True
```

Next, let us combine these two lists in a Pandas DataFrame for easy manipulation. This is achieved by wrapping the two lists in a dictionary and passing it to the pd.DataFrame() function:

```
return_df = pd.DataFrame({"Asset1":asset_return1, "Asset2":asset_return2})
>>> return_df
```

Printing out the return_df variable generates the following, where the two lists now appear as the two columns in the DataFrame:

```
   Asset1 Asset2
0    0.05    0.5
1    0.30   -0.2
2   -0.10    0.3
3    0.35    0.5
4    0.20   -0.3
```

To facilitate visual analysis, let us plot the two return series in a bar chart using the .plot.bar() method:

```
>>> return_df.plot.bar()
```

Running this command generates Figure 4-2. The figure suggests that despite having the same mean return, these two assets clearly have different risk profiles. Specifically, asset 2 (orange bars) is more volatile than asset 1 (blue bars).

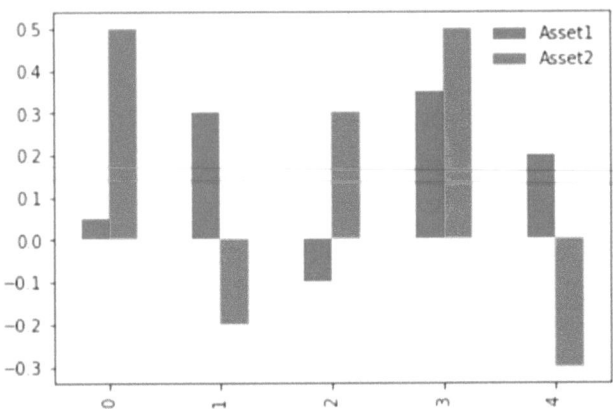

Figure 4-2. *Visualizing the returns as bar charts*

Again, this notion of higher volatility will be more concrete when we introduce its precise definition later. For now, we can simply call the std() function to calculate the standard deviation (another name for volatility) of the two columns:

```
>>> return_df.std()
Asset1    0.185068
Asset2    0.384708
dtype: float64
```

Note that the std() is applied column-wise. Similarly, we can call the mean() function to calculate the mean value of each column:

```
>>> return_df.mean()
Asset1    0.16
Asset2    0.16
dtype: float64
```

The result aligns with our previous calculations using np.mean(). This example shows that merely looking at the average return of an asset is not enough. In fact, it could be misleading if we just report the average return of an asset without its volatility.

To see the difference, assume we have an initial investment of $100 in both assets. To calculate the running asset value at each period in a sequential manner, we first add one to the percentage return values, forming the 1+R format. Take asset 1, for example.

As shown in the following, after running the following code snippet, we can use 1.05 to calculate the asset value after the first period as $100 × 1.05, the asset value after the second period as $100 × 1.05 × 1.30, and so on:

```
>>> return_df + 1
     Asset1 Asset2
0     1.05   1.5
1     1.30   0.8
2     0.90   1.3
3     1.35   1.5
4     1.20   0.7
```

Instead of multiplying these percentage returns cumulatively, a convenient function called cumprod() does the work for us. Therefore, we can obtain the period-wise asset value by applying this function on the previous 1+R formatted DataFrame and multiplying by $100, as shown in the following code snippet:

```
init_investment = 100
cum_value = (return_df + 1).cumprod()*100
>>> cum_value
       Asset1      Asset2
0     105.0000     150.0
1     136.5000     120.0
2     122.8500     156.0
3     165.8475     234.0
4     199.0170     163.8
```

We can similarly plot the evolution of asset values as a line chart:

```
>>> cum_value.plot.line()
```

Running this command generates Figure 4-3. Although asset 2 looks more profitable in most of the periods, it actually ends with a lower return in the last period. Thus, a key takeaway from this chart is that two assets with equal average returns may end up with a totally different terminal return.

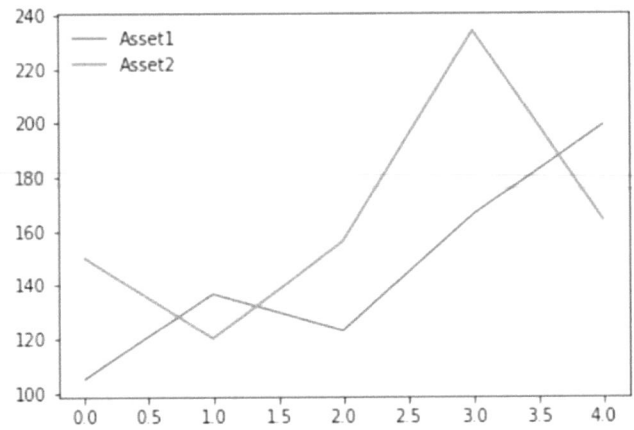

Figure 4-3. *Visualizing the evolution of asset values*

The 1+R Format

Recall that to calculate the return $R_{t-1,t}$ from the period $t-1$ to t, we need asset prices S_{t-1} and S_t in both periods. With simple manipulation, we can express the return as follows:

$$1 + R_{t-1,t} = \frac{S_t}{S_{t-1}}$$

This is the so-called 1+R format, where we use $1 + R_{t-1,t}$ to denote the percentage of current-period asset price S_t over previous-period asset price S_{t-1}. We can then easily calculate the return $R_{t-1,t}$ after obtaining the 1+R return $1 + R_{t-1,t}$:

$$R_{t-1,t} = \frac{S_t}{S_{t-1}} - 1$$

One reason why we use this format is the convenience in the calculation. Since the prices are arranged along a column from start to end, we can simply shift the price column upward by one row to obtain the next-period price and then calculate the ratio $\frac{S_t}{S_{t-1}}$ (i.e., $1 + R_{t-1,t}$) in a separate column. We could then subtract one to obtain $R_{t-1,t}$ for each period.

Figure 4-4 illustrates the benefits of using the 1+R formatted return. The extra step involved is to create a shifted column by moving the price column upward by one unit. Calculating the 1+R formatted return is straightforward and fast, as this is a direct division between two columns that are performed simultaneously across all the rows. This avoids a for loop. We will then minus one to recover the same return.

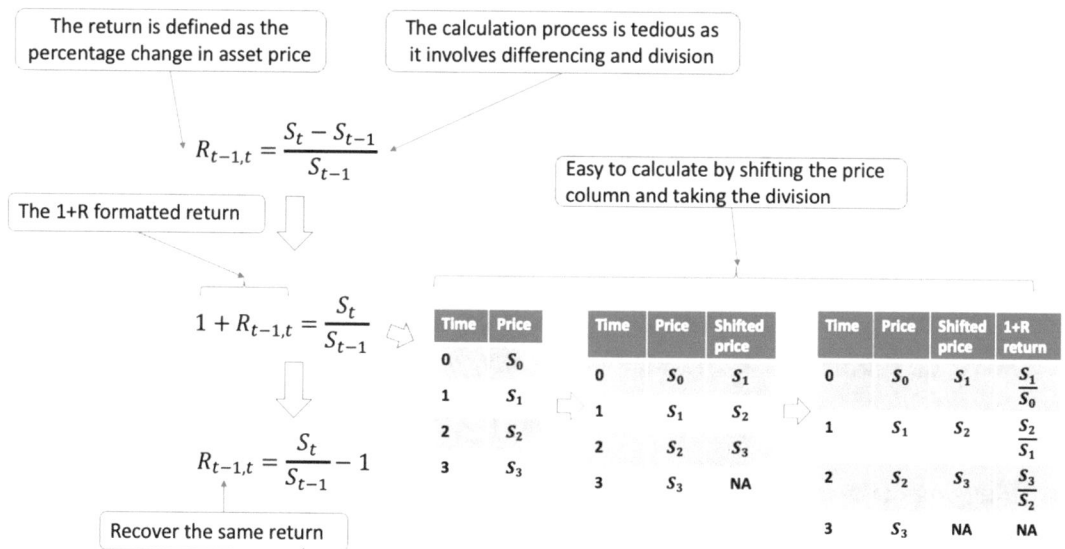

Figure 4-4. *Illustrating the calculation process of return using the 1+R format that gives a more convenient way to calculate the return*

Also, note that the last row in the shifted column is NA, which is due to the fact that there is no more future price available at the last time point. This also makes the 1+R return column NA. We will demonstrate the calculation process in code later. For now, it is good to digest and accept the 1+R formatted return as an equivalent way of describing asset returns.

The Terminal Return

Terminal return refers to the return at the last time period as compared to the initial return, that is, $R_{0,T}$. Suppose we have price data from period $t = 0$ to $t = T$. To calculate the terminal return $R_{0,T}$ at period T, we can take the initial price S_0 and terminal price S_T, take the ratio, and subtract one, giving

$$R_{0,T} = \frac{S_T}{S_0} - 1$$

This approach essentially ignores the intermediate returns and only considers the initial and terminal asset prices. By focusing solely on the initial and terminal asset prices, this metric offers a simplified view of the investment's growth or decline over time, disregarding intermediate fluctuations. This can be particularly useful when assessing the long-term performance of an investment or comparing the growth of different assets over an extended period. However, note that the terminal return does not provide insights into the volatility or risk associated with the investment, as it only considers the initial and terminal asset prices.

There is another way to calculate this value. Instead of focusing only on the initial and terminal prices, we view the whole price evolution process as sequential, changing from one price point to another. Therefore, the terminal return at period T (or an arbitrary period t) is the result of multiplying all previous 1+R formatted returns, followed by a subtraction of one. Mathematically, we have

$$R_{0,T} = \left(1 + R_{0,1}\right)\left(1 + R_{1,2}\right)\ldots\left(1 + R_{T-1,T}\right) - 1$$

Plugging in the definition of 1+R formatted return gives the following:

$$R_{0,T} = \frac{S_1}{S_0}\frac{S_2}{S_1}\ldots\frac{S_T}{S_{T-1}} - 1$$

which is nothing more than the initial equation we presented, after canceling like terms. By doing so, we acknowledge the compound effect of each period's return on the overall investment performance. This approach is more comprehensive, as it takes into account all price changes during the investment period.

Figure 4-5 illustrates the calculation process of the terminal return.

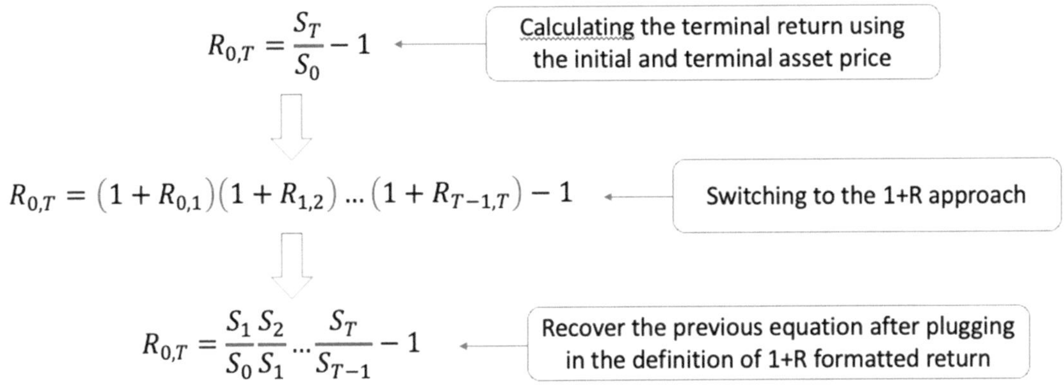

Figure 4-5. *Calculating the terminal return via different approaches*

Stock Return with Dividends

Note that dividends also need to be considered when calculating the asset return. This means that we own the stock at its current price and also enjoy the dividends it brings. The previous definition of return is called the price return, which only considers the price movements of the stock. Adding dividends together with the current stock price is referred to as the total return, which is more realistic. When analyzing stock performance, the total return is almost always used. The difference between the total return and the price return gives the dividends.

The total return of a stock is calculated as follows:

$$R_{t-1,t} = \frac{S_t + D_{t-1,t}}{S_{t-1}} - 1 = \frac{S_t + D_{t-1,t} - S_{t-1}}{S_{t-1}}$$

In this equation, the total return is denoted by $R_{t-1,t}$, which is the return from time $t-1$ to time t. S_t and S_{t-1} represent the stock prices at time t and time $t-1$, respectively. $D_{t-1,t}$ represents the dividend paid out during the period from $t-1$ to t.

The total return provides a more comprehensive assessment of an investment's performance by incorporating both capital appreciation (i.e., the increase in the stock's price) and dividend income. It is particularly relevant for income-oriented investors, who are focused on maximizing their returns through a combination of capital gains and dividends.

To calculate the total return of a stock, the formula takes into account the stock price at the beginning of the period, the stock price at the end of the period, and any dividends paid out during the period. By dividing the sum of the stock price at the end of the period and the dividends by the stock price at the beginning of the period, and then subtracting one, we obtain the total return as a percentage.

Multiperiod Return

The terminal return can also be considered as the multiperiod return, or the return over a combined period of time. Since the evolution process is sequential, we need to compound the returns in each period, sequentially. When we have the 1+R formatted returns, it is easy to calculate the multiperiod return by multiplying/compounding the intermediate 1+R returns followed by a subtraction of one.

The multiperiod return is a measure of an investment's performance over a series of consecutive periods. Recall that the terminal return can be calculated via $R_{0,T} = (1 + R_{0,1})(1 + R_{1,2})...(1 + R_{T-1,T}) - 1$. When we calculate the two-period return $R_{t,t+2}$, the formula becomes

$$R_{t,t+2} = \left(1 + R_{t,t+1}\right)\left(1 + R_{t+1,t+2}\right) - 1$$

This method allows us to calculate the overall return over the two periods while considering the compounding effect of each period's return on the next. The compounded return is thus easy to calculate using the 1+R formatted returns for both periods. Figure 4-6 illustrates the process of compounding the two-period return.

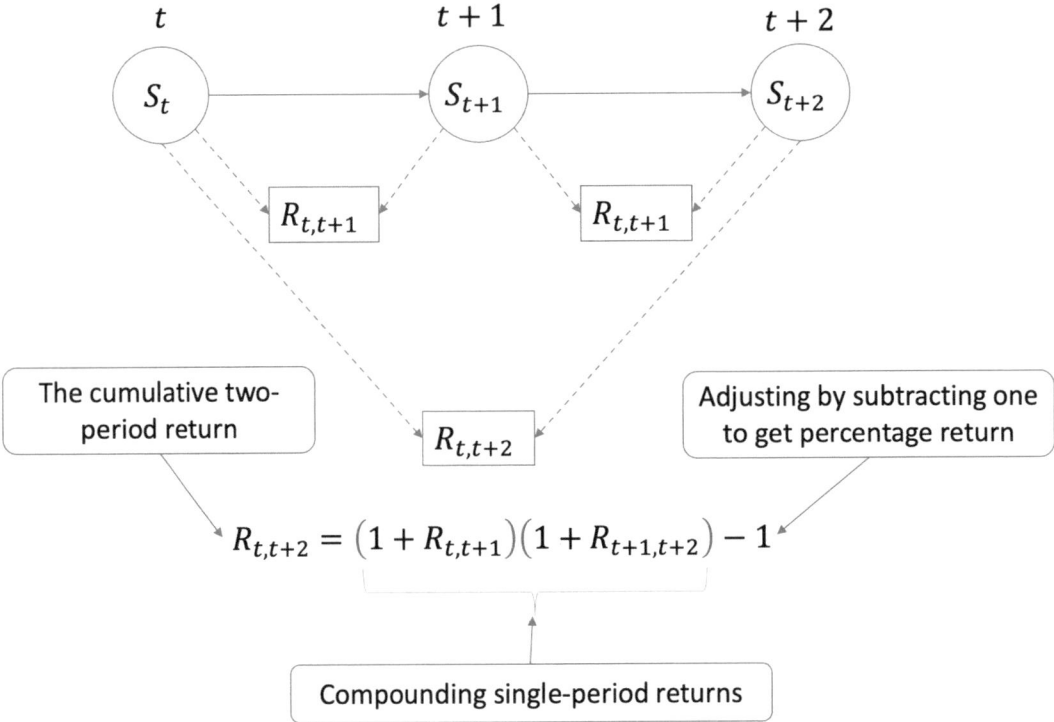

Figure 4-6. *Calculating the two-period return by compounding the two single-period returns in 1+R format, followed by an adjustment of subtraction by one*

Similarly, for an n-period return, the formula can be generalized as

$$R_{t,t+n} = \left(1 + R_{t,t+1}\right)\left(1 + R_{t+1,t+2}\right)...\left(1 + R_{t+n-1,t+n}\right) - 1$$

By multiplying the 1+R formatted returns for all n periods and then subtracting one, we can determine the compounded return over the entire n-period investment horizon.

Let us look at a simple example. Suppose we invest in an asset for two periods, where the first-period return is 10%, and the second-period return is –2%. To calculate the compounded return, our first step is to convert both single-period returns to the 1+R format, giving 1.1 and 0.98, respectively. We would then multiply these two numbers and subtract by one:

$$(1+0.1)(1-0.02)-1 \approx 0.078 = 7.8\%$$

Note that we should not calculate the two-period terminal return as (10% – 2%) = 8%, which ignores the compounding effect. Working through the calculations sequentially by multiplying the 1+R returns in each period ensures we obtain the correct result. These multiplications give the terminal return in the 1+R format, and we subtract by one to get the return itself.

Annualizing Returns

Once we know how to calculate the terminal return of any asset, the next question is comparing assets with different periods of time. For example, some returns are daily, while other returns are monthly, quarterly, or yearly. The answer is annualization, where we annualize the returns to the same time scale of a year for a fair comparison.

Annualizing returns is a crucial step in comparing the performance of assets with different investment horizons. By converting returns to an annualized basis, we can more easily evaluate and compare the performance of various assets on a standardized time scale. This process helps to level the playing field and facilitate informed decision-making.

The overall process for annualizing returns is as follows:

- Calculate the 1+R formatted return for the given period.

- Raise the 1+R formatted return to the power of the number of periods per year.

- Subtract one to convert the result from the 1+R format back to the return itself.

Let us look at an example. Suppose we have an asset that generates a monthly return of 1%. To calculate the annualized return, we need to enlarge the time horizon to a year. However, simply multiplying 12 by 1% is incorrect. To proceed with the sequential compounding process, we would construct the 1+R formatted return $(1 + 0.01)$ for each month, multiply across all 12 months to reach $(1 + 0.01)^{12}$, and finally subtract by one to give $(1 + 0.01)^{12} - 1 \approx 12.68\%$, which is higher than 12%. Calculating the annualized return thus involves deriving the 1+R formatted return, multiplying these returns by the number of periods per year, and subtracting by one to convert from 1+R to R.

This calculation shows that the annualized return is 12.68%, which is higher than simply multiplying the 1% monthly return by 12. This difference is due to the compounding effect, which is an essential factor to consider when annualizing returns.

Calculating Single-Period Returns from Price Data

We often start with the price data of an asset, and there is a process to calculate the returns. This section will demonstrate how to achieve this.

The following command creates a list of three price points, which will be used to calculate different returns similar to the previous two-period return example:

```
prices = [0.1, 0.2, -0.05]
```

The first-period return can be calculated based on the first two price points. We would first obtain the 1+R formatted return and then subtract by one to switch to the normal return:

```
>>> prices[1]/prices[0] - 1
1.0
```

Similarly, we can calculate the second-period normal return as follows:

```
>>> prices[2]/prices[1] - 1
-1.25
```

When the list gets large, it would be inconvenient to calculate these single-period returns by hand. A more convenient approach is to borrow the idea of shifting the prices. Shifting can be done via proper indexing in a list. For example, the following code snippet subsets the last two and first two prices, respectively:

```
>>> print(prices[1:])
[0.2, -0.05]
>>> print(prices[:-1])
[0.1, 0.2]
```

Now we can do division for the corresponding elements in one shot. However, we need to convert both lists to NumPy arrays in order for the element-wise multiplication to work:

```
>>> print(np.array(prices[1:])/np.array(prices[:-1])-1)
[ 1.    -1.25]
```

Another approach is to rely on the Pandas ecosystem, which implements a lot of NumPy calculations under the hood. Let us convert the list to a Pandas DataFrame by converting a dictionary, the same technique used earlier:

```
prices_df = pd.DataFrame({"price":prices})
>>> prices_df
price
0     0.10
1     0.20
2    -0.05
```

A common method to subset a Pandas DataFrame is via the iloc() method, which returns the elements based on the positional indexes at both row and column levels. The following code snippet selects the last two and first two elements, respectively:

```
>>> prices_df.iloc[1:]
     price
1     0.20
2    -0.05
>>> prices_df.iloc[:-1]
     price
0     0.1
1     0.2
```

Pay attention to the indexes in the first column here. These are the default row-level indexes assigned upon creating the Pandas DataFrame, and these indexes remain unchanged even after the subsetting operation. Having misaligned indexes could easily lead to problems when trying to combine two DataFrames. In this case, we would end up with an unwanted result when we divide these two DataFrames:

```
>>> prices_df.iloc[1:]/prices_df.iloc[:-1]
price
0    NaN
1    1.0
2    NaN
```

The reason behind this seemingly irregular behavior is that both DataFrames are trying to locate the corresponding element with the *same* index. When the counterparty cannot be found, a NaN value shows up.

To correct this, we can extract the value attribute only from these DataFrames. We only need to do this for one DataFrame as the other will be converted to the format of the value automatically. The following code snippet shows the way to go, where the result is the same as before:

```
>>> prices_df.iloc[1:].values/prices_df.iloc[:-1] - 1
price
0     1.00
1    -1.25
>>> prices_df.iloc[1:]/prices_df.iloc[:-1].values - 1
   price
1     1.00
2    -1.25
```

Let us stay with the shifting operation a bit longer. It turns out that there is a function with the same name. For example, to shift the prices downward by one unit, we can pass one to the shift() function of the Pandas DataFrame object as follows:

```
>>> prices_df.shift(1)
   price
0    NaN
1    0.1
2    0.2
```

Notice that the first element is filled with NaN since there is no value before the first price. We can then divide the original DataFrame by the shifted DataFrame to obtain the sequence of single-period 1+R formatted returns and subtract by one to get the normal return:

```
>>> prices_df/prices_df.shift(1) - 1
     price
0    NaN
1    1.00
2    -1.25
```

Finally, we have one more utility function that helps us perform these calculations in one shot. The function is pct_change(), which calculates the percentage change between two consecutive values in the DataFrame:

```
returns_df = prices_df.pct_change()
>>> returns_df
     price
0    NaN
1    1.00
2    -1.25
```

Again, the first entry is NaN as there is no prior price point.

Next, we move on to calculating the cumulative two-period terminal return.

Calculating Two-Period Terminal Return

The terminal return comes from compounding the previous single-period returns. In the case of a single-period horizon, the terminal return is the same as the single-period return. In the following example, we are calculating the two-period terminal return using a simple DataFrame (returns_df) containing single-period returns. The process involves the following steps:

- Convert the single-period returns to the 1+R format by adding one.

- Calculate the product of the 1+R formatted returns.

- Subtract one to convert the result back to the terminal return.

Specifically, to calculate the two-period terminal return, we first obtain the 1+R formatted single-period returns:

```
>>> returns_df + 1
      price
0     NaN
1     2.00
2    -0.25
```

We then call the prod() function from NumPy to multiply all elements in an array, ignoring the NaN value. This gets us the 1+R formatted terminal return, from which we subtract one to convert to the normal terminal return:

```
>>> np.prod(returns_df + 1) - 1
price    -1.5
dtype: float64
```

There is also a corresponding Pandas way, which gives the same result:

```
>>> (returns_df+1).prod() - 1
price    -1.5
dtype: float64
```

Calculating Annualized Returns

We consider three scenarios where the return frequencies are different, including a daily return of 0.0001, a monthly return of 0.01, and a quarterly return of 0.05. The calculation process is the same as calculating the multiperiod terminal return at a yearly mark:

- Convert the normal return to the 1+R format for each period.

- Raise the 1+R formatted return to the power of the number of periods in a year.

- Subtract one to convert the result back to the normal return.

For the daily return, we assume a total of 252 trading days in a year, which is a typical assumption when working with daily prices. We follow the same recipe here: convert normal return to 1+R return for every single period, compound/multiply these single periods until reaching a year, and minus one to convert back to the normal terminal return:

```
r = 0.0001
>>> (1+r)**252-10
0.025518911987694626
```

For the monthly return, since there are 12 months in a year, we would compound it 12 times:

```
r = 0.01
>>> (1+r)**12-1
0.12682503013196977
```

And lastly, there are four quarters in a year, so we compound it four times:

```
r = 0.05
>>> (1+r)**4-1
0.21550625000000023
```

Now we switch to analyzing risk in the following section.

Analyzing Risk

The risk of an asset is related to volatility, which is of equal or higher importance than the reward. Volatility is a crucial metric in assessing the risk of an investment, as it represents the level of uncertainty or fluctuations in the asset's returns. A higher volatility implies a higher risk, as the asset's price can experience more significant ups and downs. To quantify the risk associated with an investment, we must understand the concept of volatility and how to calculate it.

Recall the returns of two assets in Figure 4-3. Despite having the same average reward, asset 2 is more volatile than asset 1. Asset 2 deviates from the mean more often and more significantly than asset 1. Volatility thus measures the degree of deviation from the mean. We will formalize the notion of volatility in this section.

Before looking at volatility, let us first introduce the concept of variance and standard deviation.

Introducing Variance and Standard Deviation

Variance and standard deviation are two widely used statistical measures that describe the spread of the data around its mean value. Suppose we have a total of N returns $\{R_i\}_{i=1}^{N}$. We know the mean return R_P is calculated by averaging all returns:

$$R_P = \frac{\sum_{i=1}^{N} R_i}{N}$$

Here, the mean return R_P describes the central tendency of the returns for the asset or portfolio. That is, on average, the return is R_P. It is also called the arithmetic mean of the returns.

Now comes the measure of the deviation from the mean. For any return R_i, its distance with R_P is $R_i - R_P$. However, this distance may be positive or negative. Since we have a total of N returns and, therefore, N distances, aggregating these N distances by summing them up does not seem to be a good idea, as positive and negative distances will cancel out each other. Instead of directly summing up these distances, the variance measure says that we can square the distances first and then take the average of these squared distances. Mathematically, the variance of the returns is expressed as follows:

$$\sigma_P^2 = \frac{\sum_{i=1}^{N} \left(R_i - R_P\right)^2}{N}$$

Here, $R_i - R_P$ also means to de-mean the original return R_i, that is, subtract the mean return R_P from the original return R_i. This gives deviation from the mean. Also, by squaring these deviations, the problem of canceling out positive and negative terms no longer exists; all de-meaned returns end up being positive or zero. Finally, we take the average of the squared deviations as the variance of the return series. A visual inspection of Figure 4-3 also suggests that asset 2 has a higher variance than asset 1.

Although variance summarizes the average degree of deviation from the mean return, its unit is the squared distance from the average return, making it difficult to interpret the unit. In practice, we would often take the square root of the variance and bring it back to the same scale as the return. The result is called standard deviation, where the deviation is now standardized and comparable.

$$\sigma_P = \sqrt{\frac{\sum_{i=1}^{N} \left(R_i - R_P\right)^2}{N}}$$

This is also our measure of volatility. It measures how large the prices swing around the mean price and serves as a direct measure of the dispersion of returns. The higher the volatility, the higher the deviations from the mean return. Figure 4-7 summarizes the definitions of common statistical measures such as the mean, variance (both population and sample), and standard deviation, also called volatility in the financial context.

Mean return (arithmetic mean)
$$R_P = \frac{\sum_{i=1}^{N} R_i}{N}$$

Variance (population)
$$\sigma_P^2 = \frac{\sum_{i=1}^{N}(R_i - R_P)^2}{N}$$

Variance (sample)
$$\sigma_P^2 = \frac{\sum_{i=1}^{N}(R_i - R_P)^2}{N-1}$$

Standard deviation (volatility)
$$\sigma_P = \sqrt{\frac{\sum_{i=1}^{N}(R_i - R_P)^2}{N}}$$

Figure 4-7. *Summarizing the common statistical measures, including the mean, variance (population and sample), and standard deviation (also called volatility)*

In summary, variance and standard deviation are essential statistical measures for understanding the risk associated with an investment. They describe the dispersion or spread of returns around their mean value, which helps estimate the potential volatility of an asset or portfolio. These statistical measures also play an important role in assessing the risk tolerance in a portfolio allocation.

Annualizing Volatility

Similar to return, the volatility also needs to be annualized to warrant a fair comparison. Without annualizing the volatility, it is difficult to compare the volatility of monthly data with that of daily data.

The formula for annualizing the volatility relies on the fact that the volatility increases with the square root of the time period T. The annualized return $\sigma_{P,T}$ can be calculated as

$$\sigma_{P,T} = \sqrt{T}\sigma_P$$

where σ_P is our single-period volatility, which can be daily, monthly, or quarterly. This expression relies on the assumption that the returns are normally distributed and independent of each other. We are only going to build intuition on this formula instead of delving into the technical details.

The time period T is the full time period. Therefore, daily returns give $T = 252$, monthly returns give $T = 12$, and quarterly returns give $T = 4$. We would simply multiply the square root of this time period with the original single-period volatility to obtain the annualized volatility.

To recap, we can follow these steps to calculate the annualized volatility:

- Calculate the single-period volatility (σ_P) for the given data (daily, monthly, or quarterly returns).

- Determine the number of periods per year (T). For daily returns, T = 252 (trading days in a year); for monthly returns, T = 12; and for quarterly returns, T = 4.

- Multiply the single-period volatility (σ_P) by the square root of the number of periods per year (T) to obtain the annualized volatility; that is, $\sigma_{P,T} = \sqrt{T}\sigma_P$.

Keep in mind that the assumption of normally distributed and independent returns is critical for this method to hold true. Annualizing volatility using this method allows us to compare the volatility of assets with different return frequencies on a common scale, making it easier to evaluate and manage the risks associated with different investments.

When the single-period volatility σ_P is fixed, our annualized return $\sigma_{P,T}$ will grow as T increases. Such growth in $\sigma_{P,T}$ is a nonlinear function of T due to the square root operation. As the time period T increases, the annualized volatility will also increase, but at a decreasing rate because of the square root function. This means that when the daily return and monthly return have the same single-period volatility, the daily return will have a higher annualized volatility. This makes intuitive sense as it captures short-term fluctuations that are smoothed out when using longer time frames like monthly data, and we expect to see more variations in the daily data compared to the monthly data.

We can also view the formula from another perspective. Squaring both sides gives us the annualized variance on both sides, as shown in the following:

$$\sigma_{P,T}^2 = T\sigma_P^2$$

Now the annualized variance $\sigma_{P,T}^{2}$ grows linearly with the time T. Figure 4-8 illustrates the subtlety here.

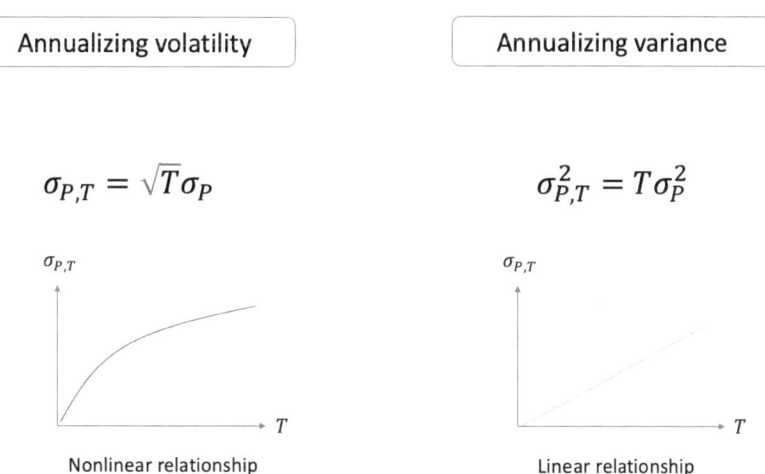

Figure 4-8. *Comparing the differences when annualizing volatility and variance. When given a fixed single-period volatility or variance, the annualized volatility grows nonlinearly with time, while the annualized variance grows linearly with time*

Let us look at a simple example. Suppose the standard deviation of a stock's daily return series is 0.1%. The annualized volatility can be calculated as

$$0.001 * \sqrt{252} \approx 1.59\%$$

Combining Risk and Return via the Sharpe Ratio

Now we have two measures for a particular asset: return and risk; both can be annualized. One asset may display a low return and a low risk, while another asset may deliver a higher return but comes with a higher risk as well. We would like to combine these two measures and create a single risk-adjusted return.

One way is to divide the average return R_P by the volatility σ_P, giving $\dfrac{R_P}{\sigma_P}$. However, the average return R_P gives no information on the overall market conditions. We are unsure if a higher ratio of $\dfrac{R_P}{\sigma_P}$ is due to the portfolio itself or the booming market. It would be good to account for the overall market benchmark in the numerator. This is where the Sharpe ratio comes in.

The Sharpe ratio is a measure that is calculated by dividing the portfolio's excess return by its volatility to assess risk-adjusted performance. Here, excess return means the return that is above an industry benchmark, typically using the risk-free rate of return such as the Treasury bill or bond. With this standardized measure, we can now compare different assets or portfolios while taking into account the overall market conditions. We will then choose the assets or portfolio with a higher Sharpe ratio.

Mathematically, the Sharpe ratio is defined as follows:

$$Sharpe\ ratio = \frac{R_P - R_f}{\sigma_p}$$

where R_P is the average return of the portfolio, R_f is the risk-free rate, and σ_p is the volatility of the portfolio. A higher Sharpe ratio indicates that the investment generates higher returns for the same level of risk compared to other investments or the overall market. When comparing different investments, an investment with a higher Sharpe ratio is considered to be more attractive because it offers a better risk-adjusted return. By incorporating the risk-free rate, the Sharpe ratio provides a more accurate assessment of an investment's performance relative to the overall market conditions.

Let us look at one example. Suppose we have two portfolios whose returns and volatilities are $(5\%, 20\%)$ and $(10\%, 50\%)$. Clearly, portfolio 2 is more profitable and also more volatile than portfolio 1. Such volatility will discount the attractiveness of portfolio 2. To compare these two portfolios using a single metric, we calculate $\frac{R_P}{\sigma_P}$ as follows:

$$\frac{0.05}{0.2} = 0.25 > \frac{0.1}{0.5} = 0.2$$

Thus, portfolio 1 is more attractive using the risk-adjusted measure. Now suppose the risk-free interest rate in the market is 3%. Now we focus on the excess return of both portfolios and compare them using the Sharpe ratio:

$$\frac{0.05 - 0.03}{0.2} = 0.1 < \frac{0.1 - 0.03}{0.5} = 0.14$$

Now portfolio 2 has become more attractive. This is because portfolio 2 did provide a better return than portfolio 1 after considering the market benchmark. Listing 4-2 demonstrates the comparison in this example.

Listing 4-2. Calculating the Sharpe ratio

```
p1_ret = 0.05
p1_vol = 0.2
p2_ret = 0.1
p2_vol = 0.5
risk_free_rate = 0.03

>>> p1_ret / p1_vol
0.25
>>> p2_ret / p2_vol
0.2
>>> (p1_ret - risk_free_rate) / p1_vol
0.1
>>> (p2_ret - risk_free_rate) / p2_vol
0.14
```

Figure 4-9 summarizes the different measures of the risk-adjusted return.

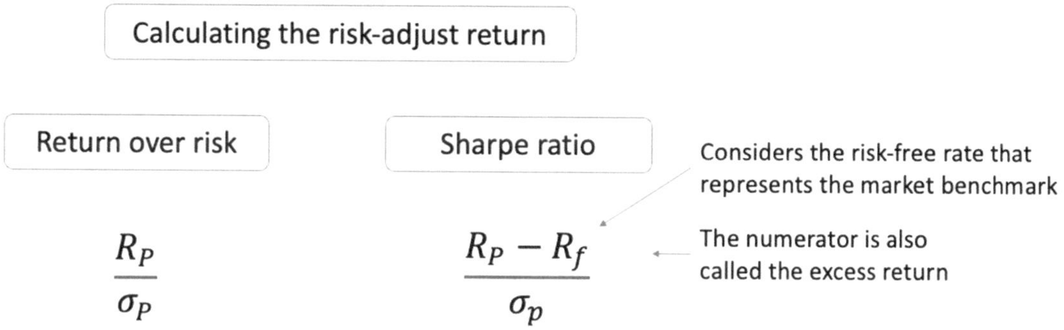

Calculating the risk-adjust return

Return over risk

$$\frac{R_P}{\sigma_P}$$

Sharpe ratio

$$\frac{R_P - R_f}{\sigma_p}$$

Considers the risk-free rate that represents the market benchmark

The numerator is also called the excess return

Figure 4-9. *Different risk-adjusted returns. Subtracting the risk-free rate from the (annualized) return gives the excess return, which considers the market benchmark performance*

Let us work with some real data to calculate the aforementioned metrics in the next section.

Working with Stock Price Data

In this section, we will download the year-to-date stock price data for Apple (AAPL) and Google (GOOG). In Listing 4-3, we specify the starting date to be "2023-01-01," with the default end date automatically determined by the system's current date, which is January 20, 2023, at the time of writing.

Listing 4-3. Downloading stock data using yfinance

```
import yfinance as yf
prices_df = yf.download(["AAPL","GOOG"], start="2023-01-01")
>>> prices_df.head()
```

Running the code generates Figure 4-10. Note the multilevel columns here. There are two levels of columns, with the first level indicating the price type and the second one denoting the ticker symbol. Also, the index of the DataFrame follows a datetime format.

Date	Adj Close		Close		High		Low		Open		Volume	
	AAPL	GOOG	AAPL	GOOG	AAPL	GOOG	AAPL	GOOG	AAPL	GOOG	AAPL	GOOG
2023-01-03 00:00:00-05:00	125.070000	89.699997	125.070000	89.699997	130.899994	91.550003	124.169998	89.019997	130.279999	89.830002	112117500	20738500
2023-01-04 00:00:00-05:00	126.360001	88.709999	126.360001	88.709999	128.660004	91.239998	125.080002	87.800003	126.889999	91.010002	89113600	27046500
2023-01-05 00:00:00-05:00	125.019997	86.769997	125.019997	86.769997	127.769997	88.209999	124.760002	86.559998	127.129997	88.070000	80962700	23136100
2023-01-06 00:00:00-05:00	129.619995	88.160004	129.619995	88.160004	130.289993	88.470001	124.889999	85.570000	126.010002	87.360001	87686600	26604400
2023-01-09 00:00:00-05:00	130.149994	88.800003	130.149994	88.800003	133.410004	90.830002	129.889999	88.580002	130.470001	89.195000	70790800	22996700

Figure 4-10. *Printing the first few rows of daily stock prices for Apple and Google*

Next, we would like to focus on the daily adjusted closing price of the two stocks, indexed by date instead of datetime. Listing 4-4 completes these two tasks.

Listing 4-4. Indexing by date and selecting the daily adjusted closing price

```
# convert datetime index to date format
prices_df.index = prices_df.index.date
# keep the adjust close
prices_df = prices_df['Adj Close']
```

```
>>> prices_df.head()
             AAPL        GOOG
2023-01-03  125.070000  89.699997
2023-01-04  126.360001  88.709999
2023-01-05  125.019997  86.769997
2023-01-06  129.619995  88.160004
2023-01-09  130.149994  88.800003
```

Here, we accessed the date attribute of the index and assigned it to the index attribute of the DataFrame. We would then calculate the 1+R formatted returns using the pct_change() utility function:

```
returns_df = prices_df.pct_change()
>>> returns_df.head()
             AAPL       GOOG
2023-01-03   NaN        NaN
2023-01-04   0.010314  -0.011037
2023-01-05  -0.010605  -0.021869
2023-01-06   0.036794   0.016019
2023-01-09   0.004089   0.007260
```

Again, the first row is empty since there is no data point before it. We can remove this row using the dropna() function:

```
returns_df = returns_df.dropna()
>>> returns_df.head()
             AAPL       GOOG
2023-01-04   0.010314  -0.011037
2023-01-05  -0.010605  -0.021869
2023-01-06   0.036794   0.016019
2023-01-09   0.004089   0.007260
2023-01-10   0.004456   0.004955
```

All rows with any NA value in a cell are removed.

Next, we calculate the mean, variance, and standard deviation of the return series for both stocks.

Calculating the Mean, Variance, and Standard Deviation

The column-wise arithmetic mean returns can be obtained by calling the `mean()` method of the returns DataFrame:

```
>>> returns_df.mean()
AAPL    0.007228
GOOG    0.004295
dtype: float64
```

It seems Apple is having a better start than Google at the beginning of the year. To calculate the standard deviation or volatility of the returns, we can use the `std()` function. However, to see the column-wise operation in action, we explicitly specify `axis=0` in the input argument, which says that the standard deviation should be taken along the columns:

```
>>> returns_df.std(axis=0)
AAPL    0.012995
GOOG    0.016086
dtype: float64
```

Google's stock prices were more volatile than Apple's in the first few days. Now let us try setting `axis=1`:

```
>>> returns_df.std(axis=1)
2023-01-04    0.015097
2023-01-05    0.007965
2023-01-06    0.014690
2023-01-09    0.002242
2023-01-10    0.000352
2023-01-11    0.009001
2023-01-12    0.002259
2023-01-13    0.000308
2023-01-17    0.011068
2023-01-18    0.000882
2023-01-19    0.016097
dtype: float64
```

The result shows the daily standard deviation calculated for the two stocks combined.

Now we show how to calculate the volatility manually by going through the exact steps described earlier. Our first step is to de-mean the daily returns and obtain the deviations from the (arithmetic) mean:

```
deviations_df = returns_df - returns_df.mean()
>>> deviations_df.head()
              AAPL       GOOG
2023-01-04   0.003086  -0.015332
2023-01-05  -0.017833  -0.026164
2023-01-06   0.029566   0.011724
2023-01-09  -0.003139   0.002964
2023-01-10  -0.002772   0.000660
```

The next step is to square these deviations so that they would not cancel each other when summing together. Squaring is the same as raising the element to the power of two, using the double asterisk notation:

```
squared_deviations_df = deviations_df**2
>>> squared_deviations_df.head()
              AAPL      GOOG
2023-01-04  0.000010  2.350688e-04
2023-01-05  0.000318  6.845668e-04
2023-01-06  0.000874  1.374582e-04
2023-01-09  0.000010  8.787273e-06
2023-01-10  0.000008  4.352158e-07
```

In the third step, we average these daily squared deviations using the mean() function:

```
variance = squared_deviations_df.mean()
>>> variance
AAPL     0.000154
GOOG     0.000235
dtype: float64
```

The last step is to take the square root of the variance to obtain the volatility:

```
volatility = np.sqrt(variance)
>>> volatility
AAPL     0.012390
GOOG     0.015337
dtype: float64
```

Notice that the result is different from the one obtained using the std() function! The cause for the difference is that the std() function calculates the sample standard deviation, which divides $N - 1$ in the denominator as opposed to N in our manual calculations.

To correct this, let us revisit step three and divide the sum of squared deviations by $N - 1$ this time. In Listing 4-5, we first get the number of rows N using the first dimension (row dimension) of the shape() function, then plug in the calculation based on the formula of variance.

Listing 4-5. Calculating the sample variance

```
num_rows = squared_deviations_df.shape[0]
variance2 = squared_deviations_df.sum() / (num_rows-1)
>>> variance2
AAPL     0.000169
GOOG     0.000259
dtype: float64
```

Taking the square root now gives the same result as using the std() function:

```
volatility2 = np.sqrt(variance2)
>>> volatility2
AAPL     0.012995
GOOG     0.016086
dtype: float64
```

Now we have the single-period volatility that measures the daily spread of the returns around its mean, the next section calculates the annualized volatility.

Calculating the Annualized Volatility

Following the formula for annualizing the single-period volatility to annual volatility, we can calculate the annualized volatility as follows, where the total length of time in a year is $T = 252$:

```
annualized_vol = returns_df.std()*np.sqrt(252)
>>> annualized_vol
AAPL    0.206289
GOOG    0.255356
dtype: float64
```

We can also calculate the square root of 252 by raising it to the power of 0.5, which returns the same result:

```
annualized_vol = returns_df.std()*(252**0.5)
>>> annualized_vol
AAPL    0.206289
GOOG    0.255356
dtype: float64
```

The next section looks at annualizing the returns.

Calculating the Annualized Returns

A note to pay attention to here is that returns follow a sequential compounding process. This means that once we have the single-period average return, we need to compound it by the corresponding frequency to reach a year's length. And, to calculate the single-period average return, we take the geometric mean of the returns. The geometric mean is a better choice than the arithmetic mean in this context because it takes into account the effects of sequential compounding.

Specifically, we first calculate the geometric mean of the returns as follows. Note that the geometric mean aligns with the sequential compounding nature when analyzing the cumulative return of an asset:

```
returns_per_day = (returns_df+1).prod()**(1/returns_df.shape[0]) - 1
>>> returns_per_day
AAPL     0.007153
GOOG     0.004178
dtype: float64
```

Let us decompose the sequence of operations here. First, we construct the 1+R returns in (returns_df+1) for each day, then perform sequential compounding using the prod() function to obtain the cumulative terminal return in 1+R format. Before subtracting one, we raise it to the power of $1/N$, where N is the number of rows in the DataFrame. This gives the geometric mean of the returns in 1+R format. We do not use the arithmetic mean here.

Now comes the annualization part. As shown in Listing 4-6, we assume a fixed daily return as the geometric mean and roll it forward by a year, corresponding to 252 trading days. Again, convert between 1+R return and the normal return.

Listing 4-6. Annualizing the daily return

```
annualized_return = (returns_per_day+1)**252-1
>>> annualized_return
AAPL     5.025830
GOOG     1.859802
dtype: float64
```

It seems Apple is doing quite well compared with Google for the first few days.

There is another way to calculate the annualized return, a faster way:

```
annualized_return = (returns_df+1).prod()**(252/returns_df.shape[0])-1
>>> annualized_return
AAPL     5.025830
GOOG     1.859802
dtype: float64
```

The key change here is that we raise the terminal return to the power of $252/N$. This is standardization, bringing the daily scale to the yearly scale.

Calculating the Sharpe Ratio

Finally, let us compute the Sharpe ratio for both stocks. We assume a risk-free interest rate of 3%, calculate the excess return by subtracting it from the annualized return, and divide it by the annualized volatility to obtain the Sharpe ratio. This is shown in Listing 4-7.

Listing 4-7. Calculating the Sharpe ratio

```
riskfree_rate = 0.03
excess_return = annualized_return - riskfree_rate
sharpe_ratio = excess_return/annualized_vol
>>> sharpe_ratio
AAPL    24.217681
GOOG     7.165694
dtype: float64
```

Thus, the Sharpe ratio as a risk-adjusted return is much higher for Apple than Google for the first few days.

Summary

In this chapter, we explored the two key characteristics of any financial asset: risk and return. Return refers to the financial reward an asset brings, while risk represents the volatility or uncertainty of that return. As investors, our goal is to maximize return while minimizing risk.

We introduced different ways to represent and calculate the returns, including the simple return, terminal return, multiperiod return, and the 1+R formatted return. It is important to understand the connections among these forms of return when translating one form to the other.

We then highlighted the risk-return trade-off, where low-return assets are typically associated with low risk and high-return assets with high risk. To better compare the risk and return for different investment vehicles, we introduced the annualized return and volatility, as well as a risk-adjusted return metric called the Sharpe ratio. We also provided examples illustrating the importance of considering both risk and return when comparing investment products.

Exercises

- How many inputs do we need to calculate a single-period return?

- What is the return if the asset price changes from $5 to $6?

- Is the total return of a popular stock typically higher or lower than its price return?

- Calculate the three-period return that consists of 10%, –5%, and 6%.

- If we buy an asset that rises by 10% on day one and drops by 10% on day two, is our return positive, negative, or zero?

- Calculate the annualized return for an asset with a quarterly (three months) return of 2%.

- Download the YTD stock data for Apple and Tesla and calculate the daily cumulative returns using the daily closing price. Plot the returns as line charts.

- Both annualized volatility and variance grow linearly with time, correct?

- Suppose the monthly volatility is 5%. Calculate the annualized volatility.

- The annualized volatility is always greater than the monthly volatility. True or false?

- The risk-free rate is the return on an investment that carries a low risk. True or false?

- If the risk-free rate goes up and the volatility of the portfolio remains unchanged, will the Sharpe ratio increase or decrease?

- Obtain monthly return data based on the median daily price per month of Apple stock in the first half of 2022. Calculate the annualized return and volatility based on the monthly returns.

CHAPTER 5

Trend-Following Strategy

Trend following is a popular investment strategy used in all types of markets, including stocks, bonds, commodities, currencies, and even cryptocurrencies. As its name suggests, this strategy is based on the assumption that prices tend to move in a particular direction (or "trend") over time, thus offering opportunities to capitalize on these movements. At its core, trend following involves analyzing historical price data to identify potential trends. The strategy then recommends taking positions that align with these trends with the expectation that they will continue. For example, if the price of an asset has been steadily rising, a trend follower would typically take a long position, expecting the upward trend to continue. Conversely, if the price has been consistently falling, the trend follower might take a short position, betting that the price will continue to drop.

However, like any trading strategy, trend following is not foolproof. Trends can reverse suddenly due to unexpected market events or changes in market sentiment, leading to potential losses. Therefore, trend-following strategies typically include overlaying risk management techniques, such as setting up stop-loss orders, to limit potential losses when the trend reverses.

Trend-following strategies use a variety of technical indicators to identify and confirm trends, such as moving averages, trend lines, and momentum indicators. This chapter introduces the working mechanism of the trend-following strategies using moving averages and then shows its implementation in Python.

Since we will be working with log returns mostly, let us start by going through an example of its calculation process.

© Peng Liu 2023

P. Liu, *Quantitative Trading Strategies Using Python*, https://doi.org/10.1007/978-1-4842-9675-2_5

Working with Log Returns

Let us build a further understanding of the logarithmic return (or log return) as we will use it to calculate the stock returns when assessing the trend-following strategy. We start with the Excel table in Figure 5-1, where we are given a set of dummy stock prices and are asked to answer questions from Q1 to Q9. We detail the questions and answers in the following.

Daily stock prices					
		Q2	Q3	Q5	Q7
Day	Price	return1	return2	return3	return4
1	100				
2	108				
3	100				
4	98				
5	106				
Q4	Q6	Q8			

Figure 5-1. *Daily dummy stock prices*

Let us go through each of these nine questions.

Q1: Why do we use percentage return?

Answer: Percentage return provides the same scale of comparison. For example, when we have the price data of another stock (stock B) in the range of 1–10, comparing it with the stock price data (stock A) given by the Excel table is difficult when using absolute terms. A $5 increase means more for stock A than stock B. By converting them to the relative percentage terms, we can put both stocks on the scale ruler and measure their performance. Thus, using percentage returns, we can accurately compare the performance of these two stocks despite their difference in price levels.

Percentage returns are also useful for comparing the performance of an investment to a benchmark or standard, such as a market index (like the S&P 500 or the Dow Jones Industrial Average). This helps investors to assess how well an investment or a portfolio is performing relative to the broader market or a sector of the market.

Q2: Calculate single-period percentage return the original way (based on the definition of return).

Answer: The single-period percentage return, also known as the simple return or the holding period return, reflects the percentage change in the value of an investment from one period to the next. It is calculated as

$$R_{t,t+1} = \frac{S_{t+1} - S_t}{S_t}$$

where $R_{t,t+1}$ is the single-period percentage return from time period t to $t+1$, and S_t and S_{t+1} are asset prices at the end of period t and $t+1$, respectively. The numerator of the formula, $S_{t+1} - S_t$, calculates the change in the price of the asset from time t to $t+1$. The denominator, S_t, is the price at the beginning of the period, which serves as the baseline for measuring the relative change. Dividing the price change by the starting price gives the relative change in price, expressed as a percentage, which is the simple return.

Applying the same formula to all cells in column return1 except for day 1 generates the result in Figure 5-2.

	A	B	C
		fx	=(B5-B4)/B4
1	Daily stock prices		
2		Q2	
3	Day	Price	return1
4	1	100	
5	2	108	8.00%
6	3	100	-7.41%
7	4	98	-2.00%
8	5	106	8.16%

Figure 5-2. *Calculating the simple returns based on the definition of percentage return*

Q3: Calculate the same returns using the 1+R way.

Answer: The 1+R approach to calculating returns is slightly different from the original method but essentially delivers the same result. This approach emphasizes the growth factor of the asset's price from one period to the next, making it easier to understand and interpret. The 1+R approach says that we rewrite the return as

$$R_{t,t+1} = \frac{S_{t+1}}{S_t} - 1$$

This requires two steps: first, calculate the ratio $\frac{S_{t+1}}{S_t}$ to obtain the so-called 1+R return. This ratio reflects the growth factor of the asset's price from the beginning of the period to the end. If this ratio is greater than one, it indicates that the asset's price has increased over the period. If it's less than one, it indicates a decrease in the asset's price. If the ratio equals one, it means the asset's price hasn't changed.

Next, we would subtract one from the 1+R return to convert it to the simple return. This step transforms the growth factor $\frac{S_{t+1}}{S_t}$ into the actual percentage return. Subtracting one essentially removes the initial investment from the calculation, leaving only the gained or lost amount relative to the initial investment, which is the return. See Figure 5-3 for an illustration, where the daily returns are the same as in the previous approach.

D5 fx =B5/B4-1

	A	B	C	D
1	Daily stock prices			
2			Q2	Q3
3	Day	Price	return1	return2
4	1	100		
5	2	108	8.00%	8.00%
6	3	100	-7.41%	-7.41%
7	4	98	-2.00%	-2.00%
8	5	106	8.16%	8.16%

Figure 5-3. *Calculating the simple returns based on the 1+R approach*

This 1+R method is often used because it is more intuitive. The growth factor $\frac{S_{t+1}}{S_t}$ easily shows how much the initial investment has grown (or shrunk), and subtracting one gives the net growth in percentage terms, which is the simple return. This method is especially useful when dealing with multiple time periods, as growth factors can simply be multiplied together to calculate the cumulative growth factor over several periods.

Q4: What is the terminal return from day 1 to day 5 without compounding?

Answer: The terminal return is the total return on an investment over a given period of time. It's a measure of the total gain or loss experienced by an investment from the start of the investment period to the end, without considering any compounding effect over the period.

To calculate the terminal return without involving the compounding process, we would resort to $R_{1,5} = \dfrac{S_5 - S_1}{S_1} = \dfrac{S_5}{S_1} - 1$, where the second formula first calculates the ratio of the asset's price on day 5 to its price on day 1 (which reflects the overall growth factor) and then subtracts one to convert the growth factor into a terminal return. See Figure 5-4 for an illustration.

A11		fx =B8/B4-1	
	A	B	C
1	Daily stock prices		
2			Q2
3	Day	Price	return1
4	1	100	
5	2	108	8.00%
6	3	100	-7.41%
7	4	98	-2.00%
8	5	106	8.16%
9			
10	Q4	Q6	Q8
11	6.00%		

Figure 5-4. *Calculating the terminal return without compounding*

Q5: What is the terminal return from day 1 to day 5 with compounding? Is it equal to the result in Q4?

Answer: Compounding returns is an important concept in finance. It reflects the fact that not only your initial investment earns a return but also the returns from previous periods. This leads to exponential growth over time, given a positive return rate.

We will fill in the "return3" column, where each cell is a product between the 1+R return of the current period and the cumulative 1+R return of the previous period, offset by one. For the first period (from day 1 to day 2), the "return3" value would be just the "1 + R" return for this period. See Figure 5-5 for an illustration.

E8		fx	=(1+D8)*(1+E7)-1	
	A	B	C	D	E
1	Daily stock prices				
2			Q2	Q3	Q5
3	Day	Price	return1	return2	return3
4	1	100			
5	2	108	8.00%	8.00%	8.00%
6	3	100	-7.41%	-7.41%	0.00%
7	4	98	-2.00%	-2.00%	-2.00%
8	5	106	8.16%	8.16%	6.00%

Figure 5-5. *Calculating the terminal return using compounding*

As it turns out, the terminal return is 6%, which is the same as previously calculated. Q6: Sum up the single-period returns in Q3. Is it equal to the result in Q4?

Answer: The result shows that it is different from 6%. In general, adding up single-period returns can lead to incorrect conclusions about the overall return on investment. The sum of the single-period returns is not equal to the terminal return (from Q4) because this approach overlooks the effect of compounding. In other words, by simply summing up single-period returns, we are effectively treating each period's return as if it was independent and earned on the initial investment amount, disregarding the fact that the investment grows with each period due to the returns earned in the prior periods. This is why we see a difference between the summed single-period returns and the terminal return calculated through the correct method that takes into account the compounding effect.

The principle of compounding acknowledges that returns accumulate over time, meaning the returns earned in one period are reinvested and can generate further returns in subsequent periods. So, while the sum of single-period returns might provide a rough estimate of the total return, it is not a correct measure, especially when the time span is long, or the return rate is high. Instead, the appropriate way to calculate the total return over multiple periods is to use the concept of compound returns, which considers both the initial investment and the reinvestment of returns. It is thus important to follow the sequential compounding process when calculating the terminal return. See Figure 5-6 for an illustration.

Figure 5-6. *Summing up all single-period returns*

Q7: Calculate the log return for each period.

Answer: The logarithmic return, or continuously compounded return, is another method of calculating returns that can simplify various calculations in finance. This method uses the natural logarithm (log) to express the rate of return, which is derived from the relative changes in price.

To calculate the log return for each period, we can use the formula:

$$\log\_\text{return} = \ln \frac{S_{t+1}}{S_t}$$

Here, S_{t+1} and S_t represent the asset price at the future time $t + 1$ and the current time t, respectively, and ln denotes the natural logarithm. See Figure 5-7 for an illustration.

Figure 5-7. *Calculating the log returns of each period*

For instance, if we have the price data in a sequence, we can compute the log return for each period using this formula. Note that the log return is a good approximation for small returns, and it also has some desirable mathematical properties, such as time additivity, which means that the log return over multiple periods is simply the sum of the log returns over each individual period.

Also, note that we need to ensure that the denominator (S_t in this case) is not zero to avoid division by zero error. This can be handled by adding a small constant to the denominator when implementing the calculation in programs.

Q8: Calculate the terminal return using the log returns. Is it equal to Q4?

Answer: The terminal return using log returns can be calculated by summing all the single-period log returns, then exponentiating the result to reverse the log operation, and finally subtracting one to convert back to the simple return format. This is because log returns are time additive, meaning that the total log return over a given period is simply the sum of the log returns over the subperiods.

In other words, if you have calculated log returns over several periods (say daily), you can get the total (terminal) log return over these periods simply by summing up all these daily log returns. This property simplifies the calculation of terminal returns over multiple periods, making it very convenient, especially for large datasets.

The result shows that it is equal to the one obtained in Q4. See Figure 5-8 for an illustration.

C11		fx =EXP(SUM(F5:F8))-1				
	A	B	C	D	E	F
1	Daily stock prices					
2			Q2	Q3	Q5	Q7
3	Day	Price	return1	return2	return3	return4
4	1	100				
5	2	108	8.00%	8.00%	8.00%	7.70%
6	3	100	-7.41%	-7.41%	0.00%	-7.70%
7	4	98	-2.00%	-2.00%	-2.00%	-2.02%
8	5	106	8.16%	8.16%	6.00%	7.85%
9						
10	Q4	Q6	Q8			
11	6.00%	6.76%	6.00%			

Figure 5-8. *Calculating the terminal return using log returns*

Q9: Discuss the advantages of using log returns.

Answer: As mentioned, the use of logarithmic returns, or "log returns," has several advantages, as detailed in the following:

- Ease of calculation and analysis: Log returns simplify mathematical calculations and statistical analyses. This simplification is particularly noticeable when dealing with compounded returns over multiple periods. Because logarithms convert multiplication and division operations into addition and subtraction, the compounded return (or "total return") over multiple periods can be calculated as the simple sum of the log returns over those periods.

- Symmetry: Log returns also exhibit a desirable symmetry property. If a price doubles and then halves, or halves and then doubles, the total log return over the two periods is zero, reflecting the fact that the price is unchanged over the two periods. This symmetry property, which is not possessed by simple returns, often simplifies analyses and improves the interpretability of results.

- Suppose a stock price S_t changes to S_{t+1} and then changes back to S_t, the resulting log returns will be symmetric around zero. For example, when the stock price changes from 100 on day 1 to 108 on day 2 and then back to 100 on day 3, the resulting log returns are 7.7% on day 2 and –7.7% on day 3. A simple mathematical analysis would immediately make sense of this:

$$\log\frac{S_{t+1}}{S_t} = -\log\left(\frac{S_{t+1}}{S_t}\right)^{-1} = -\log\frac{S_t}{S_{t+1}}$$

- Normality: In addition, financial models often assume that returns are normally distributed. However, it's been observed that simple returns have skewness and excess kurtosis, implying that they deviate from normality. On the other hand, log returns tend to have properties closer to normality which makes them a better fit for these financial models.

- Continuously compounded returns: Log returns also represent continuously compounded returns. This property makes log returns the preferred choice in certain financial applications, especially those involving options and other derivatives, where continuous compounding is commonly used.

In summary, using log returns simplifies mathematical computations and statistical analyses, enables symmetry and normality, and represents continuously compounded returns. These properties make log returns highly valuable in financial analysis and modeling.

Let us look at a concrete example to understand the calculations using log returns.

Analyzing Stock Prices Using Log Returns

We first download Google's stock price data for the first few days of 2023, as shown in Listing 5-1.

Listing 5-1. Downloading Google's stock price

```
import numpy as np
import pandas as pd
import matplotlib.pyplot as plt
import yfinance as yf
symbol = 'GOOG'
df = yf.download(symbol, start="2023-01-01", end="2023-01-08")
>>> df
              Open       High       Low      Close Adj Close      Volume
Date
2023-01-03  89.830002  91.550003  89.019997  89.699997  89.699997  20738500
2023-01-04  91.010002  91.239998  87.800003  88.709999  88.709999  27046500
2023-01-05  88.070000  88.209999  86.559998  86.769997  86.769997  23136100
2023-01-06  87.360001  88.470001  85.570000  88.160004  88.160004  26612600
```

We can use the pct_change() method to calculate the single-period percentage returns, as shown in Listing 5-2.

Listing 5-2. Calculating the single-period percentage returns

```
# single-period percentage returns
returns = df.Close.pct_change()
>>> returns
Date
2023-01-03 00:00:00-05:00         NaN
2023-01-04 00:00:00-05:00   -0.011037
2023-01-05 00:00:00-05:00   -0.021869
2023-01-06 00:00:00-05:00    0.016019
Name: Close, dtype: float64
```

Here, the first-period return is NaN as there is no prior stock price available.

Let us calculate the terminal return using the original approach by taking the first and last closing prices as the inputs (based on the definition given earlier), as shown in Listing 5-3.

Listing 5-3. Calculating the terminal return using the original approach by definition

```
# terminal return
terminal_return = df.Close[-1]/df.Close[0] - 1
>>> terminal_return
-0.01716826464354737
```

We can also calculate the same value by compounding the (1+R) returns based on the .cumprod() function, as shown in Listing 5-4.

Listing 5-4. Calculating the same cumulative terminal return by compounding 1+R formatted returns

```
# cumulative returns
cum_returns = (1+returns).cumprod() - 1
>>> cum_returns
Date
2023-01-03 00:00:00-05:00         NaN
2023-01-04 00:00:00-05:00   -0.011037
2023-01-05 00:00:00-05:00   -0.032664
2023-01-06 00:00:00-05:00   -0.017168
Name: Close, dtype: float64
```

The equality operator on both terminal returns evaluates to True:

```
# check equality on terminal return
>>> cum_returns.values[-1] == terminal_return
True
```

Now we calculate the same using log returns, starting by obtaining the single-period log returns in Listing 5-5.

Listing 5-5. Calculating the log returns

```
# log returns (1+R format)
log_returns = np.log(1+returns)
>>> log_returns
Date
2023-01-03 00:00:00-05:00          NaN
2023-01-04 00:00:00-05:00    -0.011098
2023-01-05 00:00:00-05:00    -0.022112
2023-01-06 00:00:00-05:00     0.015892
Name: Close, dtype: float64
```

We can add all log returns from previous periods together to get the cumulative log returns, convert back to the original scale via exponentiation, and, lastly, offset by one to convert from 1+R to the simple return format, as shown in Listing 5-6.

Listing 5-6. Calculating the cumulative returns using log returns

```
# get cumulative returns using log returns
cum_return2 = np.exp(log_returns.cumsum()) - 1
>>> cum_return2
Date
2023-01-03 00:00:00-05:00          NaN
2023-01-04 00:00:00-05:00    -0.011037
2023-01-05 00:00:00-05:00    -0.032664
2023-01-06 00:00:00-05:00    -0.017168
Name: Close, dtype: float64
```

Again, we verify the value of the last entry and verify that it is the same as the previous terminal return:

```
# check equality on terminal return
>>> cum_return2.values[-1] == terminal_return
True
```

The next section introduces the trend-following strategy.

Introducing Trend Trading

Trend trading, also known as trend following, is a strategy that attempts to harness the momentum of an existing trend in a financial market. It operates on the premise that securities tend to move in a relatively sustained direction over time, either upward (bullish) or downward (bearish). It is a proactive trading strategy that seeks to capitalize on the sustained directional momentum of an asset's price.

The fundamental principle behind trend trading is that a market's momentum, or the rate of acceleration of the asset's price, often continues in one direction for a period of time. This is where the two key concepts, trend and momentum, come into play. The trend represents the direction in which an asset's price is moving, while momentum indicates the strength or speed of this movement over a certain period. It refers to the capacity for the asset's price trend to sustain itself going forward. A strong momentum can continue in an upward or downward trend, which can be confirmed by a set of technical indicators.

Trend traders leverage technical analysis tools to identify potential buying and selling opportunities. They carefully analyze price charts and use various technical indicators, such as moving averages, MACD (Moving Average Convergence Divergence), and the Relative Strength Index (RSI), among others, to identify and confirm an asset's trend direction and momentum. These technical indicators provide signals that help traders to make educated decisions about when to enter and exit trades.

In an uptrend, a trend trader will enter a long position, meaning they buy the asset with the expectation that its price will continue to rise. Conversely, in a downtrend, a trend trader will enter a short position, meaning they sell the asset (or sell short) with the expectation that its price will continue to fall. The trend-following strategy aims to take advantage of these significant movements in price and to profit from both rising and falling markets based on the forward-looking uptrends with new highs or anticipated downtrends with new lows.

Let us start with the technical indicators which are used to generate trading signals.

Understanding Technical Indicators

Technical indicators are mathematical calculations based on historical price (high, low, open, close, etc.) or volume and can be used to determine entry and exit points for trades. They are integral to many trading strategies and systems, providing key insights into market behavior. They can be considered as additional features derived from the raw asset data, a practice of feature engineering in machine learning. This makes technical indicators highly security dependent: what can be a good technical indicator for a particular security might not hold the case for the other. Selecting the right features makes all the difference.

Note that these technical indicators appear as additional features for each observation in the dataset. This means that more columns are added to the price-volume table we worked with earlier, with each column representing a separate technical indicator for the specific asset and time.

When looking at the raw price data, overlaying a set of technical indicators would help clarify the market analysis for traders. For example, technical indicators help confirm if the market is following a trend or in a range-bound situation, oscillating within a price range.

Technical indicators are integral to many trading strategies and systems, providing key insights into market behavior. As you've described, they are tools derived from mathematical calculations on historical price and volume data, designed to predict future price trends or patterns.

Some of the most commonly used technical indicators include

- Moving averages (MA): Moving averages smooth out price data by creating a constantly updated average price. The two most common types are the simple moving average (SMA) and the exponential moving average (EMA). They can help identify whether a security is in an uptrend or downtrend. More on this later.

- Relative Strength Index (RSI): The RSI measures the speed and change of price movements, typically on a scale of 0 to 100. A high RSI (generally above 70) may indicate that the asset is overbought and due for a price correction, while a low RSI (generally below 30) could suggest that the asset is oversold and might rebound.

- Moving Average Convergence Divergence (MACD): This indicator is a trend-following momentum indicator that shows the relationship between two moving averages of a security's price. The MACD is calculated by subtracting the 26-day EMA from the 12-day EMA.

- Bollinger Bands: These bands are plotted two standard deviations away from a simple moving average. They help identify whether an asset is overbought or oversold and can signal the end of a trend.

- Volume-based indicators: These include indicators such as the on-balance volume (OBV), which uses volume flow to predict changes in stock price.

Each of these indicators provides a unique perspective on potential market movements. A combination of these indicators is often used to create a robust trading strategy.

Also, note that these indicators don't predict future prices with absolute certainty. Instead, they help traders identify potential trading opportunities based on statistical probabilities. Each indicator works best under specific market conditions and may not be universally applicable across different asset classes, markets, and trading horizons.

The following section provides more introduction to moving averages.

Introducing Moving Averages

Moving average, also called rolling average, is the mean or average of the specified data field (e.g., daily closing price) for a given set of *consecutive* periods. As new data becomes available, the mean of the data is computed by dropping the oldest value and adding the latest one. It is rolling along with the data, hence the name "moving average." It provides a way of smoothing out the price data of a financial asset to identify trends more clearly.

When calculating moving averages of stock prices, it works similarly to moving a fixed-size window along the time horizon, where each window reports a single number as the average of all price points within the window. And when that window does not have full price points for the initial periods, an NA value is often reported.

When working with time series data such as daily stock price, the averaging effect can also be considered as smoothening the time series, reducing short-term fluctuations and temporary variations in the data.

There are different types of moving averages, with the simple moving average and the exponential moving average being the most popular ones. The simple moving average is straightforward to calculate; we simply take the average of all the price points in the current fixed-size window, assuming an equal weightage for all the price points in this window.

The exponential moving average, or exponentially weighted moving average (EWMA), decreases the weightage for older price points. It's more complex to calculate than the SMA, as it involves a smoothing factor that needs to be computed. But the basic idea is the same: it's an average of the closing prices over a certain period.

The choice between using a simple or exponential moving average depends on the trader's preference and the specific trading strategy. In general, EMAs react more quickly to recent price changes than SMAs, making them more preferred by short-term traders or those trading volatile markets.

Moving averages can be used to identify support and resistance levels. The support level is typically a price level or zone that a stock or a market has had difficulty falling below over a specific period. The resistance level is the opposite of the support level. It's a price level or zone that a stock or a market has trouble moving above. Prices often bounce off these levels, making them useful for identifying potential trade entry and exit points.

In addition, when two moving averages (e.g., 50-day and 200-day) cross each other, it may signal a change in trend. A bullish signal is given when the shorter MA crosses above the longer MA, and a bearish signal is given when the shorter MA crosses below the longer MA. These crossover points become potential trading signals.

The following section focuses more on the simple moving averages.

Delving into Simple Moving Averages

The simple moving average SMA_t at time t is defined as follows:

$$\text{SMA}_t = \frac{S_{t-(M-1)} + \ldots + S_{t-1} + S_t}{M}$$

In other words, to calculate SMA_t, we would take M historical price points, including the current period, and then take the average of these M price points. Essentially, it involves adding up the prices of the security for the last M periods (days, hours, etc.) and then dividing by M. This provides a single output point, the SMA at time t. As new price data becomes available, the oldest data point is dropped, and the newest data point is included in the calculation. This "rolling" or "moving" calculation continues as new price data is added.

The SMA is often used in trend analysis as it smoothens out short-term fluctuations and provides a clearer picture of the overall trend. It is the unweighted mean of the previous *M* price points. Here, the choice of M (the number of periods) is crucial because it affects the sensitivity and reliability of the SMA. A smaller M will be more responsive to price changes but may also yield more false signals. A larger M will provide a slower, more reliable SMA, but it might be slower in signaling changes in trends.

Let us look at how to calculate SMA. We first download Apple's stock price data for 2022, as shown in Listing 5-7.

Listing 5-7. Downloading Apple's stock price data

```
import numpy as np
import pandas as pd
import matplotlib.pyplot as plt
import yfinance as yf
symbol = 'AAPL'
df = yf.download(symbol, start="2022-01-01", end="2023-01-01")
df.index = pd.to_datetime(df.index)
>>> df.head()
             Open        High         Low       Close  Adj Close    Volume
Date
2022-01-03  177.830002  182.880005  177.710007  182.009995  180.434296  104487900
2022-01-04  182.630005  182.940002  179.119995  179.699997  178.144302  99310400
2022-01-05  179.610001  180.169998  174.639999  174.919998  173.405685  94537600
2022-01-06  172.699997  175.300003  171.639999  172.000000  170.510956  96904000
2022-01-07  172.889999  174.139999  171.029999  172.169998  170.679489  86709100
```

Note that we have an index named Date which now assumes a datetime format to facilitate plotting.

Listing 5-8 generates a plot on the daily adjusted closing price. We will later overlay its SMA on the same plot.

Listing 5-8. Plotting the daily adjusted closing price

```
# plot the adj closing price
plt.figure(figsize=(15, 7))
df['Adj Close'].plot()
# set labels and sizes of the title and axis
plt.title('Daily adjusted closing price of Apple', fontsize=16)
plt.xlabel('Time', fontsize=15)
plt.ylabel('Price ($)', fontsize=15)
plt.xticks(fontsize=15)
plt.yticks(fontsize=15)
plt.legend(['Close'], prop={'size': 15})
# show the plot
>>> plt.show()
```

Running the commands generates Figure 5-9, suggesting a download trend overall.

Figure 5-9. *Visualizing the daily closing price of Apple in 2022*

Now we create an SMA series with a window size of three. We can create the rolling window using the `rolling()` method for a Pandas Series, followed by the `mean()` method to extract the average value from the window (a collection of price points). Listing 5-9 creates a new SMA column called `SMA-3` and subsets to keep only two columns: the adjusted closing price and the SMA column.

Listing 5-9. Creating simple moving averages

```
window = 3
SMA1 = "SMA-"+str(window)
df[SMA1] = df['Adj Close'].rolling(window).mean()
colnames = ["Adj Close",SMA1]
df2 = df[colnames]
>>> df2.head()
          Adj Close   SMA-3
Date
2022-01-03 180.434296 NaN
2022-01-04 178.144302 NaN
2022-01-05 173.405685 177.328094
2022-01-06 170.510956 174.020315
2022-01-07 170.679489 171.532043
```

Let us pause for a moment and look at how this column is generated. We see that the first two rows in the SMA column are missing. This makes sense as both of them are unable to get a full three-period moving window to calculate the average. In other words, we cannot calculate the average when there is an empty value in the window unless additional treatment is applied here, such as ignoring the empty value while calculating the average.

We note that the third entry of the SMA column is 177.844493. Let us verify through manual calculation. The following command takes the first three entries of the adjusted closing price column and calculates the average, which reports the same value:

```
>>> np.mean(df['Adj Close'][:3])
177.84449259440103
```

which verifies the calculation. Figure 5-10 summarizes the process of calculating SMA in our running example.

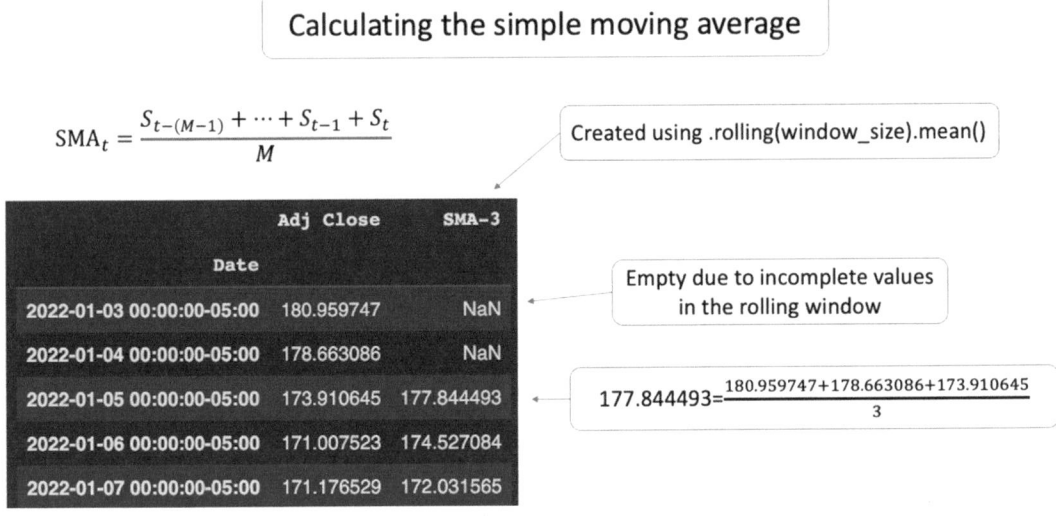

Figure 5-10. *Illustrating the process of calculating simple moving averages*

Note that we can configure the `min_periods` argument in the `rolling()` function to control the behavior at the initial windows with incomplete data. For example, by setting `min_periods=1`, the previous code will report the average value based on the *available* data in the window. See the following code snippet for a comparison:

```
df['New_SMA'] = df['Adj Close'].rolling(window, min_periods=1).mean()
>>> df[colnames + ['New_SMA']].head()
            Adj Close  SMA-3       New_SMA
Date
2022-01-03  180.434296 NaN         180.434296
2022-01-04  178.144302 NaN         179.289299
2022-01-05  173.405685 177.328094  177.328094
2022-01-06  170.510956 174.020315  174.020315
2022-01-07  170.679489 171.532043  171.532043
```

Note that the only difference is in the first two entries, where we have an incomplete set of values in the rolling window.

Next, we plot the three-period SMA alongside the original daily adjusted closing price series, as shown in Listing 5-10.

Listing 5-10. Plotting the closing price and its SMA

```
# colors for the line plot
colors = ['blue', 'red']
# line plot for original price and SMA
df2.plot(color=colors, linewidth=3, figsize=(12,6))
# modify ticks size
plt.xticks(fontsize=13)
plt.yticks(fontsize=13)
plt.legend(labels = colnames, fontsize=13)
# title and labels
plt.title('Daily adjusted closing price and its SWA', fontsize=20)
plt.xlabel('Date', fontsize=16)
plt.ylabel('Price', fontsize=16)
```

Running these commands generates Figure 5-11. Note that the three-period SMA curve in red looks less volatile than the original price series in blue. Also, the three-period SMA curve starts from the third entry.

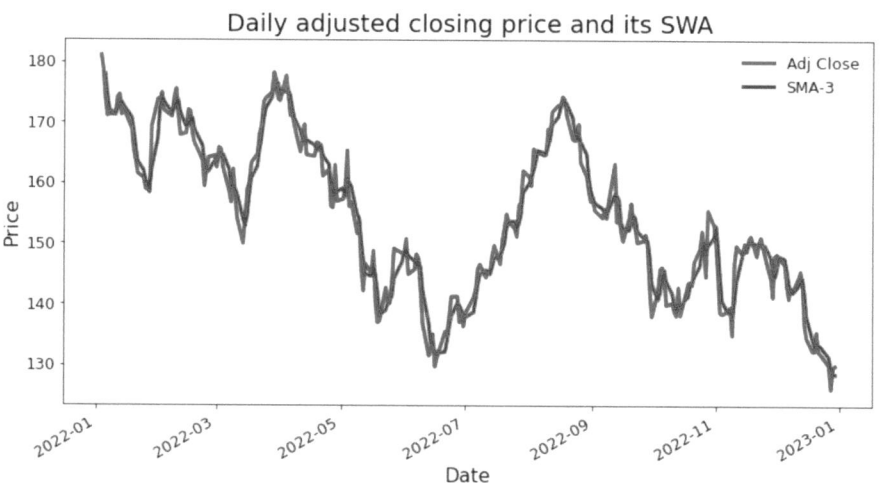

Figure 5-11. *Visualizing the original price and three-period SMA*

Now let us add another SMA with a longer period. In Listing 5-11, we add a 20-period SMA as an additional column to df2.

Listing 5-11. Creating 20-period SMA

```
window = 20
SMA2 = "SMA-"+str(window)
df2["SMA-"+SMA2] = df2['Adj Close'].rolling(window).mean()
colnames = ["Adj Close",SMA1,SMA2]
```

Next, we overlay the 20-period SMA on the previous graph, as shown in Listing 5-12.

Listing 5-12. Plotting the closing price and two SMAs

```
# colors for the line plot
colors = ['blue', 'red', 'green']
# line plot for original price and SMA
df2.plot(color=colors, linewidth=3, figsize=(12,6))
# modify ticks size
plt.xticks(fontsize=13)
plt.yticks(fontsize=13)
plt.legend(labels = colnames, fontsize=13)
# title and labels
plt.title('Daily adjusted closing price and its SWA', fontsize=20)
plt.xlabel('Date', fontsize=16)
plt.ylabel('Price', fontsize=16)
```

Running these commands generates Figure 5-12, which shows that the 20-period SMA is smoother than the 3-period SMA due to a larger window size.

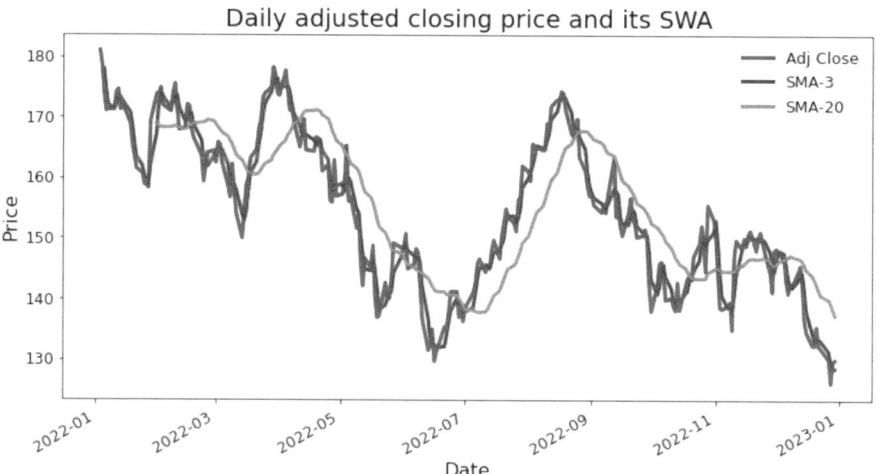

Figure 5-12. *Visualizing the daily prices together with 3-period and 20-period SMAs*

The next section focuses on the exponential moving averages (EMA).

Delving into Exponential Moving Averages

The exponential moving average (EMA), also known as an exponentially weighted moving average (EWMA), is another type of moving average that places a higher weight and significance on the most recent data points. This is a key difference compared to the simple moving average, which gives equal weight to all data points within the period.

The exponential moving average (EMA) is a widely used method to reduce the noise in the data and identify long-term trends. Each EMA entry is a weighted combination of historical prices and the current price. The weight of each price point decreases progressively over time, giving greater weight to recent data points. It is calculated using the following formula:

$$\text{EWMA}_t = \begin{cases} S_0, \ t = 0 \\ \alpha S_t + (1 - \alpha)\text{EWMA}_{t-1}, \ t > 0 \end{cases}$$

where α is the smoothing factor which ranges between zero and one. The smoothing factor α determines the weight given to the most recent price relative to the existing EMA. A higher α emphasizes recent prices more strongly.

As for the first EWMA value at time $t = 0$, a default choice is to set $EWMA_0 = S_0$. Therefore, EMA assumes that recent data is more relevant than old data. Such an assumption has its merit since EMA can react faster to changes and is thus more sensitive to recent movements as compared to the simple moving average. This also means there is no window size to be specified by the function since all historical data points are in use.

It's important to note that while EMA provides more accurate and timely signals than SMA, it might also produce more false signals as it's more responsive to short-term price fluctuations.

The EMA can be calculated by calling the ewm() method from a Pandas Series object, followed by extracting the average value via mean(). We can set the alpha argument in ewm() to directly control the importance of the current observation compared with historical ones. See Listing 5-13 for an illustration, where we set $\alpha = 0.1$ to give more weightage to historical prices.

Listing 5-13. Creating EMA series

```
alpha = 0.1
df2['EWM_'+str(alpha)] = df2['Adj Close'].ewm(alpha=alpha,
adjust=False).mean()
df2.head()
            Adj Close  SMA-3       SMA-20 EWM_0.1
Date
2022-01-03 180.434296 NaN         NaN    180.434296
2022-01-04 178.144302 NaN         NaN    180.205296
2022-01-05 173.405685 177.328094 NaN    179.525335
2022-01-06 170.510956 174.020315 NaN    178.623897
2022-01-07 170.679489 171.532043 NaN    177.829456
```

We observe that there is no missing value in the EMA series. Indeed, the first entry will simply be the original price itself due to the design of the EMA weighting scheme.

As usual, let us verify the calculations to ensure our understanding is on the right track. The following code snippet manually calculates the second EMA value, which is the same as the one obtained using the ewm() function:

```
alpha=0.1
>>> alpha*df2['Adj Close'][1] + (1-alpha)*df2['Adj Close'][0]
180.73006591796877
```

Let us continue to create another EMA series with $\alpha = 0.5$. In other words, we assign an equal weightage to the current observation and historical ones:

```
alpha = 0.5
df2['EWM_'+str(alpha)]= df2['Adj Close'].ewm(alpha=alpha,
adjust=False).mean()
df2.head()
              Adj Close  SMA-3       SMA-20 EWM_0.1     EWM_0.5
Date
2022-01-03 180.434296 NaN         NaN    180.434296 180.434296
2022-01-04 178.144302 NaN         NaN    180.205296 179.289299
2022-01-05 173.405685 177.328094 NaN    179.525335 176.347492
2022-01-06 170.510956 174.020315 NaN    178.623897 173.429224
2022-01-07 170.679489 171.532043 NaN    177.829456 172.054357
```

Let us put all these moving averages in a single chart. Here, the plot() function treats all four columns as four separate series to be plotted against the index column, as shown in Listing 5-14.

Listing 5-14. Plotting all moving averages together

```
df2.plot(linewidth=3, figsize=(12,6))
plt.title('Daily adjusted closing price with SWA and EWM', fontsize=20)
plt.xlabel('Date', fontsize=16)
plt.ylabel('Price', fontsize=16)
```

Running these commands generates Figure 5-13. We note that EWM_0.1 (red line) is close to SMA-20 (green line), both of which give more weightage to historical observations. The same is true for the other two moving averages. For EMA, a small weighting factor α results in a high degree of smoothing, while a larger value leads to a quicker response to recent changes.

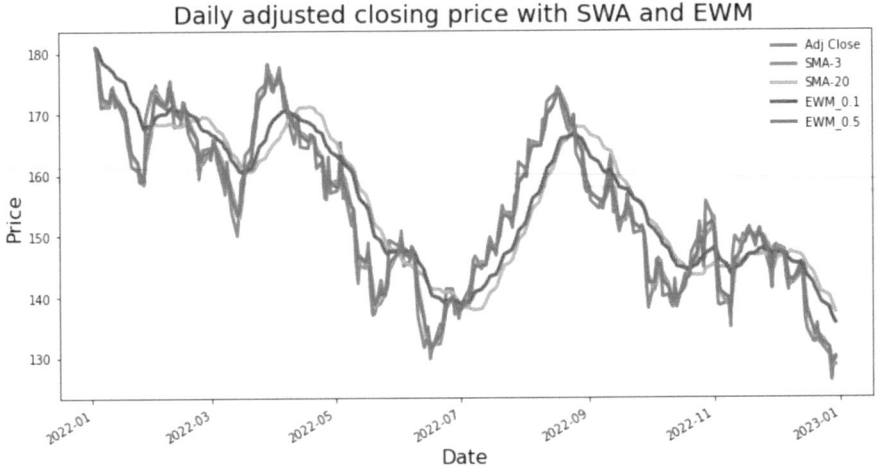

Figure 5-13. *Visualizing the daily closing prices with both SMA and EMA of different configurations*

Having looked at how to compute these moving averages, the next section shows how to use them as technical indicators to develop a trend-following strategy.

Implementing the Trend-Following Strategy

The trend-following strategy that relies on moving averages works like this. There will be two moving averages: a short-term moving average and a long-term moving average. When the short-term moving average crosses above the long-term moving average, it signals a buy action, and the trend trader enters a long position on the asset. When the short-term moving average crosses below the long-term moving average, it signals a sell action, and the trend trader enters a short position on the asset. Thus, the strategy is based on the intersection of two moving averages: one short term (quick) and one long term (slow).

Note that this framework also applies to the case when there is only one moving average series. In this case, the trend trader would buy the asset when the current price is above the moving average and sell it if the current price is below the moving average. The key justification for such trading action is, when the price is above a moving average, an uptrend may be present, and vice versa. The *crossover* between two lines generates the trading signal.

Other momentum-related technical indicators, such as the RSI and MACD, may also be used to signal entries or exits.

In the following section, we will implement a trend-following trading strategy using the long-term and short-term moving averages. Using this strategy, we are essentially searching for the trading signal at each time point. That is, we want to decide if we would buy, sell, or hold an asset at each time step. The signal is generated by a crossover between two moving averages. We assume no transaction cost will be incurred when performing a trading action, and the market is liquid (sufficient Apple stock in the market) and complete (no arbitrage opportunities).

Let us recall the main DataFrame we will work with. The following command prints out the summary information using the info() function:

```
>>> df2.info()
 <class 'pandas.core.frame.DataFrame'>
DatetimeIndex: 251 entries, 2022-01-03 00:00:00-05:00 to 2022-12-30
00:00:00-05:00
Data columns (total 5 columns):
 #    Column      Non-Null Count  Dtype
---   ------      --------------  -----
 0    Adj Close   251 non-null    float64
 1    SMA-3       249 non-null    float64
 2    SMA-20      232 non-null    float64
 3    EWM_0.1     251 non-null    float64
 4    EWM_0.5     251 non-null    float64
dtypes: float64(5)
memory usage: 19.9 KB
```

Now we will use SMA-3 and SMA-20 as the respective short-term and long-term moving averages, whose crossover will generate a trading signal. We leave it as an exercise to try both SMA with different window sizes and EMA with different weighting schemes.

Note that we can only use the information up to yesterday to make a trading decision for tomorrow. We cannot use today's information since the closing price is not yet available in the middle of the day. To enforce this requirement, we can shift the moving averages one day into the future, as shown in the following code snippet. This essentially says that the moving average for today is derived from historical information up to yesterday.

```
# Shift to the future by one day so that everyday uses the
information up to
# yesterday to make a trading decision for tmr
df2['SMA-3'] = df2['SMA-3'].shift(1)
df2['SMA-20'] = df2['SMA-20'].shift(1)
```

Now let us implement the trading rule: buy if SMA-3 > SMA-20, and sell if SMA-3 < SMA-20. Such an if-else condition can be created using the np.where() function, as shown in Listing 5-15.

Listing 5-15. Creating and identifying buy and sell signals

```
# identify buy signal
df2['signal'] = np.where(df2['SMA-3'] > df2['SMA-20'], 1, 0)
# identify sell signal
df2['signal'] = np.where(df2['SMA-3'] < df2['SMA-20'], -1, df2['signal'])
df2.dropna(inplace=True)
```

Here, a normal trading day would assume a value of either 1 or –1 in the signal column. When there is a missing value or other special cases, we set it to 0. We also use the dropna() function to ensure that the DataFrame is of good quality by dropping rows with any NA/missing value in it.

We can check the frequency distribution of the signal column as follows:

```
>>> df2['signal'].value_counts()
-1    135
 1     96
Name: signal, dtype: int64
```

The result shows that there are more declining days than inclining days, which confirms the downward trending price series shown earlier.

Next, we introduce a baseline strategy called *buy-and-hold*, which simply means we hold one share of Apple stock until the end of the whole period. Also, we will use the log return instead of the raw return to facilitate the calculations. Therefore, instead of taking the division between consecutive stock prices to get $\frac{S_{t+1}}{S_t}$, we now take the difference $\log S_{t+1} - \log S_t$ to get $\log \frac{S_{t+1}}{S_t}$, which can then be exponentiated to convert to back $\frac{S_{t+1}}{S_t}$.

The following code snippet calculates the instantaneous logarithmic single-period return, where we first take the logarithm of the adjusted closing prices and then call the `diff()` function to obtain the differences between consecutive pairs of prices:

```
df2['log_return_buy_n_hold'] = np.log(df2['Adj Close']).diff()
```

Now comes the calculation of the single-period return for the trend-following strategy. Recall the `signal` column we created earlier. This column represents whether we go long (valued 1) or short (value –1) in a position for every single period. This also shows that the logarithmic return $\log \frac{S_{t+1}}{S_t}$ is positive if $S_{t+1} > S_t$ and negative if $S_{t+1} < S_t$. This creates the following four scenarios when the asset moves from S_t to S_{t+1}:

- When we long an asset and its logarithmic return is positive, the trend-following strategy reports a positive return, that is, $1 * \log \frac{S_{t+1}}{S_t}$.
- When we long an asset and its logarithmic return is negative, the trend-following strategy reports a negative return, that is, $1 * \log \frac{S_{t+1}}{S_t}$.
- When we short an asset and its logarithmic return is positive, the trend-following strategy reports a negative return, that is, $-1 * \log \frac{S_{t+1}}{S_t}$.
- When we short an asset and its logarithmic return is negative, the trend-following strategy reports a positive return, that is, $-1 * \log \frac{S_{t+1}}{S_t}$.

Summarizing these four scenarios, we can obtain the single-period logarithmic return for the trend-following strategy by multiplying `signal` with the `log_return_buy_n_hold` (the single-period logarithmic return based on the buy-and-hold strategy), as shown in Listing 5-16.

Listing 5-16. Calculating the log return of the trend-following strategy

```
df2['log_return_trend_follow'] = df2['signal'] * df2['log_return_
buy_n_hold']
```

Compared with the buy-and-hold strategy, the key difference is the additional shorting actions generated by the trend-following strategy. That is, when the stock price drops, the buy-and-hold strategy will register a loss, while the trend-following strategy will make a profit *if* the trading signal is to go short. Creating a good trading signal thus makes all the difference.

Next, we create explicit trading actions. The `signal` column tells us whether we should go long or short in the given asset under the trend-following strategy. However, this does not mean we need to make a trade at every period. If the `signal` remains the same for two consecutive periods, we simply hold on to the position and remain seated. In other words, there is no trading action for this specific trading day. This applies in the case of two consecutive 1s or –1s in the `signal` column.

On the other hand, we will make an action when there is a sign switch in the trading signal, changing from 1 to –1 or from –1 to 1. The former means changing from longing a unit of stock to shorting it, while the latter means the reverse.

To create the trading actions, we can use the `diff()` method again on the `signal` column, as shown in the following:

```
df2['action'] = df2.signal.diff()
```

We can produce a frequency count of different trading actions using the `value_counts()` function:

```
>>> df2['action'].value_counts()
0.0     216
 2.0      7
-2.0      7
Name: action, dtype: int64
```

The result shows that the majority of the trading days do not require action. For the 14 days with a trading action, 7 days change the position from short to long, and another 7 change from long to short.

We can visualize these trading actions as triangles on the graph with stock prices and SMAs. In Listing 5-17, we indicate a buy action via the green triangle facing upward when the short-term SMA crosses above the long-term SMA. On the other hand, we use a red triangle facing downward to indicate a sell action when the short-term SMA crosses below the long-term SMA.

Listing 5-17. Visualizing trading actions

```
plt.rcParams['figure.figsize'] = 12, 6
plt.grid(True, alpha = .3)
plt.plot(df2['Adj Close'], label = 'Adj Close')
plt.plot(df2['SMA-3'], label = 'SMA-3')
plt.plot(df2['SMA-20'], label = 'SMA-20')
plt.plot(df2.loc[df2.action == 2].index, df2['SMA-3'][df2.action == 2], '^',
        color = 'g', markersize = 12)
plt.plot(df2[df2.action == -2].index, df2['SMA-20'][df2.action == -2], 'v',
        color = 'r', markersize = 12)
plt.legend(loc=1);
```

Running these commands generates Figure 5-14. Again, we denote the green triangles as acting from short to long and the red triangles as moving from long to short.

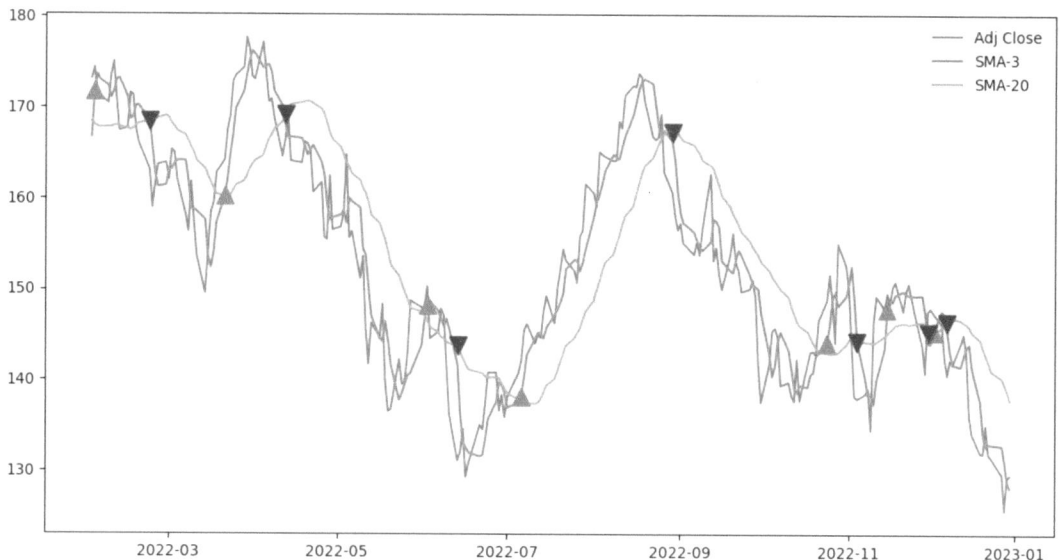

Figure 5-14. *Visualizing the trading actions, including going from short to long (green triangles) and long to short (red triangles)*

Let us analyze the cumulative returns of each period for both trading strategies. Specifically, we would like to obtain the final percentage return at the end of 2022 if we started with one unit of Apple stock at the beginning of 2022, comparing the two trading strategies.

Recall that we need to multiply the 1+R return at each period to carry out the compounding process in order to obtain the terminal return (after subtracting one). We also know that the 1+R return is the same as the division between two consecutive prices, that is, $1 + R_{t,t+1} = \dfrac{S_{t+1}}{S_t}$. Therefore, to calculate the terminal return, we first convert the returns from the logarithmic format to the usual percentage format using the np.exp() function, then carry out the compounding by performing a cumulative product operation using the cumprod() method. This is achieved via Listing 5-18, where we leave out the last step of subtracting by one and report the 1+R return.

Listing 5-18. Visualizing cumulative returns

```
plt.plot(np.exp(df2['log_return_buy_n_hold']).cumprod(),
label='Buy-n-hold')
plt.plot(np.exp(df2['log_return_trend_follow']).cumprod(), label='Trend
following')
plt.legend(loc=2)
plt.title("Cumulative return of different trading strategies")
plt.grid(True, alpha=.3)
```

Running these commands generates Figure 5-15, which shows that the trend-following strategy clearly outperforms the buy-and-hold strategy. However, note that this is a simplified setting that does not take into account transaction cost and other market factors. More analyses and tests are needed to assess the performance of this trading strategy (also many others) in the real-world environment.

Figure 5-15. *Comparing the cumulative return of buy-and-hold and trend-following strategies for one share of Apple's stock*

Lastly, we compare the terminal returns of both strategies:

```
# terminal return of buy-n-hold
>>> np.exp(df2['log_return_buy_n_hold']).cumprod()[-1] -1
-0.25156586984649587
# terminal return of trend following
>>> np.exp(df2['log_return_trend_follow']).cumprod()[-1] -1
0.0711944903093773
```

It turns out that sticking to the buy-and-hold strategy would lose by 25%, while using the trend-following strategy generates a terminal return of 7%.

Summary

In this chapter, we covered the basics of the popular trend-following strategy and its implementation in Python. We started with an exercise on working with log returns and then transitioned to different moving averages as commonly used technical indicators, including simple moving averages and exponential moving averages. Lastly, we discussed how to generate trading signals and calculate the performance metrics using this strategy, which will serve as a good baseline strategy as we delve into other candidates later on.

Exercises

- Explain why log returns are symmetric mathematically.

- How can we deal with a situation where the price point at a given day is missing when calculating its moving average?

- How does the value of the window size affect the smoothness of the SMA? What about the impact of α on the smoothness of EMA?

- Change the code to obtain a moving median instead of a moving average. Discuss the difference between the median and the mean. How about maximum and minimum over the same rolling window?

- Switch to EMA to derive the trading signals and discuss the results.

- Show mathematically why the log returns are additive over time and explain the significance of this property in the context of asset returns.

- Suppose there are multiple missing price points in your data, how would you modify the moving average calculation to handle these gaps? What are the potential issues with your approach?

- Experiment with different window sizes for SMA and different values of α for EMA. Discuss how these parameters affect the sensitivity of the moving averages to price changes. How would you choose an optimal value for these parameters?

## CHAPTER 6

Momentum Trading Strategy

Momentum trading is a strategy that makes use of the strength of price movements as a basis for opening positions, either longing or shorting a set of assets. It involves buying and/or selling a selected set of assets according to the recent strength of price trends, assuming that these trends will continue in the same direction if there is enough force behind a price move. When using momentum trading, traders intend to capitalize on the force or speed of price movements to determine investment positions. They would either initiate long or short positions in a curated selection of assets based on the recent vigor of price trends. Crucially, the key presumption underpinning this approach is that existing trends, given that their force is strong enough, will persist in the same direction.

When an asset displays an upward trend, registering higher prices, it invariably attracts more attention from a wider spectrum of traders and investors. The heightened attention garnered by the asset fuels its market price further. This momentum endures until a significant number of sellers enter and penetrate the market, supplying an abundance of the asset. Once enough sellers are in the market, the momentum changes its direction and forces an asset's price to go lower. This is essentially the price dynamics between supply and demand. At this juncture, market participants may reassess the fair price of the asset, which may be perceived as overvalued due to the recent price surge.

In other words, as more sellers infiltrate the market, the momentum alters its course, pushing the asset's price in a downward direction. This is essentially a representation of the classic supply and demand dynamics and the shift from an environment with more buyers than sellers to one where sellers outweigh buyers. Also, note that while price trends can persist for an extended period, they will inevitably reverse at some point. Thus, the ability to identify these inflection points and adjust the positions accordingly is also of equal importance.

P. Liu, *Quantitative Trading Strategies Using Python*, https://doi.org/10.1007/978-1-4842-9675-2_6

Introducing Momentum Trading

Momentum traders seek to identify the main driver assets of the trend in a given direction, taking advantage of the expected price changes and anticipated price fluctuations, rather than focusing on predicting the peak of a trend. Instead of attempting to find the top and bottom of a trend, a momentum trader focuses on the top and bottom quantiles of the price move, which implies exploitation of market herding and the tendency toward following the majority that represents the most significant price movements.

This approach essentially exploits market herding behavior, a phenomenon in which traders tend to follow the majority of the market consensus. In periods of strong upward or downward trends, many traders and investors may decide to follow the crowd to long or short popular assets, thereby initiating or augmenting the existing momentum. Thus, momentum trading is a self-reinforcing mechanism to some extent: as more traders identify an emerging trend, they contribute to the strength of the trend by adding to the buying or selling force. This, in turn, attracts more market participants, which further strengthens the identified trend. This process continues until the market dynamics shift, either due to a change in underlying fundamentals or a change in market sentiment, causing the existing trend to stall or reverse. Such a cyclical nature of trends characterizes the momentum trading strategy, although timing the beginning and end of the momentum, namely, the entry and exit points, is extremely difficult. In fact, one would use different technical indicators to attempt this task.

Diving Deeper into Momentum Trading

Momentum trading rests on the confluence of three integral elements: volume, volatility, and time frame.

- Volume: This signifies the quantity of an asset traded within a specified time frame. A high trading volume often indicates a strong interest in the asset and can be an indicator of the start of a new trend in the asset's price movement. Conversely, a low volume could signal a lack of interest in the asset, potentially leading to a reversal in trend. Hence, volume plays a crucial role in confirming the strength and sustainability of a trend.

- Volatility: Volatility represents the degree of variation in an asset's price over a short period of time. A higher volatility corresponds to larger price swings, which can provide good trading opportunities for momentum traders, if such variation is in the profitable direction. However, variability is a double-edged sword, as it also increases the risk for significant losses. Therefore, understanding and managing volatility is a critical aspect of momentum trading.

- Time frame: The time frame represents the expected duration of the identified trend. Depending on the specific time frames, momentum traders may engage in intraday trading to open and close a position within a day (called day trading) or hold positions for several weeks or months (called position trading). This choice of time frame can affect the risk and return profile of a trade, as day trading is apparently more volatile than position trading.

These factors can be quantified and aggregated together via technical analysis when developing a momentum trading strategy. The process typically involves analyzing historical price data and trading volumes, followed by applying technical indicators to identify potential trading signals. Essentially, momentum trading requires identifying potential price movements before they occur and capitalizing on these trends to generate a return.

Contrasting with the Trend-Following Strategy

The trend-following and momentum trading strategies, both grounded in the concept of momentum, aim to capture the sustained directional movement or the persistent performance of an asset. Both strategies are built upon the observation that asset prices can have a tendency to move in a particular direction over time, a phenomenon known as momentum. Despite their common underpinning, the application and focus of the two strategies differ significantly.

The momentum trading strategy, as we have discussed, is cross-sectional in nature. It involves comparing the momentum across various assets at a specific time point and investing in those that demonstrate the highest momentum. This comparative analysis occurs at a particular point in time and aims to compare the relative performance among multiple assets. Hence, momentum trading is often characterized as a type of relative momentum strategy.

In contrast, the trend-following strategy utilizes time series momentum, focusing exclusively on an asset's own historical performance over time. It analyzes the price pattern of a single asset over its own history, spanning numerous time points, to identify potential trading signals. Therefore, the trend-following strategy is an instance of an absolute momentum strategy. It emphasizes the historical trend of an individual asset and aims to capitalize on its continuation.

Observing the Role of Lookback Windows

The application of lookback windows in trend-following and momentum trading strategies varies, depending on their unique operational requirements and objectives.

The trend-following strategy, as discussed in the previous chapter, employs two lookback windows. These two windows, one short term and one long term, calculate the respective moving averages as technical indicators. The intersection or crossover of these moving averages then produces a trading signal, indicating a shift in the trend's direction and the right moment for action (for either buying or selling). Thus, the dual lookback windows in the trend-following strategy serve as the basis for decision-making, assisting traders in identifying potential shifts in market trends.

Conversely, the momentum trading strategy uses a singular, uniform lookback window to evaluate an array of assets. This window helps identify which assets have performed best over the defined lookback period. Subsequently, another uniform lookahead window is used to determine the holding period of a position once a trading decision is made. Essentially, the lookback window aids in selecting the assets to invest in based on their past performance, while the lookahead window provides a time frame for holding the investment, assuming that the asset's momentum will continue during this period.

Therefore, both lookback and lookahead windows are essential in momentum trading, helping traders identify high-momentum assets and define the investment's holding period, respectively. The strategic use of these windows provides a structured approach to navigating the ever-fluctuating market dynamics.

Let us elaborate on the difference. Figure 6-1 characterizes the selection of three stocks at regular trading intervals as indicated by the lookahead window. Each trading decision (indicated by the green box in the solid line) considers historical stock prices within the same lookback window. The trading decision could be buying the stock with the highest momentum (based on metrics such as the historical average return) and selling the stock with the lowest momentum at a specific time point. We assess all three stocks and make a trading decision at regular intervals (the lookahead window) based on a rolling lookback window.

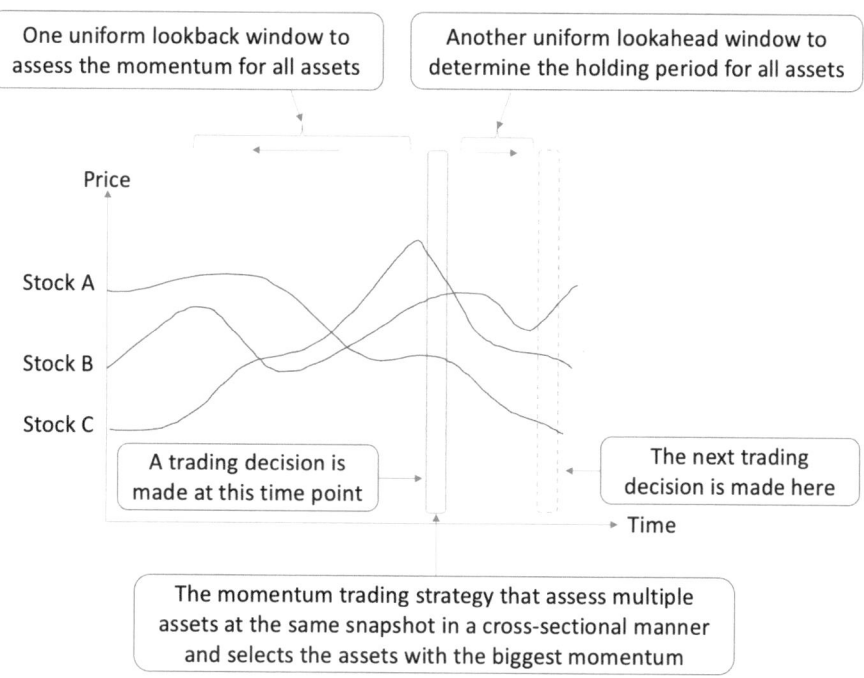

Figure 6-1. *Characterizing the momentum trading strategy for three stocks*

The momentum trading strategy is particularly effective in equities, offering a systematic approach to compare and analyze similar assets. It performs a cross-sectional analysis across the equity universe (in this case, three stocks), evaluating and rank-ordering the constituents based on their relative performances over a specified lookback period. This process enables traders to identify strong performers and potential laggards, using their recent momentum as a proxy for future performance.

In making a trading decision, the momentum strategy often embraces a two-pronged approach, establishing a portfolio with two legs. The first leg is the "long" leg, consisting of top-ranked assets projected to maintain their strong upward price momentum. Traders buy these stocks with an expectation of price appreciation, aiming to sell at a higher price in the future. The second leg is the "short" leg, made up of bottom-ranked assets showing signs of declining price momentum. Traders sell these stocks, often through short-selling, where they borrow the stock to sell in the market with the intent to buy it back at a lower price later. The idea is to profit from the anticipated price decline of these assets. By going long on assets with strong positive momentum and short on assets with negative momentum, traders can potentially benefit from both rising and falling markets, provided the identified momentum persists over the holding period.

Note that momentum strategies, grounded in the principle of relative momentum, maintain their long and short positions irrespective of the broader market trends. These strategies function on the assumption that the strongest performers and underperformers will persist in their respective trajectories, thus maintaining their relative positions in the investment universe. In other words, in a bullish market environment, the stocks with the strongest upward momentum are expected to outperform the market. Meanwhile, during bearish phases, these same high-momentum stocks may fall in price, but they are still expected to perform better than other stocks that are falling more rapidly. Conversely, the bottom-ranked stocks, showing declining momentum, are expected to underperform the market. In a rising market, these stocks may increase in value, but at a slower pace than the market. Similarly, in a falling market, these stocks are anticipated to decline more rapidly than the broader market. Thus, irrespective of whether the market is bullish or bearish, momentum strategies rely on the persistence of relative performance.

More on Trend Following

The trend-following strategy fundamentally differs from the momentum trading strategy in terms of its approach and trading frequency. Trend following is a time series–based strategy that employs moving averages over different lookback periods, one shorter and one longer, to generate the trading signals.

As depicted in Figure 6-2, the trend-following strategy calculates two moving averages at each point in time, leveraging a longer-term lookback window for one and a shorter-term lookback window for the other. A trading signal is produced when there's a crossover, which corresponds to a change in the relative position of the two moving averages from one time point to the next. For instance, when the short-term moving average crosses above the long-term moving average, it is often viewed as a bullish signal, and a bearish signal when it crosses below.

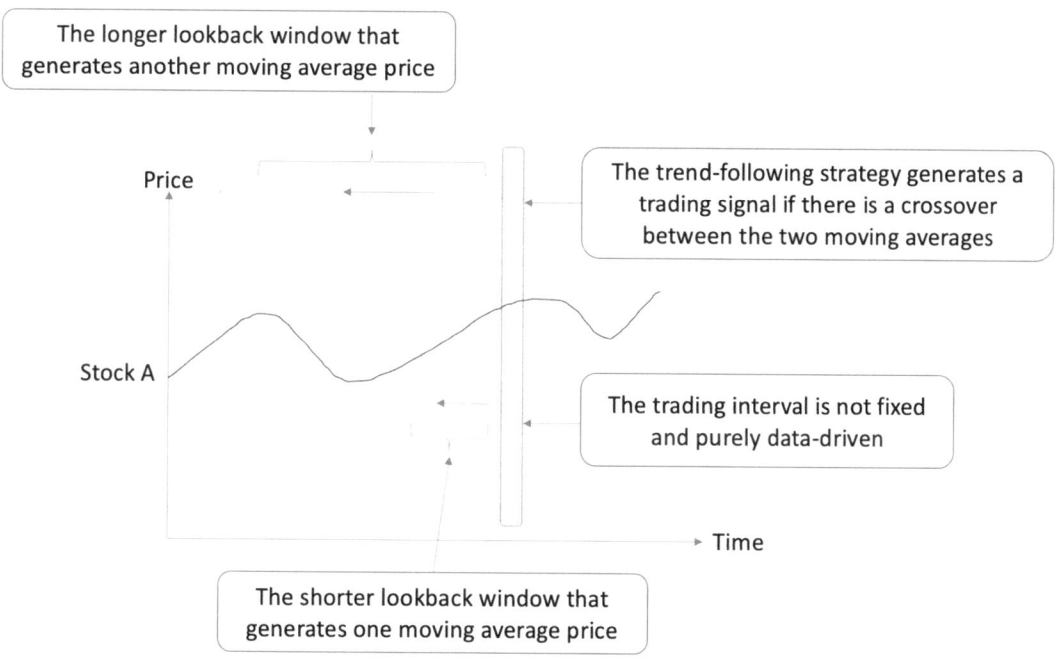

Figure 6-2. *Characterizing the trend-following strategy for a single stock*

Contrary to the momentum trading strategy, which mandates regular trading based on a predefined lookahead window, the trend-following strategy operates without a set trading frequency. Rather, it's driven entirely by the data at hand. Trading actions are informed by the moving averages' interactions, leading to potentially less frequent but more strategically timed trades. Such a mechanism makes the trend-following strategy more flexible as it adapts to the market's movements.

Note that in a trend-following strategy, the primary concern is whether an asset is on an upward or downward trend. When employing this strategy, traders do not focus on the comparative performance of different assets against each other, as in a momentum strategy. Rather, their interest lies in identifying and capitalizing on established price trends of individual assets. The underlying assumption for this strategy is that the identified asset prices that have been rising or falling steadily over a period will continue to move in the same direction. So, a trader would go long when an asset shows an upward trend and go short when it's on a downward trend. The action is to "ride the wave" as long as the trend continues. The "trendiness" of the market completely determines the trading decisions of the strategy.

In summary, while both strategies aim to exploit market momentum, the trend-following strategy involves time series analysis that relies on the absolute momentum in historical prices of the same asset, and the momentum trading strategy involves cross-sectional analysis that relies on the relative momentum across multiple assets. Thus, these two strategies are fundamentally different from each other.

The next section introduces implementing the momentum trading strategy using Python.

Implementing the Momentum Trading Strategy

The Dow Jones Industrial Average (DJIA), often referred to simply as "the Dow," is a popular equity index that comprises 30 major publicly owned companies based in the United States and covering diverse industries. The variety of sectors represented makes it a useful gauge for assessing the general trends and performance of the market. However, it is considered a relatively small pool size, as compared to other broader indices like the S&P 500, which comprises 500 of the largest publicly traded companies in the United States, making it a more accurate reflection of the market dynamics.

For the purpose of this section, we'll employ a momentum trading strategy with the DJIA constituents as our reference universe. This will involve analyzing their respective price trends and performance relative to each other over a specified period in order to identify potential investment opportunities. Our strategy will seek to capitalize on the continuing momentum of outperforming stocks while shorting those with poor performance, with the expectation that these trends will persist over the near to medium term. In other words, we are going to make trading decisions by longing top performers and shorting bottom performers of the 30 constituent stocks.

To start, we need to obtain the ticker symbols of these 30 stocks.

Obtaining DJI Stock Symbols

The Wikipedia page provides a list of these stocks at `https://en.wikipedia.org/wiki/Dow_Jones_Industrial_Average`. Instead of manually copying and pasting these symbols to our coding console, we are going to leverage a web scraping package called Beautiful Soup, a widely used Python package for parsing HTML and XML documents. We will use this package to create a parse tree and extract data from the specific HTML page.

First, as shown in Listing 6-1, we import the following packages, where the bs4 is the Beautiful Soup package, the requests package to send HTTP requests, and yfinance is used to download the financial data once the ticker symbols are obtained.

Listing 6-1. Importing relevant packages

```
import pandas as pd
import requests
from bs4 import BeautifulSoup
import os
import numpy as np
import pandas as pd
import yfinance as yf
```

Next, we write a function called fetch_info() to complete the scraping task. As shown in Listing 6-2, we first assign the web link to the url variable and store the header details in the headers variable. The headers are necessary metadata upon visiting a website. We then send a GET request to obtain information from the specified web link via the requests.get() method and pull and parse the data out of the scraped HTML file using BeautifulSoup(), stored in the soup variable. We can then find the meat in the soup by passing the specific node name (table in this case) to the find_all() function, read the HTML data into a DataFrame format using the read_html() function from Pandas, and drop the unnecessary column (the Notes column) before returning the DataFrame object. Finally, if the scraping fails, the function will print out an error message via a try-except control statement.

Listing 6-2. Fetching relevant information from the web page

```
def fetch_info():
    try:
        url = "https://en.wikipedia.org/wiki/Dow_Jones_Industrial_Average"
        headers = {
            'User-Agent': 'Mozilla/5.0 (Windows NT 10.0; Win64; x64;
            rv:101.0) Gecko/20100101 Firefox/101.0',
            'Accept': 'application/json',
            'Accept-Language': 'en-US,en;q=0.5',
        }
```

```
    #  Send GET request
    response = requests.get(url, headers=headers)
    soup = BeautifulSoup(response.content, "html.parser")
    #  Get the symbols table
    tables = soup.find_all('table')
    #  #  Convert table to dataframe
    df = pd.read_html(str(tables))[1]
    #  Cleanup
    df.drop(columns=['Notes'], inplace=True)
    return df
except:
    print('Error loading data')
    return None
```

Now let us call the function to store the result in dji_df and output the first five rows, as shown in the following:

```
# get DJI components (ticker symbols)
dji_df = fetch_info()
>>> dji_df.head()
```

	Company	Exchange	Symbol	Industry	Date added	Index weighting
0	3M	NYSE	MMM	Conglomerate	1976-08-09	2.41%
1	American Express	NYSE	AXP	Financial services	1982-08-30	3.02%
2	Amgen	NASDAQ	AMGN	Biopharmaceutical	2020-08-31	5.48%
3	Apple	NASDAQ	AAPL	Information technology	2015-03-19	2.84%
4	Boeing	NYSE	BA	Aerospace and defense	1987-03-12	3.36%

We can then take the Symbol column, extract the values, and convert it to a list format:

```
tickers = dji_df.Symbol.values.tolist()
```

With the DJI tickers available, we can now download the stock prices for these ticker symbols using the yfinance package.

Downloading Stock Prices

There are three input arguments to be specified to call the download() function: the ticker symbols, the start date, and the end date. In this case, we set the start date as 2021-01-01 and the end date as 2022-09-01, as shown in Listing 6-3.

Listing 6-3. Downloading the daily stock prices of DJI tickers

```
start_date = "2021-01-01"
end_date = "2022-09-01"
df = yf.download(tickers, start=start_date, end=end_date)
```

We will focus on the adjusted closing prices for later analysis:

```
# use the adjusted closing prices for follow-up analysis
df = df['Adj Close']
```

By now, we have stored the stock prices of the 30 DJI constituents, with each column representing one ticker and each row indicating a corresponding trading day. The index of the DataFrame follows the datetime format.

Next, we convert the daily stock prices to monthly returns.

Calculating Monthly Returns

To transition from the raw daily stock prices to monthly returns, we need to go through a few steps. The first step is to convert the prices to daily percentage returns using the pct_change() method. As introduced in the previous chapter, this function automatically calculates the simple percentage return $R_{t,t+1} = \dfrac{S_{t+1} - S_t}{S_t}$ for all trading days. As this is a daily return, we need to roll it up to the monthly return by compounding all daily returns of the same month and using the terminal return as the monthly return. Breaking it down, we need to group all trading days by month and then calculate the terminal return for each month. Listing 6-4 chains together all these operations in one shot, with the resulting monthly returns stored in mth_return_df.

Listing 6-4. Generating monthly returns from daily prices

```
mth_return_df = df.pct_change().resample("M").agg(lambda x: (x+1).prod()-1)
```

Although chaining together relevant operations looks more concise, it is not the best way to learn these operations if this is the first time we encounter them. Let us decompose these operations. The first operation is to call the `pct_change()` method, which is a convenient function widely used in many contexts. Next comes the `resample()` function, which is a convenient method for frequency conversion and resampling of time series data. Let us use some dummy data to understand this function.

The following code snippet creates a Pandas Series object with nine integers ranging from zero to eight, which are indexed by nine one-minute timestamps:

```
# creating a series with 9 one minute timestamps
index = pd.date_range('1/1/2000', periods=9, freq='T')
series = pd.Series(range(9), index=index)
>>> series
2000-01-01 00:00:00    0
2000-01-01 00:01:00    1
2000-01-01 00:02:00    2
2000-01-01 00:03:00    3
2000-01-01 00:04:00    4
2000-01-01 00:05:00    5
2000-01-01 00:06:00    6
2000-01-01 00:07:00    7
2000-01-01 00:08:00    8
Freq: T, dtype: int64
```

We then aggregate the series into three-minute bins and sum the values of the timestamps falling into a bin, as shown in the following code snippet:

```
>>> series.resample('3T').sum()
2000-01-01 00:00:00     3
2000-01-01 00:03:00    12
2000-01-01 00:06:00    21
Freq: 3T, dtype: int64
```

As we can see from the result, the `resample()` function completes the aggregation operation by the specified interval, and the following method summarizes the data within the interval.

Back to our running example, we downsample the raw daily returns into monthly returns, so each month is represented with only one data point instead of 30 (in a typical month). The aggregation works by cumulating all daily returns following the same procedure: converting to 1+R format, compounding, and then converting back to simple return.

The new thing here is the lambda function. We use the x symbol to represent a general input argument. In this case, it will be all the raw daily returns in a given month. Since this lambda function performs a customized operation, we use the agg() function to carry through the customized function, instead of using the built-in function such as sum() as before.

By now, we have converted the daily returns to monthly representations where every single monthly return represents the terminal return of the daily returns compounded within the month. Next, we calculate another metric using historical monthly returns to indicate the current month's stock performance.

Calculating the Six-Month Terminal Return

We know that making a trading decision based on the current month's return would be flawed in two ways. First, we rely too much on the current month and ignore historical performances. Second, we run into the risk of data snooping. That is, to calculate the monthly return on a given day of the month, if it does not fall on the last day of the month, we would snoop all future daily returns within the same month in order to calculate the terminal return.

We focus on the first point and come back to the second point in a moment. Obviously, we need to find a way to incorporate historical monthly returns when generating trading signals in the current month. However, different from the moving averages used for stock prices, the historical average monthly return obtained using the same arithmetic mean essentially ignores the sequential compounding process. Therefore, we need to treat historical monthly returns as a sequential process and compound these returns (up to a specific lookback window) to obtain the terminal monthly return.

This terminal monthly return will then serve as the momentum indicator for stock selection and trading initiation. This involves choosing a lookback window with a specific size. Let us assume a window size of six. Now, to calculate the six-month terminal return for each month on a rolling basis, we can use the rolling() function, which is the same function used to calculate moving averages. The only change is that, instead of taking the average using mean() after rolling the pointer backward by six months, we take the product of these 1+R monthly returns using np.prod in the apply() function to complete the compounding process, as shown in Listing 6-5.

Listing 6-5. Calculating six-month cumulative returns

```
# obtain the historical cumulative returns of past 6 months as the terminal
return of current month
past_cum_return_df = (mth_return_df+1).rolling(6).apply(np.prod) - 1
```

By now, we have calculated the six-month terminal monthly return as the cumulative return of the past six months, including the current month. This also explains why the first five months show empty values in the previous result and the cumulative monthly returns only start from the sixth month.

Next, we look at using these terminal returns to generate trading signals.

Generating Trading Signals

We have fixed the lookback window to be six months into the past. The momentum trading strategy involves another lookahead window used to fix the trading horizon in the future. Specifically, suppose we form our trading strategy and make the trading decision in the current month. These new positions will last for a full month in the next month if the lookahead horizon is one. We can then measure the performance of these positions at the end of the next month. In this case, the size of the lookahead window is set to be one.

Also, we cannot use the monthly terminal return in the formation month to generate trading signals, as it uses future daily returns within the same month. When standing in the middle of the formation month, what we can use is the terminal monthly return of the last month, which is the end of the measurement period. The measurement period represents the collection of all historically observed data and thus avoids data snooping when limiting the usable data to this period only. Figure 6-3 illustrates the subtlety here.

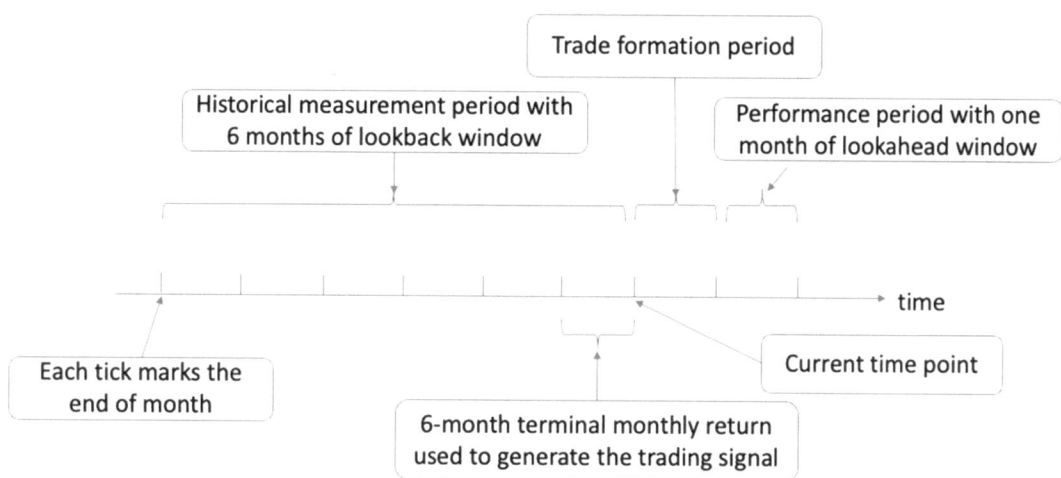

Figure 6-3. *Illustrating the measurement period, formation period, and evaluation period across the investment horizon*

Since our data lasts until 2022-08-31, we will use 2022-07-31 as the trade formation period. To generate a trading strategy, we will use the terminal monthly return from the previous month indexed at 2022-06-30 as the end of the measurement period. We resort to the datetime package to encode these two dates, as shown in Listing 6-6.

Listing 6-6. Identifying the measurement and formation periods

```
import datetime as dt

end_of_measurement_period = dt.datetime(2022,6,30)
formation_period = dt.datetime(2022,7,31)
```

These dates will then be used to slice the cumulative monthly return DataFrame stored in past_cum_return_df. In the following code snippet, we pass the end_of_measurement_period variable to the .loc[] property of past_cum_return_df to perform label-based indexing at the row level. Since the result is Pandas Series indexed by the 30 ticker symbols, we will use the reset_index() method to reset its index to zero-based integers and bring the symbols as a column in the resulting DataFrame. The following code snippet shows the resulting cumulative terminal returns at the end of the measurement period:

```
end_of_measurement_period_return_df = past_cum_return_df.loc[end_of_
measurement_period]
end_of_measurement_period_return_df = end_of_measurement_period_return_
df.reset_index()
>>> end_of_measurement_period_return_df.head()
      index        2022-06-30 00:00:00-04:00
0     AAPL         -0.227936
1     AMGN          0.099514
2     AXP          -0.144964
3     BA           -0.320882
4     CAT          -0.126977
```

These six-month terminal monthly returns of the 30 DJI constituents represent the relative momentum of each stock. We can observe the stock symbols and returns with the highest momentum in the positive and negative directions using the following code snippet:

```
# highest momentum in the positive direction
>>> end_of_measurement_period_return_df.loc[end_of_measurement_period_
return_df.iloc[:,1].idxmax()]
index                             CVX
2022-06-30 00:00:00-04:00     0.256955
Name: 7, dtype: object
# highest momentum in the negative direction
end_of_measurement_period_return_df.loc[end_of_measurement_period_return_
df.iloc[:,1].idxmin()]
index                             DIS
2022-06-30 00:00:00-04:00    -0.390535
Name: 8, dtype: object
```

Here, we used the methods idxmax() and idxmin() to return the index of the maximum and minimum values, respectively.

These two stocks would become the best choices if we were to long or short an asset. Instead of focusing on only one stock in each direction (long and short), we can enlarge the space and use a quantile approach for stock selection. For example, we can classify all stocks into five groups (also referred to as quantiles or percentiles) based on their returns and form a trading strategy that longs the stocks in the top percentile and shorts those in the bottom percentile.

To obtain the quantile of each return, we can use the qcut() function from Pandas, which receives a Pandas Series and cuts it into a prespecified number of groups based on their quantiles, thus discretizing the continuous variables into a categorical, more specifically, and ordinal one. The following code snippet provides a short example:

```
>>> pd.qcut(series, 5, labels=False)
2000-01-01 00:00:00    0
2000-01-01 00:01:00    0
2000-01-01 00:02:00    1
2000-01-01 00:03:00    1
2000-01-01 00:04:00    2
2000-01-01 00:05:00    3
2000-01-01 00:06:00    3
2000-01-01 00:07:00    4
2000-01-01 00:08:00    4
Freq: T, dtype: int64
```

Thus, the qcut() function rank-orders the series into five groups based on their quantiles. We can now similarly rank-order the returns and store the result in a new column called rank, as shown in Listing 6-7.

Listing 6-7. Rank-ordering the stocks based on cumulative terminal monthly returns

```
end_of_measurement_period_return_df['rank'] = pd.qcut(end_of_measurement_
period_return_df.iloc[:,1], 5, labels=False)
>>> end_of_measurement_period_return_df.head()
      index      2022-06-30 00:00:00-04:00      rank
0     AAPL            -0.227936                   1
1     AMGN             0.099514                   4
2     AXP             -0.144964                   2
3     BA              -0.320882                   0
4     CAT             -0.126977                   2
```

We can now use this column to select the top and bottom performers. Specifically, we will long the stocks ranked four and short the stocks ranked zero. Let us observe the stock symbols in these two groups via Listing 6-8.

Listing 6-8. Obtaining the stock tickers to long or short

```
long_stocks = end_of_measurement_period_return_df.loc[end_of_measurement_
period_return_df["rank"]==4,"index"].values
>>> long_stocks
array(['AMGN', 'CVX', 'IBM', 'KO', 'MRK', 'TRV'], dtype=object)
short_stocks = end_of_measurement_period_return_df.loc[end_of_measurement_
period_return_df["rank"]==0,"index"].values
>>> short_stocks
array(['BA', 'CRM', 'CSCO', 'DIS', 'HD', 'NKE'], dtype=object)
```

Having identified the group of stocks to be bought or sold, we will execute the trading actions and enter into these positions for a period of one month. Since the current period is 2022-07-31, we will evaluate the out-of-sample performance of the momentum strategy on 2022-08-31.

Evaluating Out-of-Sample Performance

Let us first grab the monthly return indexed at 2022-08-31 from `mth_return_df` for the long and short positions, respectively. As shown in Listing 6-9, we use the `relativedelta` function from the `dateutil` package to shift `formation_period` by one month into the future, arriving at the evaluation period. This goes to the row-level condition in the `.loc[]` property. For the column-level condition, we subset the columns to the stock symbols within the long positions using the `isin()` method. The result for the evaluation-period performance of the long position is stored in `long_return_df`.

Listing 6-9. Obtaining the performance of stocks in a long position at the evaluation period

```
from dateutil.relativedelta import relativedelta
long_return_df = mth_return_df.loc[formation_period +
  relativedelta(months=1), \ mth_return_df.columns.isin(long_stocks)]
>>> long_return_df
AMGN    -0.021474
CVX     -0.026156
IBM     -0.005517
KO      -0.038336
MRK     -0.044549
TRV      0.018526
Name: 2022-08-31 00:00:00-04:00, dtype: float64
```

The result shows that the majority of the top performers are decreasing in price, which is a direct reflection of market sentiment during that period of time. We can similarly obtain the evaluation-period performance for the bottom performances in the short position, as shown in Listing 6-10.

Listing 6-10. Obtaining the performance of stocks in a short position at the evaluation period

```
short_return_df = mth_return_df.loc[formation_period +
  relativedelta(months=1), \ mth_return_df.columns.isin(short_stocks)]
>>> short_return_df
BA       0.005900
CRM     -0.151614
CSCO    -0.014327
DIS      0.056362
HD      -0.035350
NKE     -0.073703
Name: 2022-08-31 00:00:00-04:00, dtype: float64
```

Now we calculate the return of the evaluation period based on these two positions. We assume an equally weighted portfolio in both positions. Thus, the final return is the average of all member stocks in the respective position. Also, since we hold a short position for the bottom performers, we subtract the average return from the short position in these stocks while adding the average return from the long position. Listing 6-11 completes the calculation.

Listing 6-11. Calculating the total profit

```
momentum_profit = long_return_df.mean() - short_return_df.mean()
>>> momentum_profit
0.015870799817079288
```

Therefore, the momentum trading strategy reports a final monthly return of 1.587%. Now let us compare with the buy-and-hold strategy.

Comparing with the Buy-and-Hold Strategy

We assume a buy-and-hold strategy based on DJI as the benchmark. This means entering a long position of the index at the same beginning of the trading period on 2021-01-01 and holding them all the way until 2022-09-01. We first download the data on this index by passing "^DJI" as the ticker symbol, as shown in the following code snippet:

```
df_dji = yf.download("^DJI", start=start_date, end=end_date)
```

Next, we follow the same approach to calculate the monthly terminal returns, as shown in Listing 6-12.

Listing 6-12. Calculating the monthly terminal returns of the buy-and-hold strategy

```
buy_n_hold_df = df_dji['Adj Close'].pct_change().resample("M").agg(lambda
x: (x+1).prod()-1)
>>> buy_n_hold_df.head()
Date
2021-01-31 00:00:00-05:00    -0.007983
2021-02-28 00:00:00-05:00     0.031677
2021-03-31 00:00:00-04:00     0.066247
```

```
2021-04-30 00:00:00-04:00    0.027085
2021-05-31 00:00:00-04:00    0.019324
Freq: M, Name: Adj Close, dtype: float64
```

We can then access the monthly return during the evaluation period, as shown in the following code snippet:

```
>>> buy_n_hold_df.loc[formation_period + relativedelta(months=1),]
-0.04063613884907047
```

The buy-and-hold strategy thus reports a monthly return of –4.064% in the same evaluation period. Although the momentum trading strategy performs better, we are still far from claiming victory here. More robust backtesting on the out-of-sample performance across multiple periods is still needed.

Summary

In this chapter, we looked at the momentum trading strategy and its implementation in Python. We started by comparing it with the trend-following strategy from the previous chapter, discussing their connections and differences in terms of time series and cross-sectional analysis, as well as the different use of lookback and lookahead windows. Next, we covered its implementation using monthly returns, focusing on the process of signal generation and out-of-sample performance evaluation.

In the next chapter, we will learn a systematic way of assessing different trading strategies using backtesting.

Exercises

- Play around with the parameters of the momentum trading strategy (such as the window size) and assess the performance.

- Try implementing the momentum trading strategy on a different set of assets, such as commodities, forex, or cryptocurrencies. Discuss any differences or similarities you observe in the performance of the strategy.

- Try to create a hybrid strategy that combines both momentum trading and trend following. How does this hybrid strategy perform compared to the stand-alone strategies?

- Try to incorporate volatility measures, such as Bollinger Bands or standard deviation of returns, into the momentum trading strategy. How does this impact the performance?

- Implement the strategy using other momentum indicators such as the Relative Strength Index (RSI) or the Moving Average Convergence Divergence (MACD). Compare their performance with the basic momentum strategy.

- Incorporate transaction costs into the momentum trading strategy. How do these costs impact the overall profitability of the strategy?

- Perform backtesting of the momentum trading strategy over different market periods (bull market, bear market, high volatility period, etc.). How robust is the strategy across different market conditions?

## CHAPTER 7

Backtesting a Trading Strategy

As the name suggests, backtesting refers to the process of testing a trading strategy on relevant historical data before rolling it up to the live market. It gives an indication of the likely performance in different trading scenarios. In this chapter, we delve into the intricacies of backtesting a trading strategy, starting with an understanding of why backtesting is an important component in quantitative trading.

Note that while backtesting can offer insightful results, it is only as good as the quality of the data and the assumptions underpinning the trading strategy. For example, a trading strategy might work very well in a bull market, but it's equally important to know how it performs during a bear market or during periods of high market volatility. By using backtesting, we can analyze the strategy's robustness over different market phases, which provides a more holistic view of its performance. Therefore, a good practice is to choose multiple representative trading periods and record the backtesting performances so as to obtain a robust measure of the actual performance of a specific trading strategy.

Introducing Backtesting

Backtesting allows us to simulate a trading strategy using historical data and analyze the risk and return before actually entering into a position. It refers to the process of testing a particular trading strategy backward using historical data in order to assess its performance on future data going forward. Such performance is also called the test set performance in the context of training a machine learning model, with the common constraint that the test set needs to be completely kept away when formulating a strategy or training a model. This period of historical data reserved for testing purposes allows us to assess the potential variability of the proposed trading strategy.

P. Liu, *Quantitative Trading Strategies Using Python*, https://doi.org/10.1007/978-1-4842-9675-2_7

Building on that, backtesting offers a way to measure the effectiveness of a trading strategy while keeping emotions and subjective bias at bay. It provides a scientific method to simulate the actual performance of a strategy, which then can be used to calculate various summary metrics that indicate the strategy's potential profitability, risk, and stability over time. Example metrics include the total return, average return, volatility, maximum drawdown (to be covered shortly), and the Sharpe ratio.

When carrying out a backtesting procedure, one needs to avoid data snooping (i.e., peeking into the future) and observe the sequence of time. Even if a certain period of historical data is used to cross-validate a strategy, one needs to ensure that the cross-validation periods fall outside or, more specifically, after the training period. In other words, the cross-validation period cannot exist in the middle of the training period, thus preserving the sequence of time as we move forward.

Retrospectively testing out the hypothetical performance of a trading strategy on historical data allows us to assess its variability over a set of aforementioned metrics. Since the same trading strategy may exhibit completely different behavior when backtested over various choices of investment horizons and assets, it is critical to overlay a comprehensive set of backtesting scenarios for the particular trading strategy before its adoption. It's essential to conduct a thorough and varied backtesting process, as the performance of a trading strategy can greatly vary depending on the choice of investment horizon, the selection of assets, and the specific market conditions during the testing period.

For example, we can use backtesting on the trend-following strategy we covered earlier, where we use two moving averages to generate trading signals if there is a crossover. In this process, the input consists of two window sizes: one for the short window and one for the long window. The output is the resulting return, volatility, or other risk-adjusted return such as the Sharpe ratio. Any pair of window sizes for the moving averages has a corresponding performance metric, and we would change the input parameters in order to obtain the optional performance metric on the historical data. More specifically, we can create a range of potential values for each parameter—for example, we could test short moving averages from 10 to 30 days and long moving averages from 50 to 200 days. For each combination of these parameters, we calculate the corresponding performance metric. The optimal parameters then maximize (or minimize, depending on the specific metric) this selected performance metric.

Caveats of Backtesting

Note that a good backtesting performance does not necessarily guarantee a good future return. This is due to the underlying assumption of backtesting: any strategy that did well in the past is likely to do well in the future period, and conversely, any strategy that performed poorly in the past is likely to perform poorly in the future. Since financial markets are complex adaptive systems that are influenced by a myriad of factors, including economic indicators, geopolitical events, and even shifts in investor sentiment, all these are constantly evolving and can deviate significantly from past patterns. In summary, past performance is not indicative of future results.

However, a well-conducted backtest that yields positive results gives assurance that the strategy is fundamentally sound and is likely to yield profits when implemented in reality. Backtesting can at least help us to weed out the strategies that do not prove themselves worthy. However, this assumption is likely to fail in the stock market, which typically highlights a low signal-to-noise ratio. Since financial markets keep evolving fast, the future may exhibit patterns not present in the historical data, making extrapolation a difficult task compared to interpolation.

Another issue with backtesting is the potential to overfit a strategy such that it performs well on the historical data used for testing but fails to generalize to new, unseen data. Overfitting occurs when a strategy is too complex and tailors itself to the idiosyncrasies and noise in the test data rather than identifying and exploiting the fundamental patterns that govern the data-generating process.

In addition, the backtesting period of the historical data needs to be representative and reflect a variety of market conditions. Excessively using the same dataset for backtesting is called data dredging, where the same dataset may produce an exceptionally good result purely by chance. If the backtest only includes a period of economic boom, for instance, the strategy might appear more successful than it would during a downturn or volatile market conditions. By assessing the trading strategy over a comprehensive and diverse period of historical data, we can avoid data dredging and better tell if the good performance, if any, is due to sound trading or merely a fluke.

Data dredging, or "p-hacking," is a material concern in backtesting. It involves repeatedly running different backtests with slightly modified parameters on the same dataset until a desirable result is found. The danger here lies in the fact that the positive result might just be a product of chance rather than an indication of a genuinely effective strategy. This overfitting could lead to a strategy that performs exceptionally well on the test data but fails miserably on new, unseen data.

On the other hand, the selection of the stocks used for backtesting also needs to be representative, including companies that eventually went bankrupt, were sold, or liquidated. Failing to do so produces the survivorship bias, where one cherry-picks a set of stocks and only looks at those that survived till today and ignores others that disappeared in the middle. By excluding companies that have failed or undergone significant structural changes, we could end up with an overly optimistic view of the strategy's profitability and risk profile. This is because the stocks that have survived, in general, are likely to be those that performed better than average. Ignoring companies that went bankrupt or were delisted for any reason may skew the results, creating an illusion of a successful strategy when, in reality, the strategy may not perform as well in the real environment.

Moreover, by incorporating stocks that have underperformed or failed, we are in a better position to assess the risk of the strategy and prepare for worst-case scenarios. This can lead to more accurate risk and reward assessments and better inform the decision-making process when it comes to deploying the strategy. This strategy will also be more robust and can withstand various market conditions, including periods of economic downturn or industry-specific shocks.

Lastly, a backtest should also consider all trading costs, however insignificant, as these can add up over the course of the backtesting period and drastically affect the performance of a trading strategy's profitability. These costs can include brokerage fees, bid-ask spreads, slippage (the difference between the expected price of a trade and the price at which the trade is executed), and in some cases, taxes and other regulatory fees. Overlooking these costs in backtesting can lead to an overly optimistic assessment of a strategy's performance. For example, a high-frequency trading strategy might seem profitable when backtested without trading costs. However, in reality, such strategies involve a large number of trades and, therefore, high transaction costs, which can quickly erode any potential profits. Considering these costs during the backtesting stage will present a more accurate estimate of the net profitability of the strategy. Moreover, the impact of trading costs can vary greatly depending on the specifics of the trading strategy. Strategies that involve frequent trading, narrow profit margins, or large order sizes can be particularly sensitive to the assumptions made about trading costs in the backtesting process.

Before diving into the specifics of backtesting, let us introduce a popular risk measure called the maximum drawdown, or max drawdown.

Understanding Maximum Drawdown

Previously, we introduced the Sharpe ratio, which measures the excess return per unit of volatility. There are many other measures of risk, and this section covers the max drawdown due to its popular use in practice. In particular, the max drawdown measures the impact of the downside volatility, since the upside volatility brings positive returns and is a preferred behavior. In other words, we are more concerned with deviating from the mean on the downside instead of the upside. Therefore, when we use the term risk, we often highlight more on the downside movement that leads to a lower or even negative return.

Max drawdown is defined as the maximum loss in percentage from the previous high wealth to a subsequent low wealth. Here, wealth refers to the asset value and represents the amount of money we have at hand due to holding the asset. Since it tracks the maximum loss possible, the max drawdown measures a hypothetical loss if we were to buy the asset at its peak price and sell it at its bottom price. It measures the worst return from the peak to the trough that we could have experienced, if we are unlucky enough, over the investment period. It gives an indication of how bad the worst-case scenario could be, although it does not necessarily reflect the actual returns of a trading strategy.

Max drawdown provides a valuable perspective on the potential risks associated with an investment strategy and is particularly useful in highlighting the potential extent of negative performance. By considering the maximum percentage loss that an investment strategy would have incurred in the worst-case scenario, we gain an understanding of the potential "pain" or "risk" the investor might have to endure.

To calculate the max drawdown, we first need to obtain a series of the wealth index to indicate the amount of money we have at each unit of time, assuming a hypothetical buy-and-hold strategy (or other trading strategies of interest). It is a time series that records the value of the portfolio at each point in time, taking into account all trading activities, including the reinvestment of dividends, the effect of market returns, and adjustments made to the portfolio, such as buying or selling of assets. In other words, the wealth index tracks the evolution of an initial investment amount (say $1000) that was used to buy the asset at the beginning of the investment horizon.

Next, we obtain the prior peak wealth index at any point in time. This gives the highest portfolio value that one has experienced due to the particular trading strategy at any point in time since the initiation of the position. This essentially identifies the "highest highs" of the portfolio value. The distance between the prior peak and current wealth gives the drawdown (converted to percentages), which indicates the amount of money we could have lost. This value is usually negative or zero and reflects the extent to which the current portfolio value has fallen from its most recent peak.

Lastly, the maximum distance then gives the max drawdown. This is the lowest (most negative) value of the drawdown, indicating the largest percentage loss from the peak to the trough. It signifies the worst loss the portfolio would have incurred over the backtest period if the asset is bought at the peak and sold at the lowest point thereafter.

Figure 7-1 illustrates the calculation process of max drawdown. We first obtain the raw price points of trading assets, which could typically be daily or monthly. These prices are converted to single-period returns, followed by compounding the sequential returns to obtain the wealth index. The single-period drawdown is then derived by calculating the percentage difference between the cumulative maximum wealth of each time point and the wealth value at the current time point. Finally, we report the maximum of these single-period drawdowns as the final return of the max drawdown.

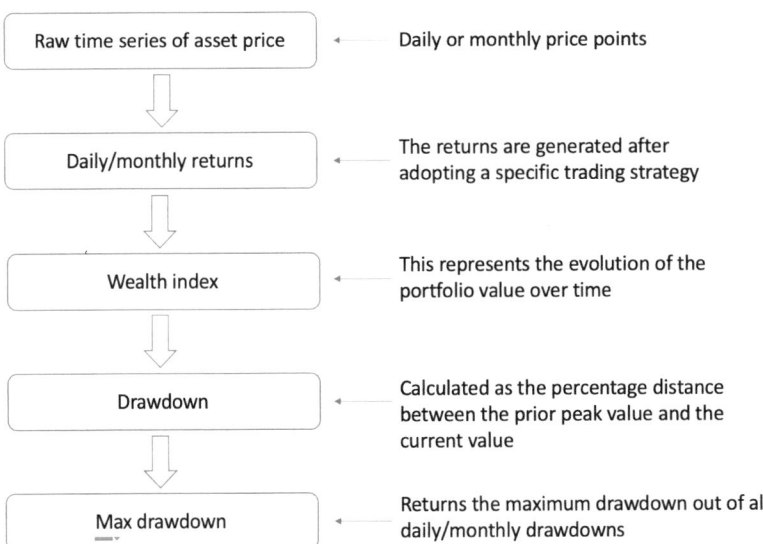

Figure 7-1. *Illustrating the process of calculating the max drawdown*

Again, the max drawdown is a risk measure that helps us understand the worst-case scenario of the trading strategy during the backtest period. Such a calculation process for the drawdown intuitively makes sense, since most people treat it as the money they have lost compared to the peak asset value they once owned in the past.

Figure 7-2 provides a sample wealth index curve and the corresponding single-period drawdowns. Based on the cumulative wealth index curve in the blue line in the left panel, we can obtain the cumulative peak value in the green line, which overlaps with the wealth index if the wealth continues to make new heights and stays flat if the wealth drops. We can thus form a new time series curve consisting of single-period drawdowns as the percentage difference between these two curves and return the lowest point as the max drawdown.

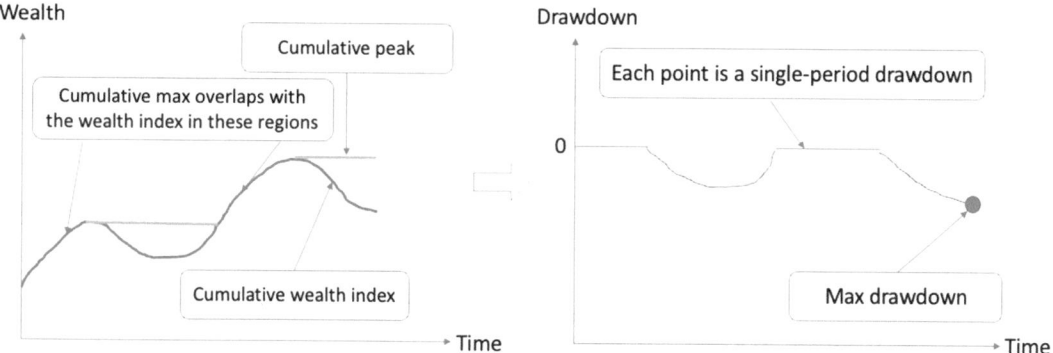

Figure 7-2. *Obtaining the max drawdown based on a sample wealth index curve*

Here, the max drawdown does not mean we are going to suffer such a loss; it simply means the maximum loss we could have suffered following the particular trading strategy. The strategy may incur such a loss if we are extremely unlucky and happen to buy the asset at its peak price and sell it at its trough price. A strategy with a high max drawdown would indicate a higher risk level, as it shows that the strategy has historically resulted in substantial losses. On the other hand, a strategy with a low max drawdown would indicate lower risk, as it has not led to significant losses in the past.

A shrewd reader may immediately wonder if there is a risk-adjusted return metric based on drawdown risk. It turns out there is, and the measure is called the Calmar ratio, which is calculated as the ratio between the annualized return of the trailing 36 months and the max drawdown over the same trailing 36 months.

The Downside of Drawdown Risk

Although the drawdown risk is a popular measure among practitioners, it is not robust and thus far from being a perfect measure of risk-adjusted return. For example, each single-period drawdown relies on two inputs: the current wealth value and the cumulative peak wealth value. The calculation then proceeds by taking the percentage difference between the two. However, when there is an outlier value in these two inputs, the resulting drawdown will be directly impacted. Its sensitivity to outliers, for instance, can skew the risk measurement and present a distorted image of the potential loss. An unusually high or low value can inflate or deflate the drawdown, leading to misleading interpretations of the strategy's riskiness. It is thus very sensitive to potential outliers in the dataset.

Another downside of using drawdown risk is its dependency on the frequency of the observations. For example, daily or weekly drawdowns exhibit a higher degree of volatility than monthly drawdowns and are thus more likely to generate a deep drawdown. However, when aggregating the data into monthly returns, such a deep drawdown may completely disappear or move to other locations. Such sensitivity to the granularity of the data further hurts the robustness of the drawdown measure.

It is also worth noting that max drawdown only provides a snapshot of the worst-case scenario observed in the past. It doesn't consider other potential unfavorable situations that didn't occur but could happen in the future.

Next, we look at calculating the max drawdown using Python.

Calculating the Max Drawdown

In this section, we will focus on the process of calculating the max drawdown for the early period of 2023 for Google and Microsoft. These two stocks are picked due to their recent introduction of large-scale language models: ChatGPT, first introduced by Microsoft, and Bard, later by Google. Both led to a relatively big shock to the stock prices, resulting in a positive uplift for Microsoft and a negative impact for Google.

Let us first download the stock price data from 2023-01-01 to 2023-02-11 via Listing 7-1.

Listing 7-1. Downloading the stock price data

```
import numpy as np
import pandas as pd
import yfinance as yf
import matplotlib.pyplot as plt

start_date = "2023-01-01"
end_date = "2023-02-11"
df = yf.download(['GOOG', 'MSFT'], start=start_date, end=end_date)
>>> df.head()
```

As shown in Figure 7-3, the DataFrame has a multilayer column structure, where the first level indicates the type of stock price and the second layer indicates the stock ticker.

	Adj Close		Close		High		Low		Open		Volume	
	GOOG	MSFT	GOOG	MSFT	GOOG	MSFT	GOOG	MSFT	GOOG	MSFT	GOOG	MSFT
Date												
2023-01-03	89.699997	239.580002	89.699997	239.580002	91.550003	245.750000	89.019997	237.399994	89.830002	243.080002	20738500	25740000
2023-01-04	88.709999	229.100006	88.709999	229.100006	91.239998	232.869995	87.800003	225.960007	91.010002	232.279999	27046500	50623400
2023-01-05	86.769997	222.309998	86.769997	222.309998	88.209999	227.550003	86.559998	221.759995	88.070000	227.199997	23136100	39585600
2023-01-06	88.160004	224.929993	88.160004	224.929993	88.470001	225.759995	85.570000	219.350006	87.360001	223.000000	26604400	43597700
2023-01-09	88.800003	227.119995	88.800003	227.119995	90.830002	231.240005	88.580002	226.410004	89.195000	226.449997	22996700	27369800

Figure 7-3. *Printing the first five rows of the downloaded stock price data*

We will use the adjusted closing prices in the follow-up analysis:

```
df2 = df['Adj Close']
```

Note that the DataFrame is indexed by a list of dates in the datetime format, as shown in the following:

```
>>> df2.index
DatetimeIndex(['2023-01-03', '2023-01-04', '2023-01-05', '2023-01-06',
'2023-01-09', '2023-01-10', '2023-01-11', '2023-01-12', '2023-01-13',
'2023-01-17', '2023-01-18', '2023-01-19', '2023-01-20', '2023-01-23',
'2023-01-24', '2023-01-25', '2023-01-26', '2023-01-27', '2023-01-30',
'2023-01-31', '2023-02-01', '2023-02-02', '2023-02-03', '2023-02-06',
'2023-02-07', '2023-02-08', '2023-02-09', '2023-02-10'],
dtype='datetime64[ns]', name='Date', freq=None)
```

We can use these date indices to subset the DataFrame by the different granularity of time periods, such as selecting at the monthly level. As an example, the following code snippet slices the data in February 2023:

```
>>> df2.loc["2023-02"]
            GOOG        MSFT
Date
2023-02-01  101.430000  252.750000
2023-02-02  108.800003  264.600006
2023-02-03  105.220001  258.350006
2023-02-06  103.470001  256.769989
```

```
2023-02-07 108.040001 267.559998
2023-02-08 100.000000 266.730011
2023-02-09 95.459999  263.619995
2023-02-10 94.860001  263.100006
```

The DataFrame we will work with contains 28 days of daily adjusted closing prices for both stocks, ranging from 2023-01-03 to 2023-02-10. We can check these details using the info() method:

```
>>> df2.info()
<class 'pandas.core.frame.DataFrame'>
DatetimeIndex: 28 entries, 2023-01-03 to 2023-02-10
Data columns (total 2 columns):
 #   Column  Non-Null Count  Dtype
---  ------  --------------  -----
 0   GOOG    28 non-null     float64
 1   MSFT    28 non-null     float64
dtypes: float64(2)
memory usage: 672.0 bytes
```

Let us visualize the price curves as line plots:

```
>>> df2.plot.line()
```

As shown in Figure 7-4, both stocks maintained an increasing trend during this period, although Google suffered a big hit in stock price near the end of the period.

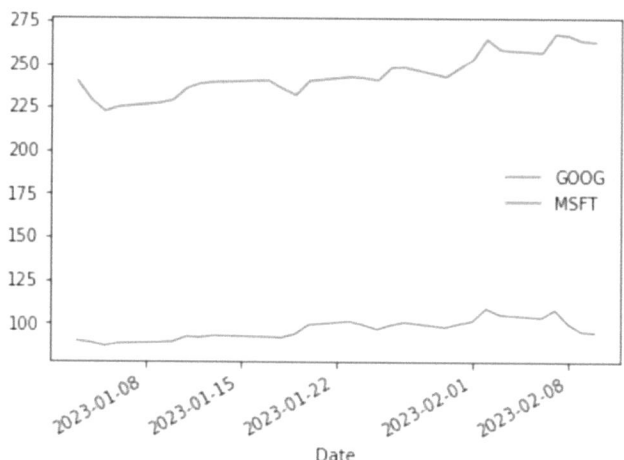

Figure 7-4. *Visualizing the stock prices as line plots*

To better understand the stock returns, let us convert the raw stock prices to single-period percentage returns using the pct_change() function:

```
returns_df = df2.pct_change()
>>> returns_df.head()
            GOOG        MSFT
Date
2023-01-03  NaN         NaN
2023-01-04  -0.011037  -0.043743
2023-01-05  -0.021869  -0.029638
2023-01-06  0.016019   0.011785
2023-01-09  0.007260   0.009736
```

Again, the first day shows an NA value since there is no prior stock price as the baseline to calculate the daily return.

The corresponding line plot for the daily returns follows in Figure 7-5.

```
>>> returns_df.plot.line()
```

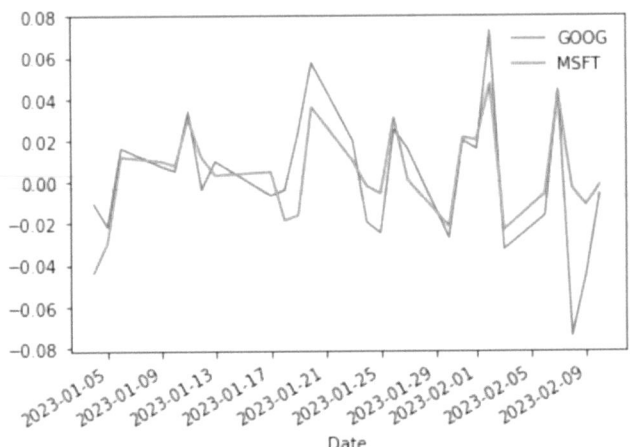

Figure 7-5. *Visualizing the stock returns*

The figure suggests that the daily returns of both stocks are highly correlated, except for the last few days when Google showed a sharp dip in price. Such a dip will reflect itself in the max drawdown measure, as we will show later. Besides, we also observe a higher volatility for Google as compared to Microsoft.

Now let us construct the wealth index time series. We assume an initial amount of $1000 for each stock, based on which we will observe the daily evolution of the portfolio value, assuming a buy-and-hold strategy. Such a wealth process relies on the sequential compounding process using the cumprod() function based on 1+R returns, as shown in Listing 7-2.

Listing 7-2. Constructing the wealth curve

```
initial_wealth = 1000
wealth_index_df = initial_wealth*(1+returns_df).cumprod()
>>> wealth_index_df.head()
            GOOG         MSFT
Date
2023-01-03  NaN          NaN
2023-01-04  988.963234   956.256801
2023-01-05  967.335558   927.915502
2023-01-06  982.831735   938.851285
2023-01-09  989.966623   947.992292
```

We can override the initial entry as 1000 in order to plot the complete wealth index curve for both stocks. This essentially tracks the money we have at each time point after we invest $1000 in each stock on day 1, that is, 2023-01-03.

```
wealth_index_df.loc["2023-01-03"] = initial_wealth
>>> wealth_index_df.head()
            GOOG          MSFT
Date
2023-01-03 1000.000000  1000.000000
2023-01-04 988.963234   956.256801
2023-01-05 967.335558   927.915502
2023-01-06 982.831735   938.851285
2023-01-09 989.966623   947.992292
```

Now we plot the wealth curve for both stocks, as shown in Figure 7-6.

```
>>> wealth_index_df.plot.line()
```

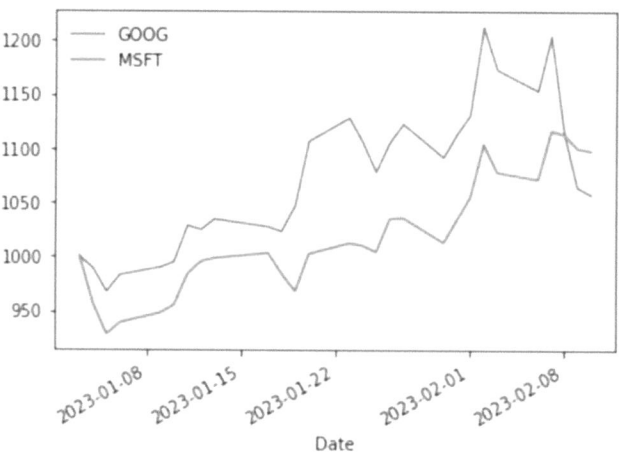

Figure 7-6. *Visualizing the wealth curves*

It appears that investing in Microsoft ends up with a higher portfolio value than in Google, despite the latter taking the lead in all of the previous trading days. As it turns out, one of the biggest drivers for the strong momentum behind Microsoft's growth is its investment in the ChatGPT model and recent integration with its search engine Bing and Edge.

With the wealth index ready, we can build a new series to indicate the cumulative peak wealth value for each trading day. This is achieved using the cummax() function shown in Listing 7-3.

Listing 7-3. Constructing the cumulative maximum wealth

```
prior_peaks_df = wealth_index_df.cummax()
>>> prior_peaks_df.head()
            GOOG    MSFT
Date
2023-01-03 1000.0 1000.0
2023-01-04 1000.0 1000.0
2023-01-05 1000.0 1000.0
2023-01-06 1000.0 1000.0
2023-01-09 1000.0 1000.0
```

Let us plot them as line charts, as shown in Figure 7-7.

```
>>> prior_peaks_df.plot.line()
```

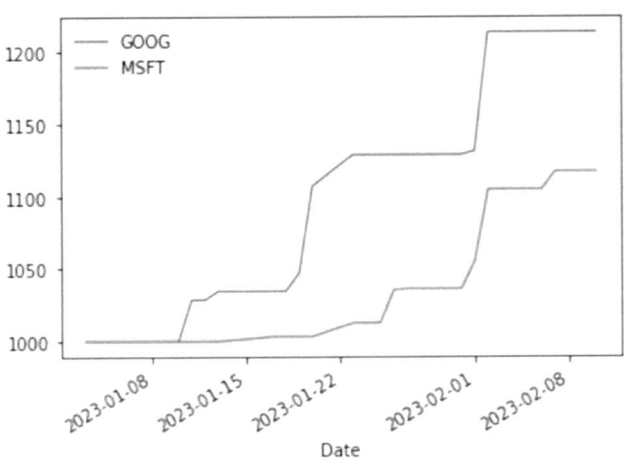

Figure 7-7. *Visualizing the cumulative maximum of the wealth curves*

Now we are in a good position to calculate the daily drawdown as the percentage difference between the current wealth and the prior peak. This is shown in Listing 7-4.

Listing 7-4. Calculating the daily drawdown

```
drawdown_df = (wealth_index_df - prior_peaks_df) / prior_peaks_df
>>> drawdown_df.head()
              GOOG       MSFT
Date
2023-01-03   0.000000   0.000000
2023-01-04  -0.011037  -0.043743
2023-01-05  -0.032664  -0.072084
2023-01-06  -0.017168  -0.061149
2023-01-09  -0.010033  -0.052008
```

The corresponding line charts are shown in Figure 7-8.

```
>>> drawdown_df.plot.line()
```

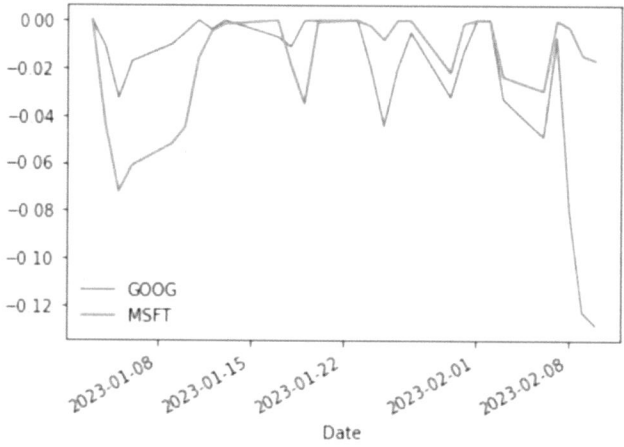

Figure 7-8. *Visualizing the daily drawdown*

The sharp dip in Google's drawdown at the end of the series becomes more noticeable now, and we can probably say something about the reason behind the steep drop. It turns out that there was a factual error in the demo when Google introduced Bard as a response to the challenge from its rival, Microsoft's ChatGPT. The error caused Google shares to tank by a drop of $100 billion in market value.

Coming back to the max drawdown, we can now collect the minimum of these daily drawdowns as the final report of the max drawdown for this trading strategy, as shown in Listing 7-5. Note that we entered a long position in both stocks at the beginning of the investment period, so the trading strategy is simply buy-and-hold.

Listing 7-5. Calculating the max drawdown

```
>>> drawdown_df.min()
GOOG    -0.128125
MSFT    -0.072084
dtype: float64
```

Here, we take the minimum of the daily drawdown as it is a negative value. In practice, we would often report it as a positive number. The result shows that Google has a much bigger max drawdown (again, expressed as a negative value and interpreted as the positive absolute value), more than double the max drawdown of Microsoft during the same trading period.

We can observe the date when the max drawdown occurs using the `idxmin()` function, which returns the date index of the minimum value across the whole column/series, as shown in the following code snippet:

```
>>> drawdown_df.idxmin()
GOOG    2023-02-10
MSFT    2023-01-05
dtype: datetime64[ns]
```

We can also limit the range of the DataFrame by subsetting using a less granular date index in the `loc()` function. For example, the following code returns the max drawdown and the corresponding date for each stock in January 2023:

```
>>> drawdown_df.loc["2023-01"].min()
GOOG    -0.044264
MSFT    -0.072084
dtype: float64
>>> drawdown_df.loc["2023-01"].idxmin()
GOOG    2023-01-25
MSFT    2023-01-05
dtype: datetime64[ns]
```

Till now, we have managed to calculate the max drawdown following the requisite steps. It turns out that a function would be extremely helpful when such steps become tedious and complex. Using a function to wrap the recipe as a black box allows us to focus on the big picture and not get bogged down by the inner workings each time we calculate the max drawdown.

We define a function called drawdown() to achieve this task, as shown in Listing 7-6. This function takes the daily returns in the form of a single Pandas Series as input, executes the aforementioned calculation steps, and returns the daily wealth index, prior peaks, and drawdowns in a DataFrame as the output.

Listing 7-6. Defining a function to calculate the wealth index, prior peak, and drawdown

```
def drawdown(return_series: pd.Series):
    """

    Input: a time series of asset returns
    Output: a DataFrame that contains:
    - the wealth index
    - the prior peaks
    - percentage drawdowns
    """

    wealth_index_series = initial_wealth*(1+return_series).cumprod()
    prior_peaks_series = wealth_index_series.cummax()
    drawdown_series = (wealth_index_series - prior_peaks_series) / prior_
    peaks_series
    return pd.DataFrame({
        "Wealth index": wealth_index_series,
        "Prior peaks": prior_peaks_series,
        "Drawdown": drawdown_series
    })
```

Note that the calculation process remains the same. The only change is the compilation of the relevant information (wealth index, prior peaks, and drawdown) in one DataFrame. Also, we explicitly specified the input type to be a Pandas Series, as this saves the need to check the input type later on.

Now let us test this function by passing Google's daily returns as the input series:

```
>>> drawdown(returns_df["GOOG"]).head()
          Wealth index  Prior peaks  Drawdown
Date
2023-01-03 NaN           NaN          NaN
2023-01-04 988.963234    988.963234   0.000000
2023-01-05 967.335558    988.963234  -0.021869
2023-01-06 982.831735    988.963234  -0.006200
2023-01-09 989.966623    989.966623   0.000000
```

The following code snippet plots the wealth index and prior peaks as line charts:

```
>>> drawdown(returns_df["GOOG"])[['Wealth index', 'Prior peaks']].
plot.line()
```

Running the command generates Figure 7-9.

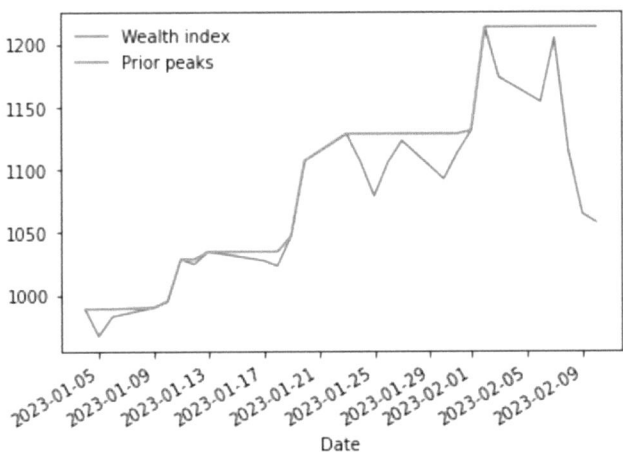

Figure 7-9. *Visualizing the wealth index and prior peaks as line charts*

We can use the loc() function to subset for a specific month. For example, the following code returns the same curves for January 2023:

```
>>> drawdown(returns_df.loc["2023-01","GOOG"])[['Wealth index', 'Prior
peaks']].plot.line()
```

Running the command generates Figure 7-10.

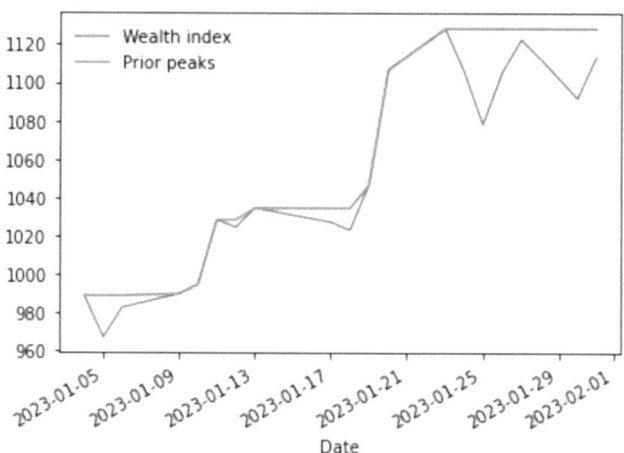

Figure 7-10. *Visualizing the wealth index and prior peaks for January 2023*

Similarly, we can obtain the max drawdown and the corresponding date for both stocks, as shown in the following code snippet:

```
>>> drawdown(returns_df["GOOG"])['Drawdown'].min()
-0.1281250188455857
>>> drawdown(returns_df["GOOG"])['Drawdown'].idxmin()
Timestamp('2023-02-10 00:00:00')
>>> drawdown(returns_df["MSFT"])['Drawdown'].min()
-0.035032299621028426
>>> drawdown(returns_df["MSFT"])['Drawdown'].idxmin()
Timestamp('2023-01-19 00:00:00')
```

The following code snippet returns the max drawdown for both stocks in January 2023:

```
>>> drawdown(returns_df.loc["2023-01","GOOG"])['Drawdown'].min()
-0.04426435893749917
>>> drawdown(returns_df.loc["2023-01","MSFT"])['Drawdown'].min()
-0.035032299621028426
```

In the next section, we will discuss the backtesting procedure using the trend-following strategy.

Backtesting the Trend-Following Strategy

In this backtesting exercise, we are going to calculate four metrics as the performance indicator: the annualized return and volatility, the Sharpe ratio, and the max drawdown. Since the trend-following strategy works on one asset only, we are going to backtest Google's stock price for the year 2022 based on its adjusted closing price.

First, let us download the dataset and store it in df_goog:

```
df_goog = yf.download(['GOOG'], start="2022-01-01", end="2023-01-01")
['Adj Close']
df_goog = pd.DataFrame(df_goog)
>>> df_goog.head()
            Adj Close
Date
2022-01-03 145.074493
2022-01-04 144.416504
2022-01-05 137.653503
2022-01-06 137.550995
2022-01-07 137.004501
```

Now we create two moving averages, a short curve with a span of 5 using the exponential moving average via the ewm() method and a long curve with a window size of 30 using the simple moving average via the rolling() method, as shown in Listing 7-7.

Listing 7-7. Calculating the short and long moving averages

```
sma_span = 30
ema_span = 5
short_ma = 'ema'+str(ema_span)
long_ma ='sma'+str(sma_span)
df_goog[long_ma] = df_goog['Adj Close'].rolling(sma_span).mean()
df_goog[short_ma] = df_goog['Adj Close'].ewm(span=ema_span).mean()
>>> df_goog.head()
            Adj Close  sma30 ema5
Date
2022-01-03 145.074493 NaN    145.074493
```

```
2022-01-04 144.416504 NaN    144.679700
2022-01-05 137.653503 NaN    141.351501
2022-01-06 137.550995 NaN    139.772829
2022-01-07 137.004501 NaN    138.710106
```

Note that the span is directly related to the α parameter we introduced earlier via the following relationship:

$$\alpha = \frac{2}{span + 1}$$

where $span \geq 1$.

Since generating the trading signal requires that both moving averages are available at each time point, we remove the rows with any NA value in the DataFrame using the dropna() method, where we set inplace=True to change within the DataFrame directly:

```
df_goog.dropna(inplace=True)
>>> df_goog.head()
          Adj Close  sma30       ema5
Date
2022-02-14 135.300003 137.335750 137.064586
2022-02-15 136.425507 137.047450 136.851559
2022-02-16 137.487503 136.816483 137.063541
2022-02-17 132.308502 136.638317 135.478525
2022-02-18 130.467499 136.402200 133.808181
```

Now let us plot these two moving averages together with the original price curve via the following code snippet:

```
fig = plt.figure(figsize=(14,7))
plt.plot(df_goog.index, df_goog['Adj Close'], linewidth=1.5, label='Daily
Adj Close')
plt.plot(df_goog.index, df_goog[long_ma], linewidth=2, label=long_ma)
plt.plot(df_goog.index, df_goog[short_ma], linewidth=2, label=short_ma)
plt.title("Trend following strategy")
plt.ylabel('Price($)')
plt.legend()
```

Running the command generates Figure 7-11.

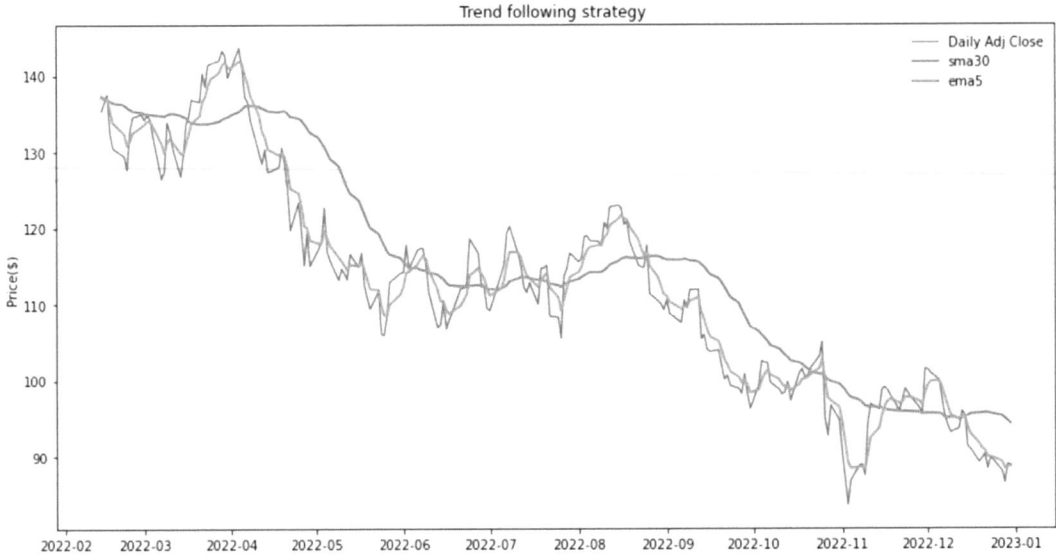

Figure 7-11. *Visualizing the moving averages together with the raw time series*

As Figure 7-11 suggests, the short moving average (green curve) tracks the raw time series more closely, while the long moving average (orange curve) displays a smoother pattern due to a stronger averaging effect.

Now let us calculate the log returns of the buy-and-hold strategy, which assumes buying one share of Google stock and holding it till the end of the investment period. This is shown in Listing 7-8.

Listing 7-8. Calculating the log returns of the buy-and-hold strategy

```
df_goog['log_return_buy_n_hold'] = np.log(df_goog['Adj Close'] / df_
goog['Adj Close'].shift(1))
```

An equivalent way of calculating the log returns is to convert the prices to logarithmic form and then take the difference, as shown in Listing 7-9.

Listing 7-9. An equivalent way of calculating the log returns

```
df_goog['log_return_buy_n_hold'] = np.log(df_goog['Adj Close']).diff()
```

Next, we identify the trading signals for the trend-following strategy, starting by creating a signal column that indicates the intended position based on the magnitude of the two moving averages. This is shown in Listing 7-10.

Listing 7-10. Creating the signal column

```
# identify buy signal
df_goog['signal'] = np.where(df_goog[short_ma] > df_goog[long_ma], 1, 0)
# identify sell signal
df_goog['signal'] = np.where(df_goog[short_ma] < df_goog[long_ma], -1, df_
goog['signal'])
df_goog.dropna(inplace=True)
>>> df_goog.head()
          Adj Close  sma30      ema5        log_return_buy_n_hold  signal
Date
2022-02-15 136.425507 137.047450 136.851559  0.008284                  -1
2022-02-16 137.487503 136.816483 137.063541  0.007754                   1
2022-02-17 132.308502 136.638317 135.478525 -0.038397                  -1
2022-02-18 130.467499 136.402200 133.808181 -0.014012                  -1
2022-02-22 129.402496 136.148800 132.339619 -0.008196                  -1
```

The periodic log returns for the trend-following strategy can be obtained by multiplying signal with log_return_buy_n_hold via Listing 7-11.

Listing 7-11. Calculating the periodic log returns of the buy-and-hold strategy

```
df_goog['log_return_trend_follow'] = df_goog['signal'] * df_goog['log_
return_buy_n_hold']
```

The terminal return can be calculated using the cumprod() function or the prod() function, as shown in Listing 7-12. The first approach calculates the compounded periodic return and accesses the last period as the final return before converting to the simple return format. The second approach directly multiplies all intermediate percentage returns to get the final return as the last period, followed by conversion to a simple return.

Listing 7-12. Calculating terminal returns of both strategies

```
# terminal return of buy-n-hold
>>> np.exp(df_goog['log_return_buy_n_hold']).cumprod()[-1] -1
-0.34419806832531474
# another way to calculate
```

```
>>> np.exp(df_goog['log_return_buy_n_hold']).prod() - 1
-0.34419806832531474
# terminal return of trend following
>>> np.exp(df_goog['log_return_trend_follow']).cumprod()[-1] -1
0.3609149965748346
# another way to calculate
np.exp(df_goog['log_return_trend_follow']).prod() - 1
0.3609149965748346
```

Although the buy-and-hold strategy is obviously no match for the trend-following strategy, we will still calculate the aforementioned backtesting measures, namely, annualized return and volatility, Sharpe ratio, and the max drawdown.

Let us start with the annualized return. As shown in Listing 7-13, the annualized return is calculated by obtaining the terminal return in 1+R format, rescaling it to an annual basis, and finally converting it back to a simple return.

Listing 7-13. Calculating the annualized return

```
# calculate annualized return of buy-n-hold
annualized_return_buy_n_hold = np.exp(df_goog['log_return_buy_n_hold']).
prod()**(252/df_goog.shape[0])-1
>>> annualized_return_buy_n_hold
-0.3818823804560594
# calculate annualized return of trend following
annualized_return_trend_follow = np.exp(df_goog['log_return_trend_
follow']).prod()**(252/df_goog.shape[0])-1
>>> annualized_return_trend_follow
0.4210313983829783
```

Note that we can also add up all the log returns and exponentiate the sum to get the same result:

```
>>> np.exp(df_goog['log_return_trend_follow'].sum())**(252/df_goog.
shape[0])-1
0.4210313983829783
```

Let us calculate the annualized volatility, as shown in Listing 7-14. Recall that the daily volatility scales up as a function of the square root of time.

Listing 7-14. Calculating the annualized volatility

```
# calculate annualized volatility of buy-n-hold
annualized_vol_buy_n_hold = (np.exp(df_goog['log_return_buy_n_hold'])-1).
std()*(252**0.5)
>>> annualized_vol_buy_n_hold
0.3896836224899977
# calculate annualized volatility of trend following
annualized_vol_trend_follow = (np.exp(df_goog['log_return_trend_
follow'])-1).std()*(252**0.5)
>>> annualized_vol_trend_follow
0.39285546408734645
```

Now we calculate the Sharpe ratio, assuming a risk-free interest rate of 3%. This is shown in Listing 7-15.

Listing 7-15. Calculating the Sharpe ratio

```
riskfree_rate = 0.03
# calculate Sharpe ratio of buy-n-hold
sharpe_ratio_buy_n_hold = (annualized_return_buy_n_hold - riskfree_rate) /
annualized_vol_buy_n_hold
>>> sharpe_ratio_buy_n_hold
-1.0569661045137495
# calculate Sharpe ratio of trend following
sharpe_ratio_trend_follow = (annualized_return_trend_follow - riskfree_
rate) / annualized_vol_trend_follow
>>> sharpe_ratio_trend_follow
0.9953569038205886
```

Lastly, we calculate the max drawdown of both strategies, as shown in Listing 7-16.

Listing 7-16. Calculating the max drawdown

```
# max drawdown of buy-n-hold
max_drawdown_buy_n_hold = drawdown(np.exp(df_goog['log_return_buy_n_
hold'])-1)['Drawdown'].min()
>>> max_drawdown_buy_n_hold
```

```
-0.41876535983781205
# max drawdown of trend following
max_drawdown_trend_follow = drawdown(np.exp(df_goog['log_return_trend_
follow'])-1)['Drawdown'].min()
>>> max_drawdown_trend_follow
-0.20685357874978227
```

Although these two strategies are quite disparate in terms of these measures in backtesting, it also shows the importance of demonstrating the superiority of a strategy among a set of common backtesting measures before its adoption. In the next chapter, we will discuss a feedback loop that optimizes the selection of trading parameters, such as the window size, in order to obtain the best trading performance given a specific trading strategy.

Summary

In this chapter, we covered the process of backtesting a trading strategy. We started by introducing the concept of backtesting and its caveats. We then introduced the maximum drawdown, a commonly used performance measure on the downside risk of a particular trading strategy, followed by its calculation process. Lastly, we provided an example of how to backtest a trend-following strategy via multiple performance measures.

In the next chapter, we will introduce statistical arbitrage with hypothesis testing, with the pairs trading strategy as the working example.

Exercises

- Asset A loses 1% a month for 12 months, and asset B gains 1% per month for 12 months. Which is the more volatile asset?

- Drawdown is a measure of only downside risk and not upside risk. True or false?

- Assume the risk-free rate is never negative. The drawdown of an investment that returns the risk-free rate every month is zero. True or false?

- The drawdown computed from a daily return series is always greater than or equal to the drawdown computed from the corresponding monthly series. True or false?

- Write a class to calculate the annualized return, volatility, Sharpe ratio, and max drawdown of a momentum trading strategy.

- How does the frequency of data sampling affect the calculated max drawdown? What might be the implications of using daily data vs. monthly data?

- Assume you have calculated a Sharpe ratio of 1.5 for your trading strategy. If the risk-free rate increases, what would happen to the Sharpe ratio, all else being equal?

- If a strategy has a positive average return but a high max drawdown, what might this suggest about the risk of the strategy?

## CHAPTER 8

Statistical Arbitrage with Hypothesis Testing

Statistical arbitrage is a market-neutral trading strategy leveraging statistical methods to identify and exploit significant relationships between financial assets. Through hypothesis testing, it discerns pricing discrepancies within correlated asset pairs due to temporary market inefficiencies. By purchasing underpriced and selling overpriced assets, the strategy ensures profit as the market corrects these inefficiencies, regardless of overall market movements.

Statistical Arbitrage

Statistical arbitrage refers to the use of statistical methods to identify statistically significant relationships underlying multiple financial assets and generate trading signals. There are two parts involved in this process: statistical analysis and arbitrage. In this context, statistical analysis mostly refers to hypothesis testing, which is a suite of statistical procedures that allows us to determine if a specific relationship among multiple financial instruments based on the observed data is statistically significant. On the other hand, arbitrage means making sure-win profits.

At its core, this strategy relies on mean reversion, which assumes that financial instruments that have deviated far from their historical relationship will eventually converge again. For instance, consider two highly correlated stocks, A and B. If, due to some short-term market factors, the price of A increases disproportionately compared to B, a statistical arbitrage strategy might involve short-selling A (which is now overpriced) and buying B (which is underpriced). As the prices of A and B revert to their historical correlation, the arbitrageur would close both positions—buy A to cover the short sell and

© Peng Liu 2023

P. Liu, *Quantitative Trading Strategies Using Python*, https://doi.org/10.1007/978-1-4842-9675-2_8

sell B to realize the gain. The net profit comes from the convergence of prices. Therefore, statistical arbitrage is essentially a market-neutral strategy, generating profits by taking advantage of temporary market inefficiencies.

Note that statistical arbitrage strategies should expect a relatively stable long-term equilibrium relationship between the two underlying assets for the strategy to work. They also operate on relatively small profit margins, necessitating high volumes of trades to generate substantial returns.

Delving deeper, the first step in the statistical arbitrage process is to identify pairs of trading instruments that exhibit a high degree of comovement. This can be achieved through statistical procedures such as correlation analysis or cointegration tests. For instance, consider stocks A and B, which typically move in sync with each other. Although perfect correlation is rare in financial markets, we can leverage historical price data to find stocks that are highly correlated, often within the same industry or sector.

However, this comovement doesn't always mean equal price changes. Short-term fluctuations driven by various factors like market sentiment, sudden news announcements, or unforeseen events like a pandemic can cause a temporary divergence in the price relationship. In the given example, if stock A increases by 10% and stock B only by 5%, it suggests a temporary mispricing where B is underpriced relative to A.

This brings us to the second step, which involves capitalizing on this mispricing through trading actions such as pairs trading. In the case of A and B, an investor could execute a long position on the underpriced stock B, expecting its price to increase and converge with the price of A.

It's important to note that statistical arbitrage relies heavily on the premise that these pricing inefficiencies are temporary and that the price relationship will revert to its historical norm. Therefore, this strategy necessitates diligent monitoring and a robust risk management system to ensure timely entries and exits.

Figure 8-1 illustrates one way of performing statistical arbitrage. We assume a perfect correlation between stocks A and B, where the same percentage change is observed for periods 0, 1, and 2. However, stock A increased by 10% in period 3, while stock B only increased by 5%. Based on the principle of statistical arbitrage, we could long stock B, which is considered to be underpriced, or short stock A, which is considered overpriced. We could also do both at the same time.

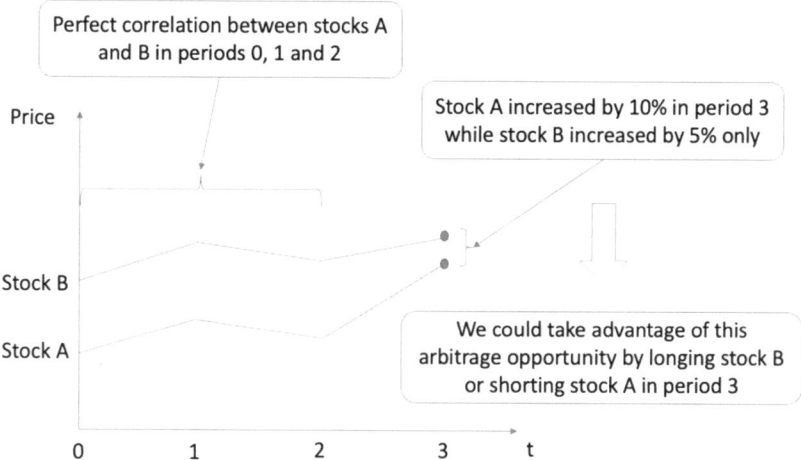

Figure 8-1. *Illustrating the concept of statistical arbitrage. After identifying a perfect correlation between stocks A and B using statistical techniques, as indicated by the prices in periods 0, 1, and 2, we would take advantage of market mispricing by longing stock B (which is underpriced) and/or shorting stock A (which is overpriced)*

Pairs Trading

Pairs trading is a market-neutral strategy that leverages statistical analysis to generate potential profits regardless of the overall market direction. The "pair" in pairs trading refers to simultaneously taking two positions: going long on one asset and short on another, with the key requirement being that these assets are highly correlated. The trading signal stems from the spread or price difference between these two assets.

An unusually large spread, in comparison to historical data, suggests a temporary divergence, and the anticipation is that this divergence will eventually correct itself, reverting to its mean or average value over time. Traders can capitalize on this mean-reverting behavior, initiating trades when the spread is abnormally wide and closing them once the spread narrows and returns to its typical range.

The determination of what constitutes an "abnormal" or "normal" spread is crucial and forms the core parameters of the pairs trading strategy. This typically involves extensive backtesting, where historical price data is analyzed to identify consistent patterns in price divergence and convergence, which then informs the thresholds for trade entry and exit points. Pairs trading, while robust in its market-neutral stance, requires a keen understanding of the long-term equilibrium relationship between the paired assets and careful management of potential risks if the expected price convergence does not materialize.

In the strategy of pairs trading, asset selection is grounded in a statistical procedure called hypothesis testing, specifically, the cointegration test. This process uses historical price data to identify pairs of financial instruments that exhibit a high level of correlation. When two assets are highly correlated, they tend to move in a synchronized manner. This means that any price change in one asset is typically mirrored proportionally by the other, resulting in relatively stable spreads that do not deviate significantly from their historical average. However, there can be moments when this spread deviates markedly from its historical norm, suggesting temporary mispricing of the assets. This divergence indicates that the assets' prices have drifted apart more than their usual correlation would predict.

Such deviations create a unique profit opportunity in pairs trading. Traders can capitalize on these large spreads by betting on their future contraction. Specifically, the strategy would be to go long on the underpriced asset and short on the overpriced one, with the anticipation that the spread will revert back to its historical average as the asset prices correct themselves. This reversion provides the opportunity to close both positions at a profit.

Figure 8-2 provides the overall workflow of implementing a pairs trading strategy. At first, we analyze a group of financial assets (such as stocks) and identify a pair that passes the cointegration test. This is a statistical test that determines if a group of assets is cointegrated, meaning their combination generates a stationary time series, despite each individual time series not exhibiting such stationarity. In other words, the historical differences, or spreads, of the two cointegrated assets form a stationary time series. We can thus monitor the current spread and check if it exceeds a reasonable range of historical spreads. Exceeding the normal range indicates a trading signal to enter two positions: long the underpriced asset and short the overpriced asset. We would then hold these positions until the current spread shrinks back to the normal range, upon which point we would exit the positions and lock in a profit before it shrinks even further (which results in a loss).

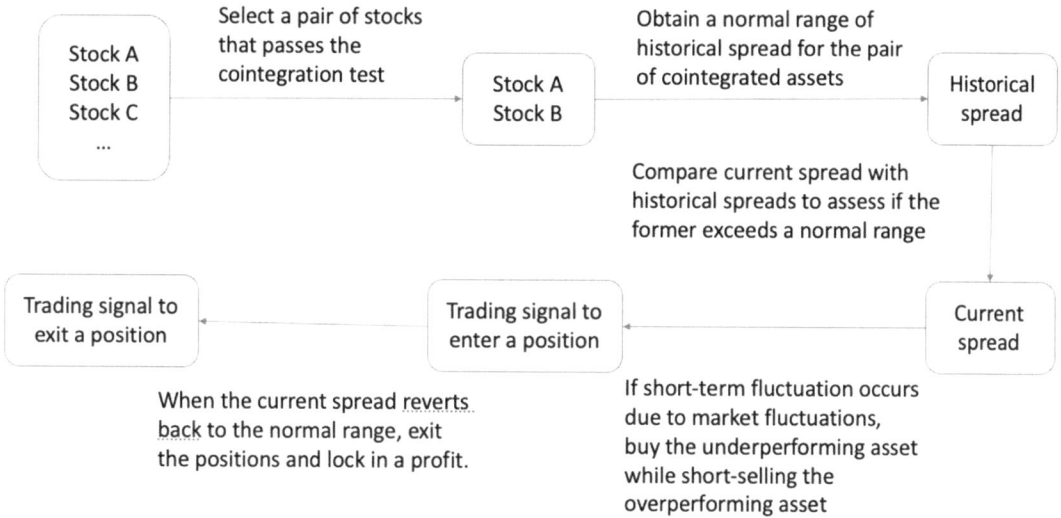

Figure 8-2. *Overall workflow of implementing the pairs trading strategy*

Cointegration

Cointegration, a concept pivotal to hypothesis testing, posits two potential scenarios: the null hypothesis, which states that two or more non-stationary time series are not cointegrated, and the alternative hypothesis, which claims the opposite, that is, these time series are cointegrated if their linear combination generates a stationary time series (more on this later).

Let's demystify some of the jargon here. A time series refers to a sequence of data points indexed (or listed or graphed) in time order, with each data point assigned a specific timestamp. This dataset can be analyzed through several summary statistics or statistical properties. These can include metrics like mean and variance computed over a certain time frame or window.

Moving this window across different periods, a stationary time series exhibits constancy in its mean and variance on average. This means that no matter when you observe it, its basic properties do not change. On the other hand, a non-stationary time series demonstrates a trend or a drift, signifying a changing mean and variance across varying time periods. These time series are dynamic, with their basic properties shifting over time, often due to factors like trends and seasonality.

Hence, the process of cointegration examines whether there is a long-term equilibrium relationship between non-stationary time series despite short-term fluctuations. Such long-term equilibrium manifests as a stationary time series as a linear combination of the two non-stationary time series.

Many traditional statistical methods, including ordinary least squares (OLS) regression, are based on the assumption that the variables under analysis—which are also time series data points—exhibit stationarity. This implies that their fundamental statistical characteristics remain consistent over time. However, when dealing with non-stationary variables, this stationarity assumption gets violated. As a result, different techniques are needed to perform the modeling. One common strategy is to difference the non-stationary variable (deriving a new time series by taking the difference in the observed values of two consecutive time points) to eliminate any observable trend or drift.

A non-stationary time series might possess a unit root, which signifies a root of one in its autoregressive (AR) polynomial. To put it differently, the value in the next time period is strongly impacted by the present period value. This dependency reflects a form of serial correlation, where values from previous periods exert influence on subsequent ones, thereby potentially leading to non-stationary behavior.

The unit root test, therefore, is a method to examine whether a time series is non-stationary and possesses a unit root. Identifying and addressing the presence of a unit root is a critical step in the process of time series modeling, especially when the aim is to understand long-term trends and forecasts.

In essence, a cointegration test examines the assumption that, although individual time series may each have a unit root and hence be non-stationary, a linear combination of these time series might result in a stationary series. This forms the alternative hypothesis for the test.

To be precise, the alternative hypothesis states that the aggregate time series, derived from a linear combination of individual time series, achieves stationarity. Should this be the case, it would imply a persistent long-term relationship among these time series variables. Such long-term relationships will get obscured by temporary fluctuations in the market from time to time, due to factors such as mispricing. Hence, the cointegration test aids in revealing these hidden long-term relationships among time series variables.

When assets are determined to be cointegrated—meaning that the alternative hypothesis is upheld—they are fed into the trading signal generation phase of the pairs trading strategy. Here, we anticipate the long-term relationship between the two time series variables to prevail, regardless of short-term market turbulence.

Therefore, cointegration serves as a valuable tool in statistical analysis, exposing the underlying long-term relationship between two non-stationary and seemingly unrelated time series. This long-term association, difficult to detect when these time series are analyzed independently, can be discovered by combining these individual non-stationary assets in a particular way. This combination is typically done using the Johansen test, yielding a new, combined time series that exhibits stationarity, characterized by a consistent mean and variance over different periods. Alternatively, the Engle-Granger test can be employed to generate a spread series from the residuals of a linear regression model between the two assets.

Figure 8-3 illustrates the process of cointegration and strategy formulation. The purpose of cointegration is to convert individual non-stationary time series data into a combined stationary series, which can be achieved via the Johansen test with a linear combination, the Engle-Granger test via a linear regression model, or other test procedures. We would then derive another series called the spread to indicate the extent of short-term fluctuation from the long-term equilibrium relationship. The spread is used to generate trading signals in the form of entry and exit points based on the extent of deviation at each time point, with the help of entry and exit thresholds defined in advance.

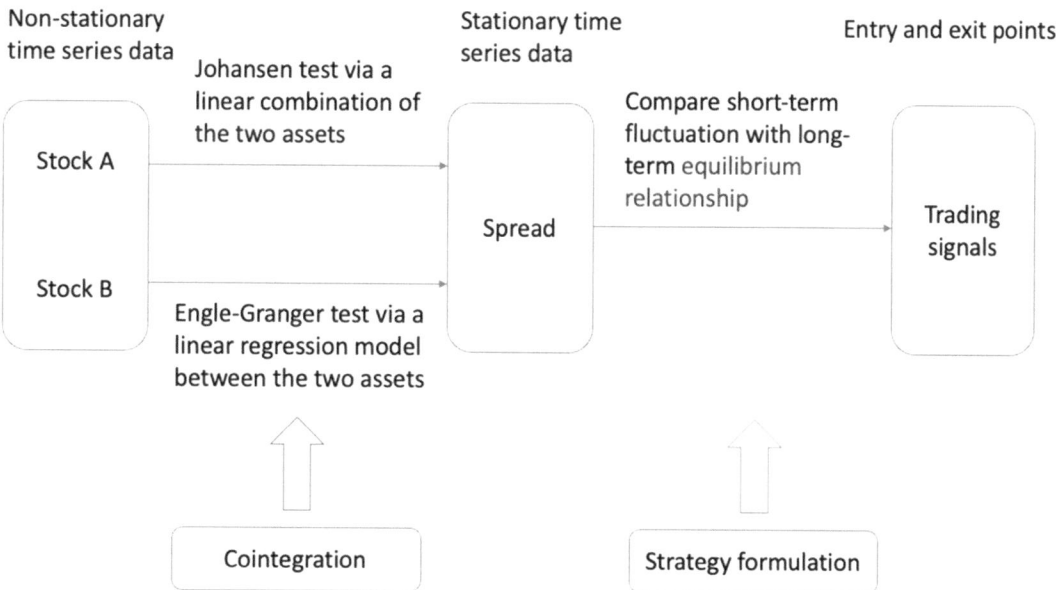

Figure 8-3. *Illustrating the process of cointegration using different tests and strategy formulation to generate trading signals*

The next section covers a more in-depth discussion on stationarity.

Stationarity

Stock prices are time series data. A stationary time series is a time series where the statistical properties of the series, including the mean, variance, and covariance at different time points, are constant and do not change over time. A stationary time series is thus characterized by a lack of observable trends or cycles in the data.

Let us take the normal distribution as an example. A normal distribution $y = f(x; \mu, \sigma)$ is a probability density function that maps an input x to a probability output y, assuming a fixed set of parameters: the mean μ as the central tendency and standard deviation σ as the average deviation from the mean. The specific form of the probability distribution is as follows:

$$y = f(x; \mu, \sigma) = \frac{1}{\sqrt{2\pi\sigma^2}} e^{-\frac{(x-\mu)^2}{2\sigma^2}}$$

A widely used normal distribution is the standard normal, specifying $\mu = 0$ and $\sigma = 1$. The resulting probability density function is

$$y = f(x; \mu, \sigma) = \frac{1}{\sqrt{2\pi}} e^{-\frac{x^2}{2}}$$

We can generate random samples following this specific form using the `random.normal()` function from NumPy. In Listing 8-1, we define a function `generate_normal_sample()` that generates a normally distributed random sample by passing in the input parameter μ and σ in a list.

Listing 8-1. Generating normal samples

```
# generate random samples from normal distribution
def generate_normal_sample(params):
    """
    input: params, including mean in params[0] and standard deviation in
    params[1]
    output: a random sample from the normal distribution parameterized by
    the input
```

```
    """
    mean = params[0]
    sd = params[1]
    return np.random.normal(mean, sd)
```

Now we generate a sample by specifying a standard normal distribution:

```
# generate sample from standard norml
>>> print(generate_normal_sample([0,1]))
0.09120471661981977
```

To see the impact on the samples generated from a non-stationary distribution, we will specify three different non-stationary distributions. Specifically, we will generate 100 samples that follow a distribution with either an increasing mean or standard deviation. Listing 8-2 performs the random sampling for 100 rounds and compares them with the samples from the standard normal distribution.

Listing 8-2. Generating samples from stationary and non-stationary normal distributions

```
# generate 100 random samples for both stationary and non-stationary
distribution
T = 100
stationary_list, nonstationary_list1, nonstationary_list2 = [], [], []

for i in range(T):
    # generate a stationary sample and append to list
    stationary_list.append(generate_normal_sample([0,1]))
    # generate a non-stationary sample with an increasing mean and
    append to list
    nonstationary_list1.append(generate_normal_sample([i,1]))
    # # generate a non-stationary sample with an increasing mean and sd and
    append to list
    nonstationary_list2.append(generate_normal_sample([i,np.sqrt(i)]))

x = range(T)
# plot the lists as line plots with labels for each line
plt.plot(x, stationary_list, label='Stationary')
```

```
plt.plot(x, nonstationary_list1, label='Non-stationary with
increasing mean')
plt.plot(x, nonstationary_list2, label='Non-stationary with increasing mean
and sd')

# set the axis labels
plt.xlabel('Sample index')
plt.ylabel('Sample value')
# add a legend
plt.legend()
# show the plot
plt.show()
```

Running the code generates Figure 8-4, where the impact of a changing mean and standard deviation becomes more pronounced as we increase the magnitude in later rounds.

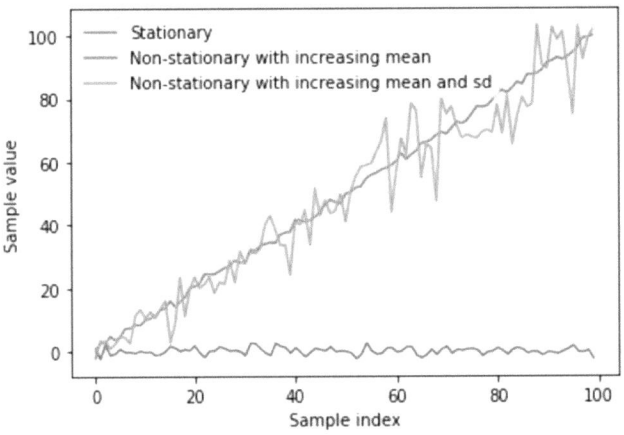

Figure 8-4. *Generating normally distributed random samples from non-stationary distributions with different parameter specifications*

Note that we can use the augmented Dickey-Fuller (ADF) test to check if a series is a stationary. The function `stationarity_test()` defined in Listing 8-3 accepts two inputs: the time series to be tested for stationarity and the significant level used to compare with the p-value and determine the statistical significance. Note that the p-value is accessed as the second argument from the test result object using the `adfuller()` function. This is shown in Listing 8-3.

Listing 8-3. Testing stationarity of a time series

```
# test for stationarity
def stationarity_test(x, threshold=0.05):
    """

    input:
      x: a list of scalar values
      threshold: significance level
    output: print out message on stationarity
    """

    pvalue = adfuller(x)[1]
    if pvalue < threshold:
        return 'p-value is ' + str(pvalue) + '. The series is likely
        stationary.'
    else:
        return 'p-value is ' + str(pvalue) + '. The series is likely non-
        stationary.'
```

Let us apply this function to the previous time series data. The result shows that the ADF is able to differentiate if a time series is stationary (with fixed parameters) based on a preset significance level:

```
>>> print(stationarity_test(stationary_list))
>>> print(stationarity_test(nonstationary_list1))
>>> print(stationarity_test(nonstationary_list2))
p-value is 1.2718058919122438e-12. The series is likely stationary.
p-value is 0.9925665941220737. The series is likely non-stationary.
p-value is 0.9120355459829741. The series is likely non-stationary.
```

Let us look at a concrete example of how to test for cointegration between two stocks.

Test for Cointegration

This section provides an example of performing the cointegration test using the Engle-Granger two-step method. Here's a general overview of the steps involved:

- Estimate the coefficients of the linear regression model between one stock (as the dependent variable) and the other stock (as the independent variable) using ordinary least squares (OLS).

- Calculate the residuals from the linear regression model.

- Test the residuals for stationarity using a unit root test, such as the augmented Dickey-Fuller (ADF) test.

- If the residuals are stationary, the two stocks are cointegrated. If the residuals are non-stationary, the two stocks are not cointegrated.

Let us illustrate the procedure using two stocks: Google and Microsoft. Listing 8-4 imports necessary packages and downloads the daily stock prices for the whole year of 2022. We will use the adjusted closing price for the cointegration test.

Listing 8-4. Importing packages and downloading stock data

```
import os
import random
import numpy as np
import yfinance as yf
import pandas as pd
from statsmodels.tsa.stattools import adfuller
from statsmodels.regression.linear_model import OLS
import statsmodels.api as sm
from matplotlib import pyplot as plt
%matplotlib inline

SEED = 8
random.seed(SEED)
np.random.seed(SEED)

# download data from yfinance
start_date  = "2022-01-01"
```

```
end_date   = "2022-12-31"
stocks = ['GOOG','MSFT']
df = yf.download(stocks, start=start_date, end=end_date)['Adj Close']
>>> df.head()
             GOOG        MSFT
Date
2022-01-03 145.074493 330.813873
2022-01-04 144.416504 325.141357
2022-01-05 137.653503 312.659882
2022-01-06 137.550995 310.189301
2022-01-07 137.004501 310.347382
```

Now we dig into the linear regression model between these two stocks. We will treat Google stock as the (only) independent variable and Microsoft stock as the dependent variable to be predicted. The model assumes the following form:

$$y = \beta_0 + \beta_1 x + \epsilon$$

where β_0 denotes the intercept and β_1 is the slope of the linear line fitted between these two stocks. ϵ represents the random noise that is not modeled by the predictor x. Note that we are assuming a linear relationship between x and y, which is unlikely to be the case in a real-world environment. Another name for ϵ is the residual, which is interpreted as the (vertical) distance between the predicted value $\beta_0 + \beta_1 x$ and the target value y. That is, $\epsilon = y - (\beta_0 + \beta_1 x)$.

Our focus would then shift to these residuals, with the intention of assessing if the residual time series would be stationary. Let us first obtain the residuals from the linear regression model.

In Listing 8-5, we assign the first stock as the target variable Y and the second stock as the predictor variable X. We then use the add_constant() function to add a column of ones to the X variable, which can also be considered as the bias trick to incorporate the intercept term β_0. Next, we construct a linear regression model object using the OLS() function, perform learning by invoking the fit() function, and calculate the residuals as the difference between the target values and the predicted values, obtained via the predict() method.

Listing 8-5. Extracting residuals from OLS

```
# build linear regression model
# Extract prices for two stocks of interest
# target var: Y; predictor: X
Y = df[stocks[0]]
X = df[stocks[1]]

# estimate linear regression coefficients of stock1 on stock2
X_with_constant = sm.add_constant(X)
model = OLS(Y, X_with_constant).fit()
residuals = Y - model.predict()
```

The model object is essentially a collection of the model weights (also called parameters) and the architecture that governs how the data flow from the input to the output. Let us access the model weights:

```
# access model weights
>>> print(model.params)
const    -47.680218
MSFT       0.610303
dtype: float64
```

We have two parameters in the model: const corresponding to β_0 and MSFT corresponding to β_1.

Besides using the predict() method to obtain the predicted values, we can also construct the explicit expression for the predictions and calculate them manually. That is, we can calculate the predicted values $\{\hat{y}\}_{i=1}^{N}$ as follows:

$$\hat{y}_i = \beta_0 + \beta_1 x_i, i \in \{1, \ldots, N\}$$

The following code snippet implements this expression and calculates the model predictions manually. We also check if the manually calculated residuals are equal to the previous values using the equals() function:

```
# alternative approach
residuals2 = Y - (model.params['const'] + model.params[stocks[1]] * X)
# check if both residuals are the same
print(residuals.equals(residuals2))
```

Lastly, we test the stationarity of the residual series, again using the augmented Dickey-Fuller (ADF) test. The test can be performed using the `adfuller()` function from the `statsmodels` package. There are two metrics that are relevant to every statistical test: the test statistic and the p-value. Both metrics convey the same information on the statistical significance of the underlying hypothesis, with the p-value being a standardized and, thus, more interpretable metric. A widely used threshold (also called the significance level) is 5% for the p-value. That is, if the resulting p-value from a statistical test is less than 5%, we can safely (up to a confidence level of 95%) reject the null hypothesis in favor of the alternative hypothesis. If the p-value is greater than 5%, we fail to reject the null hypothesis and conclude that the two stocks are not cointegrated.

The null hypothesis often represents the status quo. In the case of the cointegration testing using the Engle-Granger test, the null hypothesis is that the two stocks are not cointegrated. That is, the historical prices do not exhibit a linear relationship in the long run. The alternative hypothesis is that the two stocks are cointegrated, as exhibited by a linear relationship between the two and a stationary residual series.

Now let us carry out the ADF test and use the result to determine if these two stocks are cointegrated using a significance level of 5%. In Listing 8-6, we apply the `adfuller()` function to the prediction residuals and print out the test statistic and p-value. This is followed by an if-else statement to determine if we have enough confidence to reject the null hypothesis and claim that the two stocks are cointegrated.

Listing 8-6. Testing stationarity of the residuals

```
# test stationarity of the residuals
adf_test = adfuller(residuals)
print(f"ADF test statistic: {adf_test[0]}")
print(f"p-value: {adf_test[1]}")

if adf_test[1] < 0.05:
    print("The two stocks are cointegrated.")
else:
    print("The two stocks are not cointegrated.")
ADF test statistic: -3.179800920038961
p-value: 0.021184058997635733
The two stocks are cointegrated.
```

The result suggests that Google and Microsoft stocks are cointegrated due to a small p-value of 2%. Indeed, based on our previous analysis of calculating the max drawdown, Google and Microsoft stock prices generally tend to move together. However, with the introduction of ChatGPT in Bing search, the overall picture may start to change. Such cointegration (comovement) may gradually weaken as the tool gives everything for Microsoft to win (due to a small revenue from web search) and for Google to lose (majority revenue comes from web search).

Next, we touch upon another closely related but different statistical concept: correlation.

Correlation and Cointegration

Both correlation and cointegration are important statistical measures used to analyze the relationship between two time series datasets. Correlation quantifies the degree of linear association between two time series. In essence, it reveals whether the two variables increase or decrease in tandem and the strength of this relationship. The correlation coefficient can vary between –1 and 1. A coefficient of 1 denotes a perfect positive linear relationship, –1 signifies a perfect negative linear relationship, while 0 suggests the absence of any linear relationship.

In contrast, cointegration is concerned with the long-term equilibrium relationship between two potentially non-stationary time series. If two time series are cointegrated, it signifies that they share a common long-term trend, regardless of their short-term variations. Consequently, while the two time series may not exhibit short-term linear correlation, they can display a long-term stationary pattern when suitably combined. This enables analysts to uncover persistent relationships masked by transitory market volatility.

The following code snippet provides an example of two correlated time series that are not cointegrated. We first sample two series of 100 random values following normal distributions with a different mean and the same variance. This is followed up by a cumulative summation operation stored as a Pandas Series object. Finally, we plot both series as lines after combining them horizontally in a DataFrame and calling the plot() function:

```
np.random.seed(123)
X = np.random.normal(1, 1, 100)
Y = np.random.normal(2, 1, 100)
```

```
X = pd.Series(np.cumsum(X), name='X')
Y = pd.Series(np.cumsum(Y), name='Y')

pd.concat([X, Y], axis=1).plot()s
```

Running the code generates Figure 8-5. Series Y has a higher drift than series X as designed and also exhibits a high degree of correlation (or comovement) across the whole history of 100 points.

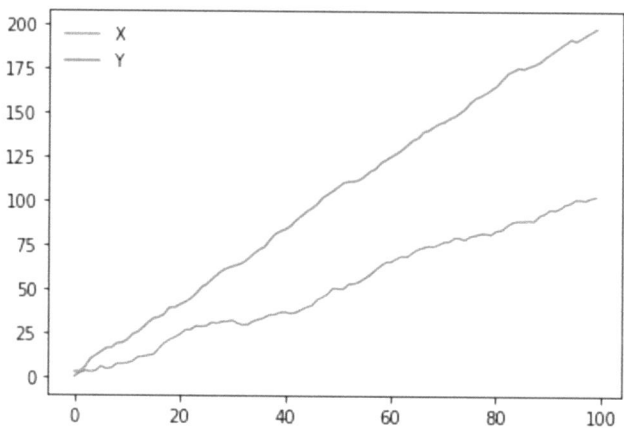

Figure 8-5. *Illustrating the evolution of two series that are highly correlated but not cointegrated*

Let us calculate the exact correlation coefficient and cointegration p-value. In the following code snippet, we call the corr() method to obtain the correlation of X with Y and use the coint() function from the statsmodels package to perform the cointegration test and retrieve the resulting p-value. The coint() function performs the augmented Engle-Granger two-step cointegration test, similar to how to manually carry out the two-step process earlier. The result shows that these two series are highly correlated but not cointegrated.

```
from statsmodels.tsa.stattools import coint
# calculate the correlation coefficeint
>>> print('Correlation: ' + str(X.corr(Y)))
# perform in cointegration test
score, pvalue, _ = coint(X,Y)
>>> print('Cointegration test p-value: ' + str(pvalue))
Correlation: 0.994833254077976
Cointegration test p-value: 0.17830098966789126
```

In the next section, we dive deep into the implementation of the pairs trading strategy.

Implementing the Pairs Trading Strategy

As a market-neutral trading strategy, pairs trading identifies two cointegrated stocks based on a specific statistical test procedure using historical data. It takes a long and a short position in these two stocks simultaneously. Therefore, no matter whether the market moves up or down for these two stocks, there is no impact on the pairs trading strategy, so long as their relative spread remains the same. Instead, the strategy monitors the spread between the two stocks, which should remain relatively constant over time, and makes a move in case of short-term price movements based on preset thresholds.

Let us first download the stock price data. We will focus on a few stock symbols of major tech giants: Google, Microsoft, Apple, Tesla, Meta, and Netflix. The following code snippet downloads the historical stock prices for the full year of 2022 and extracts the adjusted closing prices to the df variable:

```
# download data from yfinance
stocks = ['GOOG','MSFT','AAPL','TSLA','META','NFLX']
df = yf.download(stocks, start=start_date, end=end_date)['Adj Close']
```

Next, we analyze each unique pair of stocks and perform the cointegration test to look for those with a long-term equilibrium relationship.

Identifying Cointegrated Pairs of Stocks

There are a total of six stocks in our search space, leading to a total of $C_6^2 = 15$. Generating the list of unique pairs of stocks can be performed via the combinations() function from the itertools package, as shown in Listing 8-7.

Listing 8-7. Generating all unique pairs of stocks

```
from itertools import combinations

# get all pairs of stocks
stock_pairs = list(combinations(df.columns, 2))
```

```
>>> stock_pairs
[('AAPL', 'GOOG'),
 ('AAPL', 'META'),
 ('AAPL', 'MSFT'),
 ('AAPL', 'NFLX'),
 ('AAPL', 'TSLA'),
 ('GOOG', 'META'),
 ('GOOG', 'MSFT'),
 ('GOOG', 'NFLX'),
 ('GOOG', 'TSLA'),
 ('META', 'MSFT'),
 ('META', 'NFLX'),
 ('META', 'TSLA'),
 ('MSFT', 'NFLX'),
 ('MSFT', 'TSLA'),
 ('NFLX', 'TSLA')]
```

These 15 unique pairs of stocks are stored as tuples in a list. Each tuple will go through the cointegration test in the following section.

Testing Pairwise Cointegration

In Listing 8-8, we loop through each pair of stocks and perform the Engle-Granger test using the `coint()` function. For each unique pair of stocks, we first extract the corresponding DataFrame via subsetting by column names and then perform the cointegration test using the two series to obtain the test score and p-value. We will then compare the p-value with a preset threshold and print out the result to assess if the test result is statistically significant.

Listing 8-8. Performing a cointegration test for each unique pair of stocks

```
threshold = 0.1
# run Engle-Granger test for cointegration on each pair of stocks
for pair in stock_pairs:
    # subset df based on current pair of stocks
    df2 = df[list(pair)]
```

```
# perform test for the current pair of stocks
score, pvalue, _ = coint(df2.values[:,0], df2.values[:,1])
# check if the current pair of stocks is cointegrated
if pvalue < threshold:
    print(pair, 'are cointegrated')
else:
    print(pair, 'are not cointegrated')
```

Note that the threshold is set as 10% instead of 5% as before, since the test would show no cointegrated pair of stocks when setting the threshold as the latter. As it turns out, the coint() function is slightly different from our manual implementation of the test procedure earlier. For example, the order of the time series assumed by the coint() function may not be the same.

Running the code generates the following result:

```
('AAPL', 'GOOG') are not cointegrated
('AAPL', 'META') are not cointegrated
('AAPL', 'MSFT') are not cointegrated
('AAPL', 'NFLX') are not cointegrated
('AAPL', 'TSLA') are not cointegrated
('GOOG', 'META') are not cointegrated
('GOOG', 'MSFT') are cointegrated
('GOOG', 'NFLX') are not cointegrated
('GOOG', 'TSLA') are not cointegrated
('META', 'MSFT') are not cointegrated
('META', 'NFLX') are not cointegrated
('META', 'TSLA') are not cointegrated
('MSFT', 'NFLX') are not cointegrated
('MSFT', 'TSLA') are not cointegrated
('NFLX', 'TSLA') are not cointegrated
```

It turns out that only Google and Microsoft stock prices are cointegrated using the 10% threshold on the significance level. These two stocks will be the focus of our pairs trading strategy in the following, starting by identifying the stationary spread between the two stocks.

Obtaining the Spread

As introduced earlier, the spread is a time series derived from the historical data of the two stocks in the pairs trading strategy. There are many ways to calculate the spread, and we will go with the one employed in the cointegration test procedure. Specifically, we define the spread as the residuals from the linear regression model between the two stocks. If they pass the cointegration test, we have confidence (up to 90% confidence level) that these two stocks, when linearly combined, generate a stationary time series in the spread.

Listing 8-9 generates the spread time series and visualizes it in a line plot. As before, we first extract the predictor X and target Y, apply the bias trick by adding a column of constant ones to X, run the linear regression model, and finally obtain the spread as the residual between the target and the prediction.

Listing 8-9. Calculating the spread

```
# calculate the spread for GOOG and MSFT
Y = df["GOOG"]
X = df["MSFT"]
# estimate linear regression coefficients
X_with_constant = sm.add_constant(X)
model = OLS(Y, X_with_constant).fit()
# obtain the spread as the residuals
spread = Y - model.predict()
spread.plot(figsize=(12,6))
```

Running the code generates Figure 8-6. The spread now appears as white noise, that is, following a normally distributed Gaussian distribution. Since different stocks have different scales of spread, it would be recommended to standardize them into the same scalar for ease of comparison and strategy formulation. The next section covers the conversion process that turns the spread into z-scores.

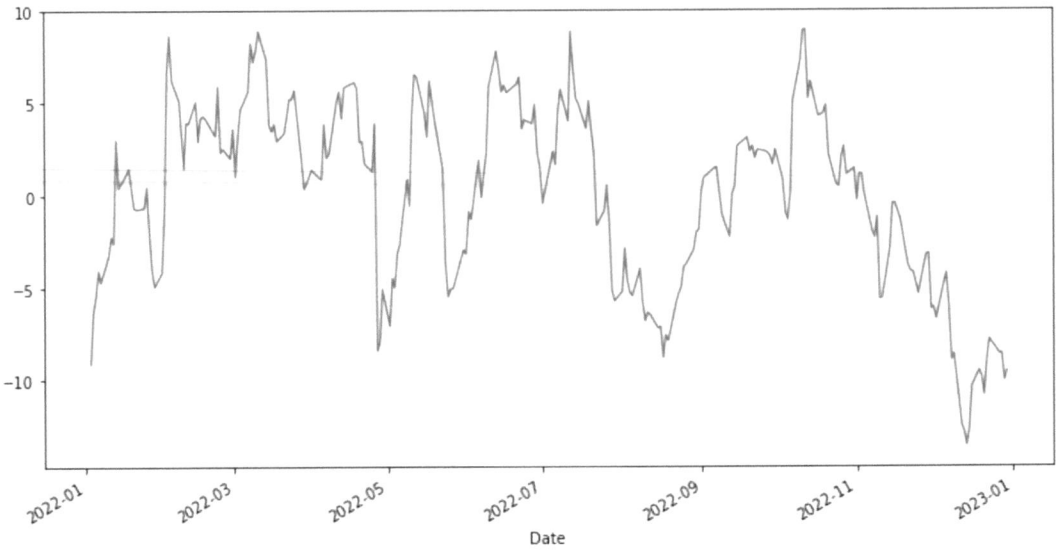

Figure 8-6. *Visualizing the spread as the residuals of the linear regression model*

Converting to Z-Scores

A z-score is a measure of how many standard deviations the daily spread is from its mean. It is a standardized score that we can use to compare across different distributions. Denote x as the original observation. The z-score is calculated as follows:

$$z = \frac{x - \mu}{\sigma}$$

where μ and σ denote the mean and standard deviation of the time series, respectively.

Therefore, the magnitude of the z-score indicates how far away the current observation deviates from the mean in terms of the unit of standard deviations, and the sign of the z-score suggests whether the deviation is above (a positive z-score) or below (a negative z-score) the mean.

For example, assume a distribution with a mean of 10 and a standard deviation of 2. If an observation is valued at 8, the z-score for this observation would be $\frac{10 - 8}{2} = 1$.

In other words, this observation is one standard deviation away from the mean of the distribution.

The z-score is often used to assess the statistical significance of observation in hypothesis testing. A z-score of greater than or equal to 1.96 (or smaller than or equal to –1.96) corresponds to a p-value of 0.05 or less, which is a common threshold for assessing the statistical significance.

In Listing 8-10, we visualize the probability density function (PDF) of a standard normal distribution with a mean of 0 and a standard deviation of 1. We first generate a list of equally spaced input values as the z-scores using the np.linspace() function and obtain the corresponding probabilities in the PDF of standard normal distribution using the norm.pdf() function with a location parameter of 0 (corresponding to the mean) and scale of 1 (corresponding to the standard deviation). We also shade the areas before –1.96 and after 1.96, where a z-score of 1.96 corresponds to a 95% significance level in a statistical test. In other words, z-scores greater than or equal to 1.96 account for 5% of the total probability, and z-scores lower than or equal to –1.96 account for 5% as well.

Listing 8-10. Calculating the z-score

```
# illustrate z score by generating a standard normal distribution with mu 0
and sd 1
from scipy.stats import norm
# input: unbounded scalar, assumed to be in the range of [-5,-5] in this case
x = np.linspace(-5, 5, 100)
# output: probability between 0 and 1
y = norm.pdf(x, loc=0, scale=1)
# set up the plot
fig, ax = plt.subplots()
# plot the pdf of normal distribution
ax.plot(x, y)
# shade the area corresponding to a z-score of >=1.96 and <=-1.96
z_critical = 1.96
x_shade = np.linspace(z_critical, 5, 100)
y_shade = norm.pdf(x_shade, loc=0, scale=1)
ax.fill_between(x_shade, y_shade, color='red', alpha=0.3)
z_critical2 = -1.96
x_shade2 = np.linspace(-5, z_critical2, 100)
y_shade2 = norm.pdf(x_shade2, loc=0, scale=1)
ax.fill_between(x_shade2, y_shade2, color='red', alpha=0.3)
```

```
# add labels and a title
ax.set_xlabel('Z-score')
ax.set_ylabel('Probability density')
# add a vertical line to indicate the z-score of 1.96 and -1.96
ax.axvline(x=z_critical, linestyle='--', color='red')
ax.axvline(x=z_critical2, linestyle='--', color='red')
# display the plot
plt.show()
```

Running the code generates Figure 8-7.

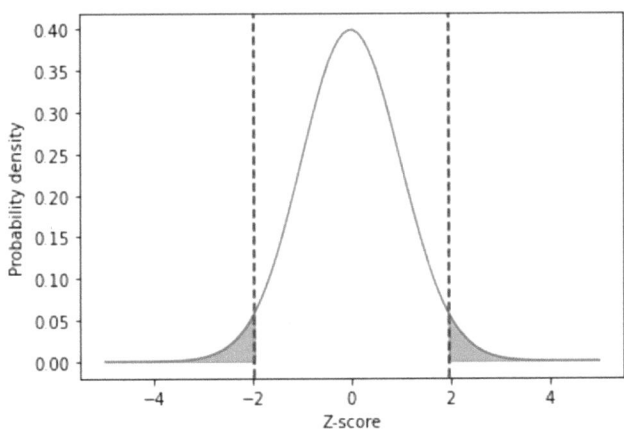

Figure 8-7. *Visualizing the probability density function of a standard normal distribution, with the 5% significance level shaded at both the left and right sides*

In the context of hypothesis testing, the shaded area represents the probability of observing a z-score greater than 1.96 under the null hypothesis. Performing the statistical test would give us a z-score. If the z-score is above 1.96 or below –1.96 in a one-sided test, we would reject the null hypothesis in favor of the alternative hypothesis at the 0.05 significance level, since the probability of observing the phenomenon under the null hypothesis would simply be too small.

In summary, we use the z-score as a standardized score to measure how many standard deviations an observation is from the mean of a distribution. It is used in hypothesis testing to determine the statistical significance of an observation, that is, the probability of an event happening under the null hypothesis. The significance level is often set at 0.05. We can use the z-score to calculate the probability of observing a value as extreme as the observation under the null hypothesis. Finally, we make a decision on whether to reject or fail to reject the null hypothesis.

Now let us revisit the running example. Since stock prices are often volatile, we switch to the moving average approach to derive the running mean and standard deviation. That is, each daily spread would have a corresponding running mean and standard deviation based on the collection of spreads in the rolling window. In Listing 8-11, we derive the running mean and standard deviation using a window size of ten and apply the transformation to derive the resulting z-scores as the standardized spread.

Listing 8-11. Converting to z-scores based on moving averages

```
# convert to z score
# z-score is a measure of how many standard deviations the spread is from
its mean
# derive mean and sd using a moving window
window_size = 10
spread_mean = spread.rolling(window=window_size).mean()
spread_std = spread.rolling(window=window_size).std()
zscore = (spread - spread_mean) / spread_std
zscore.plot(figsize=(12,6))
```

Running the code generates Figure 8-8, where the standardized spreads now look more normally distributed as white noise.

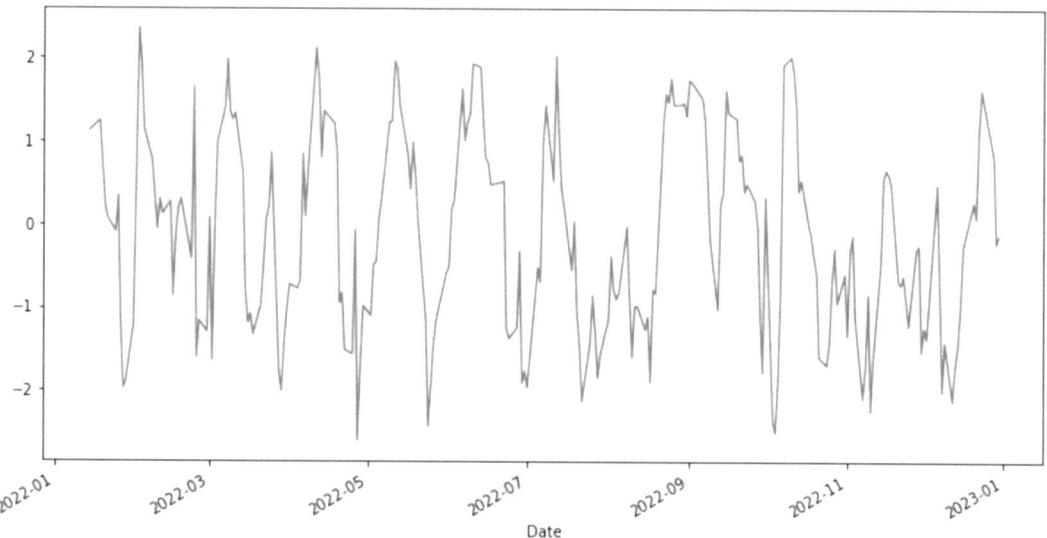

Figure 8-8. *Visualizing the z-scores after standardizing the spreads using the running mean and standard deviation*

Since we used a window size of ten, the first nine observations will appear as NA in the moving average series. Let us get rid of the initial NA values by first identifying the first valid index using the `first_valid_index()` function and then subsetting the z-score series, as shown in the following code:

```
# remove initial days with NA
first_valid_idx = zscore.first_valid_index()
zscore = zscore[first_valid_idx:]
>>> zscore
Date
2022-01-14    1.123748
2022-01-18    1.245480
2022-01-19    0.742031
2022-01-20    0.211878
2022-01-21    0.064889
                ...
2022-12-23    1.618937
2022-12-27    0.977235
2022-12-28    0.807607
2022-12-29   -0.230086
2022-12-30   -0.137035
Name: GOOG, Length: 242, dtype: float64
```

The next section formulates the trading strategy using the z-scores.

Formulating the Trading Strategy

As introduced earlier, the pairs trading strategy utilizes the z-scores to generate trading signals in the face of short-term fluctuations in the spread, taking long and short positions in two cointegrated assets and profiting from the long-term mean reversion of the spread.

The trading signals are generated when the z-score obtained from the previous section crosses over a specific threshold. For example, we can long the first stock and short the second stock when the z-score is below –2, meaning that the spread is more negative than usual, and there is a good chance that the spread will revert back to its mean in the long run. Similarly, we can short the first stock and long the second stock when the z-score is above 2, suggesting that the spread is more positive than usual and there is a good chance that the spread will go back to its mean. These constitute our entry signals.

On the other hand, when we are in an open position, the stock may move in an adverse direction in a very small amount of time. To protect our profit and stop the loss, we can place an exit signal that serves as a stop-loss order. For example, assume we entered a long position when the z-score was below –2 in the previous step. We can set up another threshold to exit the position when the z-score returns to a small value, say –1. Crossing this threshold indicates that the spread has reverted back to its mean.

The following list summarizes the formulation of trading signals for entering and exiting the long and short positions:

- Long entry: Enter a long position in the first stock when the z-score is below a preset negative threshold value (say –2).

- Long exit: Exit the long position in the first stock when the z-score crosses above another preset negative threshold value (say –1).

- Short entry: Enter a short position in the second stock when the z-score is above a preset positive threshold value (say 2).

- Short exit: Exit the short position in the second stock when the z-score crosses below another preset positive threshold value (say 1).

To manage these four types of signals in implementation, we could maintain a Pandas Series object for each stock, where each value is either 1 (for long), –1 (for short), or 0 (for exit position). To simplify the process, we also assume that the long and short positions for each stock are also entered and exited together. In other words, upon entering a long position for one stock, we would enter a short position in the other stock at the same time.

Figure 8-9 overlays these four trading signals in the previous z-score time series. The outer thresholds 2 and –2 represent entry signals for long and short positions, and the inner thresholds 1 and –1 represent the exit signals for existing positions. In between these two thresholds, we simply maintain the current position.

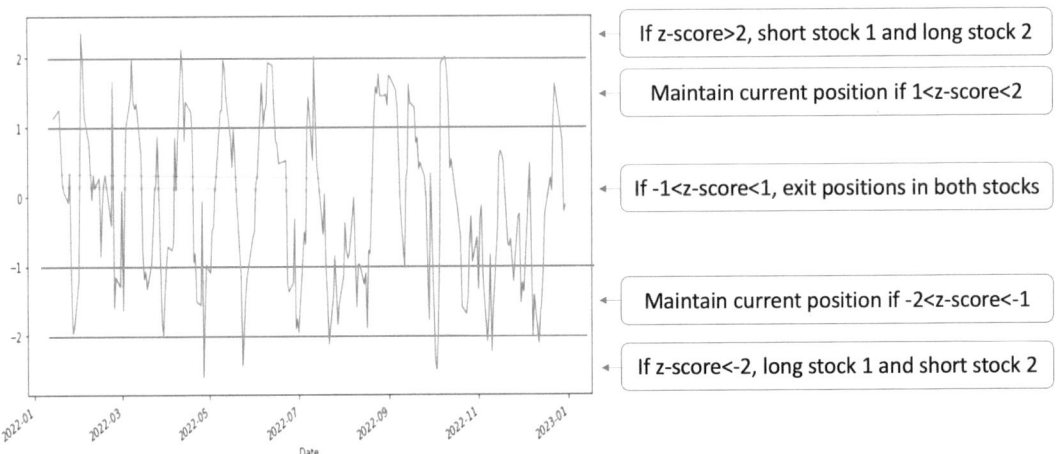

Figure 8-9. *Illustrating the process of formulating trading signals based on preset entry and exit thresholds for the z-scores*

In Listing 8-12, we first initialize the entry and exit thresholds, respectively. We create two Pandas Series objects (`stock1_position` and `stock2_position`) to store the daily positions for each stock. Based on the current z-score and present thresholds for entering and exiting long or short positions, we check the daily z-score in a loop and match it to one of the four cases for signal generation based on the following rule:

- Long stock 1 and short stock 2 if the z-score is below –2 and stock 1 has no prior position.

- Short stock 1 and long stock 2 if the z-score is above 2 and stock 2 has no prior position.

- Exit the position in both stock 1 and stock 2 if the z-score is between –1 and 1.

- Maintain the position in both stock 1 and stock 2 for the rest of the cases, that is, the z-score is between –2 and –1 or between 1 and 2.

Listing 8-12. Implementing pairs trading

```
# set the threshold values for entry and exit signals
entry_threshold = 2.0
exit_threshold = 1.0
# initialize the daily positions to be zeros
stock1_position = pd.Series(data=0, index=zscore.index)
```

```
stock2_position = pd.Series(data=0, index=zscore.index)
# generate daily entry and exit signals for each stock
for i in range(1, len(zscore)):
    # zscore<-2 and no existing long position for stock 1
    if zscore[i] < -entry_threshold and stock1_position[i-1] == 0:
        stock1_position[i] = 1 # long stock 1
        stock2_position[i] = -1 # short stock 2
    # zscore>2 and no existing short position for stock 2
    elif zscore[i] > entry_threshold and stock2_position[i-1] == 0:
        stock1_position[i] = -1 # short stock 1
        stock2_position[i] = 1 # long stock 2
    # -1<zscore<1
    elif abs(zscore[i]) < exit_threshold:
        stock1_position[i] = 0 # exit existing position
        stock2_position[i] = 0
    # -2<zscore<-1 or 1<zscore<2
    else:
        stock1_position[i] = stock1_position[i-1] # maintain existing
        position
        stock2_position[i] = stock2_position[i-1]
```

We can now calculate the overall profit of the pairs trading strategy. In Listing 8-13, we first obtain the daily percentage changes using the pct_change() function for each stock, starting from the index with a valid value. These daily returns will be adjusted according to the position we held from the previous trading day. In other words, multiplying the shifted positions with the daily returns gives the strategy's daily returns for each stock, filling possible NA values with zero. Finally, we add up the daily returns from the two stocks, convert them to 1+R returns, and perform the sequential compounding procedure using the cumprod() function to obtain the wealth index.

Listing 8-13. Calculating the cumulative return

```
# Calculate the returns of each stock
stock1_returns = (df["GOOG"][first_valid_idx:].pct_change() * stock1_
position.shift(1)).fillna(0)
stock2_returns = (df["MSFT"][first_valid_idx:].pct_change() * stock2_
position.shift(1)).fillna(0)
```

```
# calculate the total returns of the strategy
total_returns = stock1_returns + stock2_returns
cumulative_returns = (1 + total_returns).cumprod()
# plot the cumulative returns
>>> cumulative_returns.plot()
```

Running the code generates Figure 8-10.

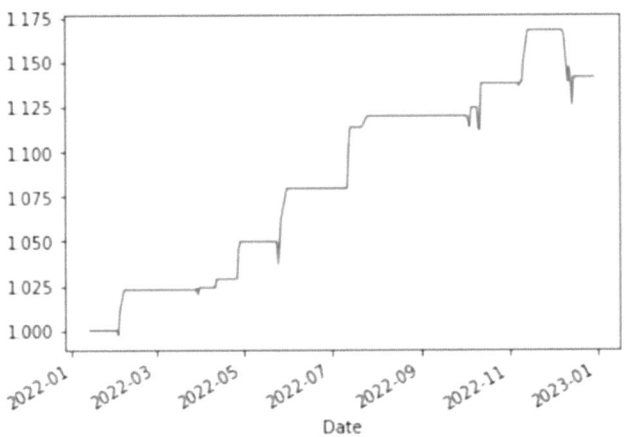

Figure 8-10. *Cumulative returns of the pairs trading strategy*

The terminal return, extracted via the following code, shows that the pairs trading strategy delivers a total of 14.1% profit at the end of the trading year.

Again, this result is subject to more rigorous backtesting in terms of the selection of investment assets, trading periods, and evaluation metrics.

Summary

In this chapter, we covered the concept of statistical arbitrage and hypothesis testing, as well as the implementation details based on the pairs trading strategy. We first walked through the overall process of developing a pairs trading strategy and introduced new concepts such as cointegration and stationarity. Next, we compared cointegration and correlation, both closely related but drastically different. Last, we introduced a case study on calculating the cumulative return using the pairs trading strategy.

In the next chapter, we will introduce Bayesian optimization, a principled way to search for optimal parameters of a trading strategy.

Exercises

- Evaluate the cointegration of selected stock pairs during bull and bear market periods separately. Do the results vary significantly? If so, discuss possible reasons.

- Implement rolling cointegration tests on a pair of time series data and observe how cointegration status (cointegrated or not) evolves over time.

- For a given pair of stocks, test the stationarity of the spread between them using the ADF test. If the spread is stationary, what does it imply for the pairs trading strategy?

- Given the time series data of spreads for a pair of stocks, perform a hypothesis test to check whether the mean of spreads is equal to zero.

- Calculate the z-scores of the spread for different lookback periods (e.g., 30, 60, and 90 days). How does changing the lookback period affect the distribution of z-scores and the performance of your pairs trading strategy?

## CHAPTER 9

Optimizing Trading Strategies with Bayesian Optimization

Financial trading employs numerous strategies in order to maximize returns. The effectiveness of these strategies can often hinge on the fine-tuning of the respective parameters, a task that can be both time-consuming and computationally expensive. Bayesian optimization comes into play as a highly efficient method for strategy optimization. It is a model-based optimization algorithm that uses the past evaluation results (in the form of a training set) to form a probabilistic surrogate model, which it exploits to determine the next point to evaluate using the so-called acquisition function. This approach is particularly useful in trading strategy optimization, where the objective function is often noisy, nonconvex, and expensive to evaluate.

In this chapter, we will explore the principles of Bayesian optimization and its use in trading strategy optimization. By the end of this chapter, readers will have a solid understanding of how Bayesian optimization can be used to fine-tune parameters and therefore enhance trading strategies, leading to potentially higher returns and more efficient use of computational resources.

Optimizing Trading Strategies

We aim to maximize terminal profitability via a specific trading strategy, which often comes with a set of parameters. When properly located, the optimal set of parameters can generate the highest profit (if the goal is to maximize the terminal return) during the backtesting period. Since different testing periods likely exhibit different characteristics in terms of the asset price curve, a robust approach is to backtest a specific set of

© Peng Liu 2023
P. Liu, *Quantitative Trading Strategies Using Python*, https://doi.org/10.1007/978-1-4842-9675-2_9

parameters over different test periods that cover most representative scenarios. The optimal set of parameters thus consistently produces the highest terminal return over multiple backtesting periods.

The optimal set of parameters is the one that consistently produces the highest terminal return over multiple backtesting periods. This means that the strategy performs well not just in one specific market condition, but across a variety of typical scenarios. This approach helps to ensure that the strategy is robust and adaptable, capable of delivering strong returns regardless of market fluctuations.

However, manually fine-tuning a trading strategy by setting different parameter values is an extremely time-consuming process. On the one hand, the number of possible parameter values to test out may simply be too large. When there are too many alternative configurations to be tested, carrying out a grid search (search over each unique configuration) may look too prohibitive, especially when each parameter has multiple alternative values, and there are many such parameters. In particular, a continuous parameter will render such manual search infeasible due to infinitely many values. Yet, on the other hand, backtesting each specific set of parameters is not instantaneous. Instead, each round of execution may take very long, thus further exacerbating the challenge in the global search for the optimal strategy and making the process of manually fine-tuning a trading strategy a daunting task.

This is where automated optimization techniques, such as Bayesian optimization, come into play. These methods can efficiently navigate the search space (also referred to as the domain), intelligently choosing the next set of parameters to test based on previous results. This allows for more efficient sampling of the parameter space, saving both time and computational resources.

It turns out that there are many optimization techniques that aim at locating the optimal set of parameters for a specific trading strategy. Let us first understand the optimization problem that occurs upon searching for the optimal trading strategy.

Parametric Trading Strategies

The parameters serve as the input variables to a specific trading strategy. A typical trading strategy has one or more parameters, each assuming a particular value within the prespecified range. Each parameter can vary within its defined ranges, allowing for a wide array of possible strategy configurations. Upon accepting these input parameters, the strategy will generate the resulting trading signals, from which the terminal return over a specific backtesting period could be calculated as an indicator of the "goodness" of these parameters. The input parameters do not assume fixed values; instead, they are variables that can vary within predefined ranges.

Let us look at a concrete example. Recall the trend-following strategy covered earlier. This trading strategy relies on two moving averages to generate a trading signal: a short-term moving average and a long-term moving average. We would enter into a long position if the short-term moving average crosses above the long-term moving average, after closing the existing short position, if any. Alternatively, we would enter into a short position if the short-term moving average crosses below the long-term moving average, after closing the existing long position, if any.

This strategy thus depends on two input parameters: the window lengths l_1 and l_2 for the short-term and long-term moving averages, respectively. Each set of parameters would correspond to a number of performance metrics, such as the terminal return or the Sharpe ratio. Each set of parameters (l_1 and l_2) will generate a unique series of trading signals, which in turn will result in a specific terminal return or Sharpe ratio. These performance metrics serve as indicators of the "goodness" or effectiveness of the chosen parameters.

To proceed with the search for the optimal set of window length parameters, we would need a single-number metric to optimize over. Such scalar objective serves as the feedback signal on how good or bad the current set of input parameters is. This objective serves as a feedback signal, indicating the effectiveness of a given set of input parameters. For example, suppose we choose the Sharpe ratio as the objective to be maximized. This results in an objective function, where the output is the Sharpe ratio S over a specific backtesting period, the input parameters are window lengths l_1 and l_2, and we can represent the objective function as $S = f(l_1, l_2)$. Here, f represents a black-box function, which means we do not have its explicit mathematical form or its derivative information. A black-box function is one where we do not have explicit knowledge of its mathematical form or its derivative information. This means that we can evaluate the function (i.e., we can determine the Sharpe ratio for a given set of parameters), but we don't have a simple formula that allows us to directly calculate the optimal parameters. This makes global optimization extremely difficult since we know very little about the characteristics of this function while our goal is to find its global maximum point.

Such a lack of explicit knowledge about the function makes the optimization problem challenging. We are essentially searching for the global maximum of a function that we know very little about. However, this is precisely the type of problem that Bayesian optimization is designed to tackle.

More formally, we could frame the question as this: for a given stock, locate the values of l_1 and l_2 in the range of $[1,10]$ and $[11,20]$ (note that we need to ensure $l_1 < l_2$) that maximizes the Sharpe ratio within the backtesting period of a whole year. Figure 9-1 summarizes the characteristics of the optimization problem. Note that different trading strategies correspond to a different unknown black-box function f. Even if the strategy is the same, varying the backtesting period also yields a different function realization of the objective function f.

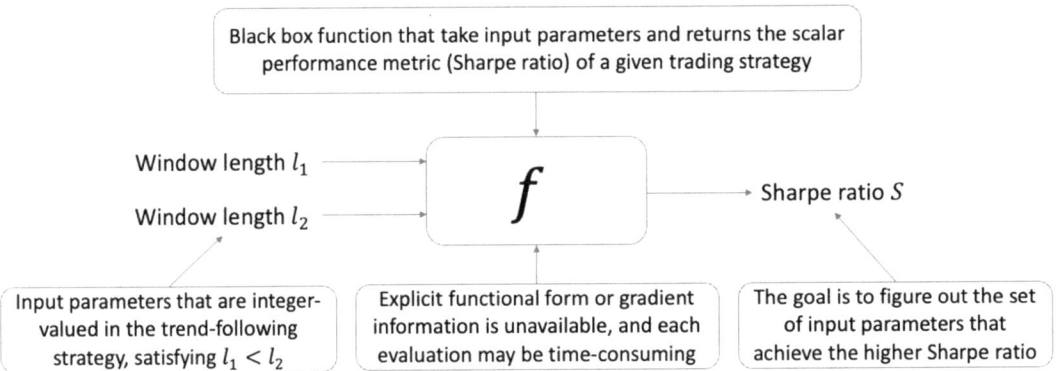

Figure 9-1. *Illustrating the optimization problem. The selected trading strategy manifests as an unknown function, and our goal is to search for the optimal set of window lengths that deliver the highest performance metric, the Sharpe ratio in this case*

The next section provides more perspectives on the overall optimization process.

More on Optimization

Optimization aims at locating the optimal value $f^* = f(x^*)$ or its maximizer $x^* = \text{argmax}_{x \in \mathcal{X}} f$ for all the input values $x \in \mathcal{X}$ in a maximization setting, which could also be a minimization problem. The procedure that carries out the optimization process is called the optimizer. There are multiple types of optimizers, with stochastic gradient descent (SGD) being the most popular optimizer in the space of deep learning. In the context of backtesting a trading strategy, we are mostly interested in optimizing the risk-adjusted return, represented by the Sharpe ratio or other risk measures such as the max drawdown. Plus, we have the additional challenge that the inputs are not continuous values; instead, they are discrete such as window sizes or trading volumes.

The optimizer takes a function f and figures out the desired optimum value f^* or its corresponding input parameter x^*. Being an optimum value means that $f(x^*)$ is greater (or less, in the case of minimization) than any other values in the neighborhood. Here, f^* may be either a local optimum or a global optimum. A local optimum means $f(x^*)$ is at the top of a mountain, and global optimum means the highest point of all mountains in the region. That is, in a maximization setting, we could take all the local maxima, compare each other, and report the maximum of them as the global maximum. Both are characterized by having a zero gradient at the point x^*, yet the global optimum is often what we aim for. The optimizer needs a strategy to escape from these local optima and continue its search for the global optimum. There are various techniques to handle this issue, including using different initial values via the multistart procedure, applying random jumps in the parameter space, and using complex algorithms like simulated annealing or genetic algorithms that employ specific mechanisms to escape local optima.

In the context of developing a trading strategy, we are interested in the global maximizer (optimal input parameters) that gives the maximal Sharpe ratio. This is a complex task as there may be many sets of parameters that yield good results (local maxima), but we want to find the absolute best (global maximum).

Note that using the gradient information to identify an optimum represents a huge improvement in our understanding of optimization problems, as first proposed by Isaac Newton. Prior to his time, we would make the manual comparison for each unique pair, which is a combinatorial problem that requires the most time-consuming work. When the function form is available, such as $y = x^2$, we could invoke the tool of calculus and solve for the point whose gradient is zero, that is, $y' = 2x = 0$, giving $x = 0$. We could then calculate the second derivative or apply the sign chart method to ascertain if this is a maximum or minimum point.

The next section introduces more on the global optimization problem.

Global Optimization

Optimization aims to locate the optimal set of parameters of interest across the whole search domain, often by carefully allocating limited resources. For example, when searching for the car key at home before leaving for work in two minutes, we would naturally start with the most promising place where we would usually put the key. If it is not there, think for a little while about the possible locations and go to the next most promising place. This process iterates until the key is found. In this example, the search policy is, in a way, behaving intelligently. It digests the available information on previous searches and proposes the following promising location, so as to use the limited resource wisely. The resource could be the limited number of trials we could run before a project deadline approaches tomorrow or the two-minute budget to search for the key in this case. The unknown function is the house itself, a binary value that reveals if the key is placed at the proposed location upon each sampling at the specific location.

This intelligent search policy represents a cornerstone concept in optimization, especially in the context of derivative-free optimization where the unknown function does not reveal any derivative information. Here, the policy needs to balance exploration, which probes the unknown function at various locations in the search domain, and exploitation, which focuses on promising areas where we have already identified a good candidate value. This trade-off is usually characterized by a learning curve showing the function value of the best-found solution over the number of function evaluations.

The key search example is considered an easy one since we are familiar with the environment in terms of its structural design. However, imagine locating an item in a totally new environment. The optimizer would need to account for the uncertainty due to unfamiliarity with the environment while determining the next sampling location via multiple sequential trials. When the sampling budget is limited, as is often the case in real-life searches in terms of time and resources, the optimizer needs to argue carefully on the utility of each candidate input parameter value.

This process is characterized by sequential decision-making under uncertainty, a problem that lies at the heart of the field of optimization. When faced with such a situation, optimizers need to develop an intelligent search policy that effectively manages the trade-off between exploration (searching new areas) and exploitation (capitalizing on known, promising locations). In the context of searching for an item in an unfamiliar environment, exploration involves searching in completely new areas where the item could potentially be located, while exploitation involves focusing the search around areas where clues or signs of the item have already been found. The challenge is to balance these two approaches, as focusing too much on exploration could lead to a waste of time and resources, while focusing too much on exploitation could result in missed opportunities.

In the world of trading strategies, this situation amounts to a search in a high-dimensional parameter space where each dimension represents a different aspect of the trading strategy. Exploration would involve trying out completely new sets of parameters, while exploitation would involve fine-tuning the most promising sets of parameters already discovered. The optimizer aims to effectively navigate this high-dimensional space and find the set of parameters that yields the best possible performance in terms of the Sharpe ratio or other preset metrics.

Let us formalize this sequential global optimization using mathematical terms. We are dealing with an unknown scalar-valued objective function f based on a specific domain $\mathcal{X}$. In other words, the unknown subject of interest f is a function that maps a certain candidate parameter in $\mathcal{X}$ to a real number in $\mathbb{R}$, that is, $f : \mathcal{X} \to \mathbb{R}$. We typically place no specific assumption about the nature of the domain $\mathcal{X}$ other than that it should be a bounded, compact, and convex set.

A bounded set $\mathcal{X}$ means that it has upper and lower limits, and all values of the parameters contained within $\mathcal{X}$ fall within these bounds. A compact set is one that is both bounded and closed, meaning that it includes its boundary. And a convex set is one in which, for any two points within the set, the set contains the whole line segment that joins them. These assumptions make our problem mathematically tractable and realistic in the real-world scenario.

Unless otherwise specified, we focus on the maximization setting instead of minimization since maximizing the objective function is equivalent to minimizing the negated objective, followed by another negation to recover the original maximum value. The optimization procedure thus aims at locating the global maximum f^* or its corresponding location x^* in a principled and systematic manner. Mathematically, we wish to locate f^* where

$$f^* = \max_{x \in \mathcal{X}} f\left(x\right) = f\left(x^*\right)$$

Or equivalently, we are interested in its location x^* where

$$x^* = \operatorname{argmax}_{x \in \mathcal{X}} f\left(x\right)$$

The argmax operation is used in mathematics to denote the argument of the maximum or the set of points in the domain $\mathcal{X}$ that maximizes the function f. When used in this optimization problem, it means that we are looking for the specific values of the input parameters that yield the maximum value of the function.

Again, note that $f(x)$ is unknown and only indirectly observable through sampling, and $\mathcal{X}$ could be a set in a high-dimensional space. So, we are looking for the best parameters in a high-dimensional space that we can only explore one sample at a time. This is what makes the global optimization problem challenging in practice.

Figure 9-2 provides an example one-dimensional objective function with its global maximum f^* and its location x^* highlighted. The goal of global optimization is thus to systematically reason about a series of sampling decisions within the total search space $\mathcal{X}$, so as to locate the global maximum as fast as possible, that is, sampling as few times as possible, instead of conducting random trials or grid search. Besides, when the optimizer makes a sequence of decisions about where in the parameter space to sample next, each decision is influenced by the results of previous samples (also referred to as the training set) and is aimed at improving the estimated optimum.

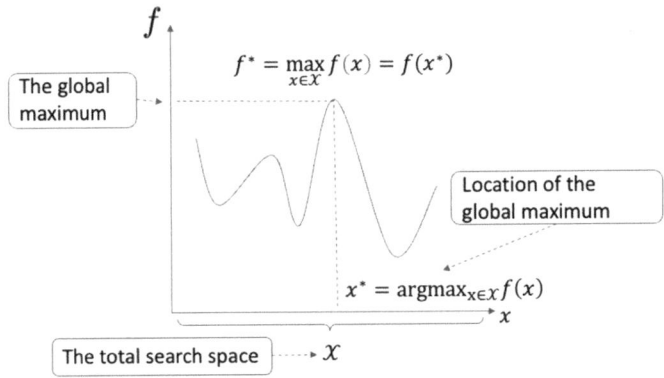

Figure 9-2. *An example objective function with the global maximum f^* and its location x^*. The goal of global optimization is to systematically reason about a series of sampling decisions so as to locate the global maximum as fast as possible*

Note that this is a nonconvex function, as is often the case in real-life functions we are optimizing. A nonconvex function means that there are multiple local optima in the function. Thus, we could not resort to first-order gradient-based methods to reliably search for the global optimum, as we did for the convex function $y = x^2$. Using the gradient-based method, such as solving for the solution that makes the gradient of the original function equal to zero, will likely converge to a local optimum. This is also one of the advantages of Bayesian optimization, introduced as a global optimization technique later, compared with other gradient-based optimization procedures for local search.

The next covers more on the objective function.

The Objective Function

The objective function governs how the quantity of interest is generated. The whole chapter would be finished if we knew its explicit expression, and the problem would be considered solved if we could access its underlying mathematical form. Unfortunately, many objective functions in real life are black boxes to us: the stock price of a given company the next day, the weather two days from now, or the exact time point when the interest rate starts to go down. Even though the objective function is a black box, we can still use optimization techniques to find the best possible solution given the available data and resources.

There are different types of objective functions. For example, some functions are wiggly shaped, while others are smooth; some are convex, while others are nonconvex. Many complex functions are almost impossible to be expressed using an explicit expression. For the specific type of objective functions that govern the performance of trading strategies, we summarize the following common attributes:

- We do not have access to the explicit expression of the objective function, making it a "black-box" function. This means we can only interact with the objective function by sampling at a specific location to perform a functional evaluation.

- The returned value by probing at a specific input parameter value is highly sensitive to the choice of backtesting period. In other words, it is often corrupted by noise and does not represent the exact true value of the objective function at that location. Due to the indirect evaluation of its actual value, we need to account for such noise embedded in the actual observations from the functional evaluation.

- Each functional evaluation is costly, thus ruling out the option for an exhaustive probing exercise. We need a sample-efficient method to minimize the number of evaluations of the trading strategy while trying to locate its global optimum. In other words, the optimizer needs to fully utilize the existing observations and systematically reason about the next sampling decision so that the limited resource is well spent on promising candidate parameter values.

- We do not have access to its gradient. When the functional evaluation is relatively cheap, and the functional form is smooth, it would be very convenient to compute/estimate the gradient and optimize using the first-order procedure such as gradient descent. Access to the gradient is necessary for us to understand the adjacent curvature of a particular evaluation point. With gradient evaluations, the follow-up direction of travel is easier to determine.

The black-box function, such as the one that calculates the Sharpe ratio based on two window length parameters, is challenging to optimize for the preceding reasons. To further elaborate on the possible functional form of the objective, we list three representative examples in a minimization setting, as shown in Figure 9-3. On the left is a convex function with only one global minimum; this is considered easy for global optimization, since we could just set the derivative of the function to zero and solve for the optimal value of the input variable. In the middle is a nonconvex function with multiple local optima; it is difficult to ascertain if the current local optimum is also globally optimal. It is also difficult to identify whether this is a flat region vs. a local optimum for a function with a flat region full of saddle points, as shown on the right panel. Such nonconvexity makes it difficult to perform global optimization efficiently.

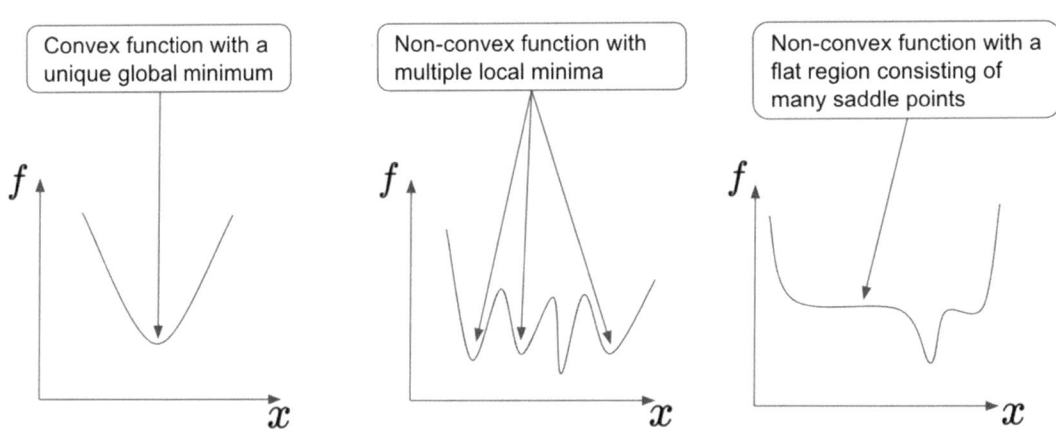

Figure 9-3. *Three possible functional forms. On the left is a convex function whose optimization is easy. In the middle is a nonconvex function with multiple local minima, and on the right is also a nonconvex function with a wide flat region full of saddle points. Optimization for the latter two cases takes a lot more work than for the first case*

Let us look at one example of hyperparameter tuning when training machine learning models. A machine learning model is a function that involves a set of parameters to be optimized given the input data. These parameters are automatically tuned via a specific optimization procedure, typically governed by a set of corresponding meta parameters called hyperparameters, which are fixed before the model training starts. For example, when training deep neural networks using the gradient descent algorithm, a learning rate that determines the step size of each parameter update needs to be manually selected in advance. If the learning rate is too large, the model may diverge and eventually fails to learn. If the learning rate is too small, the model may converge very slowly as the weights are updated by only a small margin in this iteration. See Figure 9-4 for a visual illustration of the two scenarios.

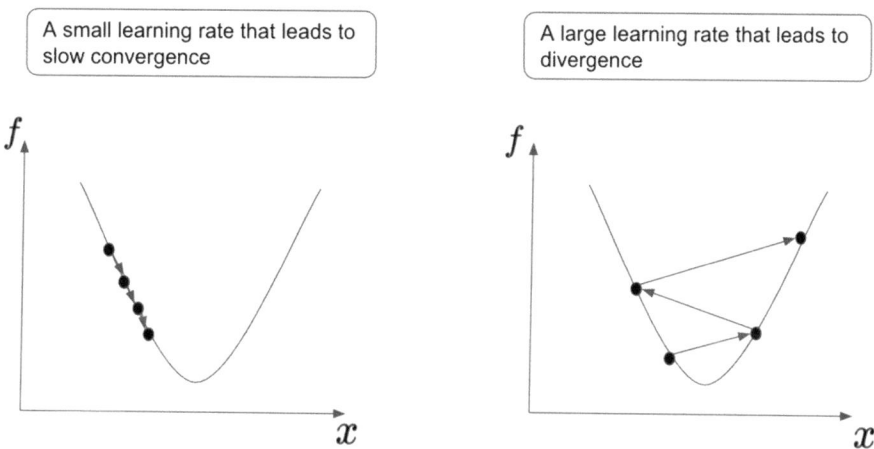

Figure 9-4. *Slow convergence due to a small learning rate on the left and divergence due to a large learning rate on the right*

Choosing a reasonable learning rate as a preset hyperparameter thus plays a critical role in training a good machine learning model. Locating the best learning rate and other hyperparameters is an optimization problem that fits the purpose of Bayesian optimization (introduced later). In the case of hyperparameter tuning, evaluating each learning rate is a time-consuming exercise. The objective function would generally be the model's final test set loss (in a minimization setting) upon model convergence. A model needs to be fully trained in order to do reasonably well on the training set, which typically involves hundreds of epochs of training to reach a stable convergence. Here, one epoch is a complete pass of the entire training dataset.

The functional form of the test set loss or accuracy may also be highly nonconvex and multimodal for the hyperparameters. Upon convergence, it is not easy to know whether we are in a local optimum, a saddle point, or a global optimum. Besides, some hyperparameters may be discrete, such as the number of nodes and layers when training a deep neural network. We could not calculate its gradient in such a case since it requires continuous support in the domain.

The Bayesian optimization approach is designed to tackle all these challenges. It has been shown to deliver good performance in locating the best hyperparameters under a limited budget (i.e., the number of evaluations allowed). It is also widely and successfully used in other fields, such as chemical engineering.

Bayesian Optimization

As the name suggests, Bayesian optimization is an area that studies optimization problems using the Bayesian approach. Optimization aims at locating the optimal objective value (i.e., a global maximum or minimum) of all possible values or the corresponding location of the optimum over the search domain, also called the environment. The search process starts at a specific initial location and follows a particular policy to iteratively guide the following sampling locations, collect new observations, and refresh the guiding search policy.

At its core, Bayesian optimization uses a probabilistic model (such as Gaussian processes) to represent the unknown function and a utility function (also called the acquisition function) to decide where to sample next. It iteratively updates the probabilistic model with new sample points and uses this updated model to select the next sampling location.

As shown in Figure 9-5, the overall optimization process consists of repeated interactions between the policy (the optimizer) and the environment (the unknown objective function). The policy is a mapping function that takes in a new input parameter (plus historical ones) and outputs the next parameter value to try out in a principled way. Here, we are constantly learning and improving the policy as the search continues. A good policy guides our search toward the global optimum faster than a bad one. In arguing which parameter value to try out, a good policy would spend the limited sampling budget on promising candidate values.

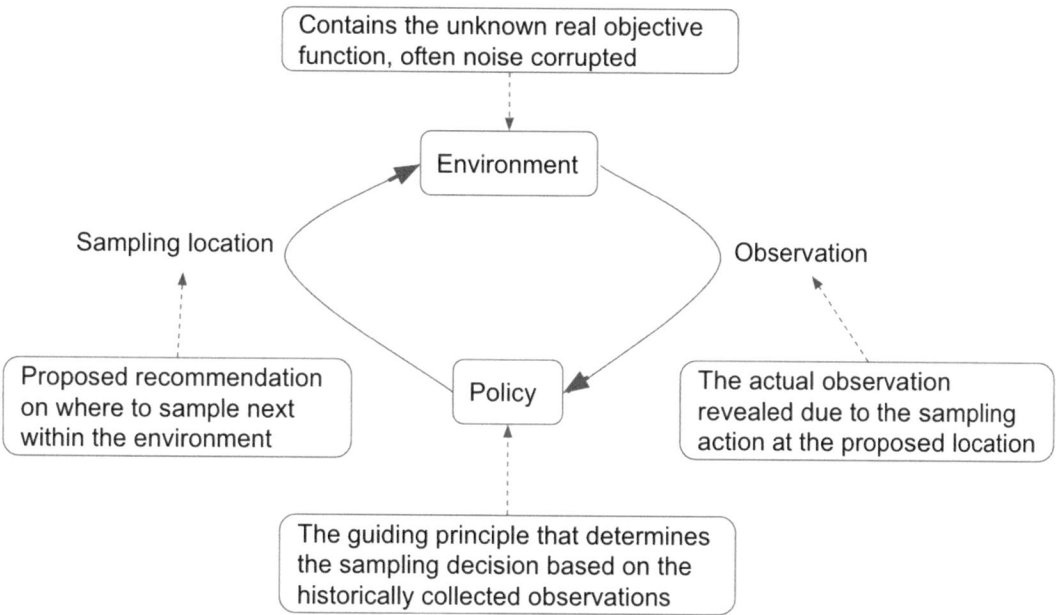

Figure 9-5. *The overall Bayesian optimization process. The policy digests the historical observations and proposes a new sampling location. The environment governs how the (possibly noise-corrupted) observation at the newly proposed location is revealed to the policy. Our goal is to learn an efficient and effective policy that could navigate toward the global optimum as quickly as possible*

On the other hand, the environment contains the unknown objective function to be learned by the policy within a specific boundary (maximum and minimum values of the parameter value). When probing the functional value as requested by the policy, the actual observation revealed by the environment to the policy is often corrupted by noise due to the choice of the backtesting period, making the learning even more challenging. Thus, Bayesian optimization, a specific approach for global optimization, would like to learn a policy that can help us efficiently and effectively navigate toward the global optimum of an unknown, noise-corrupted objective function as quickly as possible.

When deciding which parameter value to try next, most search strategies face the exploration and exploitation trade-off. Exploration means searching within an unknown and faraway area, and exploitation refers to searching within the neighborhood visited earlier in the hope of locating a better functional evaluation. Bayesian optimization also faces the same dilemma. Ideally, we would like to explore more at the initial phase to increase our understanding of the environment (the black-box function) and gradually shift toward the exploitation mode that taps into the existing knowledge and digs into known promising regions.

Bayesian optimization achieves such a trade-off via two components: a Gaussian process (GP) used to approximate the underlying black-box function and an acquisition function that encodes the exploration-exploitation trade-off into a scalar value as an indicator of the sampling utility across all candidates in the domain. Let us look at each component in detail in the following sections.

Gaussian Process

As a widely used stochastic process (able to model an unknown black-box function and the corresponding uncertainties of modeling), the Gaussian process takes the finite-dimensional probability distributions one step further into a continuous search domain that contains an infinite number of variables, where any finite set of points in the domain jointly forms a multivariate Gaussian distribution. It is a flexible framework to model a broad family of functions and quantify their uncertainties, thus being a powerful surrogate model used to approximate the true underlying function. Let us look at a few visual examples to see what it offers.

Figure 9-6 illustrates an example of a "flipped" prior probability distribution for a single random variable selected from the prior belief of the Gaussian process. Every single point represents a parameter value, although it is now modeled as a random variable and thus has randomness in its realizations. Specifically, each point follows a normal distribution. Plotting the mean (solid line) and 95% credible interval (dashed lines) of all these prior distributions gives us the prior process for the objective function regarding each location in the domain. The Gaussian process thus employs an infinite number of normally distributed random variables within a bounded range to model the underlying objective function and quantify the associated uncertainty via a probabilistic approach.

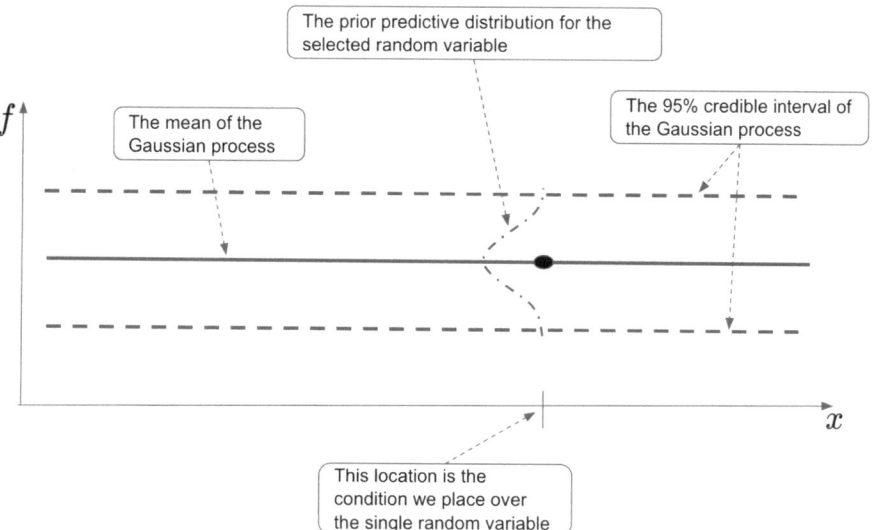

Figure 9-6. *A sample prior belief of the Gaussian process represented by the mean and 95% credible interval for each location in the domain. Every objective value is modeled by a random variable that follows a normal prior predictive distribution. Collecting the distributions of all random variables and updating these distributions as more observations are collected could help us quantify the potential shape of the true underlying function and its probability*

The prior process can thus serve as the surrogate data-generating process of the unknown black-box function, which can also be used to generate samples in the form of functions, an extension of sampling single points from a probability distribution. For example, if we were to repeatedly sample from the prior process, we would expect the majority (around 95%) of the samples to fall within the credible interval and a minority outside this range. Figure 9-7 illustrates three functions sampled from the prior process.

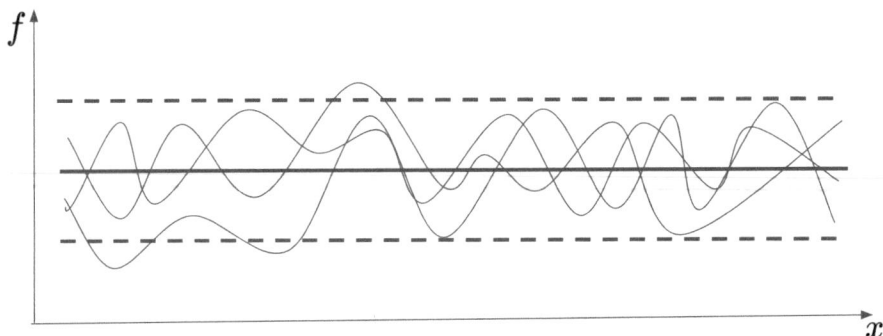

Figure 9-7. *Three example functions sampled from the prior process, where the majority of the functions fall within the 95% credible interval*

In a Gaussian process, the uncertainty on the objective value of each location (i.e., the parameter value of a trading strategy) is quantified using a credible interval. As we start to collect observations and assume a noise-free and exact observation model, the uncertainties at the collection locations will be resolved, leading to zero variance and direct interpolation at these locations. Besides, the variance increases as we move further away from the observations, which is a result of integrating the prior process (the prior belief about the unknown black-box function) with the information provided by the actual observations. Figure 9-8 illustrates the updated posterior process after collecting two observations. The posterior process with updated knowledge based on the observations will thus make a more accurate surrogate model and better estimate the objective function.

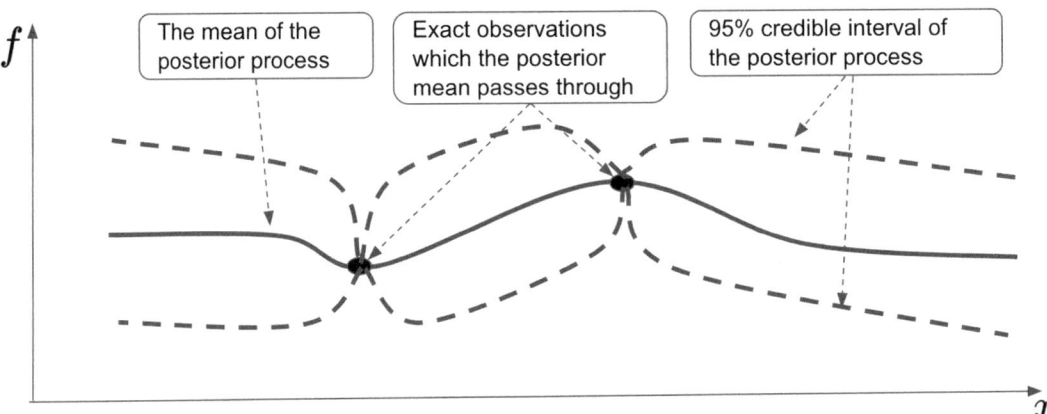

Figure 9-8. *Updated posterior process after incorporating two exact observations in the Gaussian process. The posterior mean interpolates through the observations, and the associated variance reduces as we move nearer the observations*

Mathematically, for a new sampling location $\mathbf{x}_* \in \mathcal{X}$, the corresponding functional evaluation f_* following the Gaussian process would assume a conditional normal distribution:

$$p\left(f_*; \mathbf{x}_*, D_n\right) = N\left(f_* | \mu_*, \sigma_*^2\right)$$

where $D_n = \left\{\left(\mathbf{x}_i, \mathbf{f}_i\right)\right\}_{i=1}^n$ contains the historical observed in pairs of sampling locations and scalar observations. The closed form of the posterior mean and variance functions can be derived by invoking the multivariate Gaussian theorem, giving

$$\mu_* = \mathbf{k}\left(\mathbf{x}_{1:n}, \mathbf{x}_*\right) \mathbf{K}\left(\mathbf{x}_{1:n}, \mathbf{x}_{1:n}\right)^{-1} \mathbf{f}_{1:n}$$

$$\sigma_*^2 = k\left(\mathbf{x}_*, \mathbf{x}_*\right) - \mathbf{k}\left(\mathbf{x}_{1:n}, \mathbf{x}_*\right) \mathbf{K}\left(\mathbf{x}_{1:n}, \mathbf{x}_{1:n}\right)^{-1} \mathbf{k}\left(\mathbf{x}_{1:n}, \mathbf{x}_*\right)$$

Therefore, we can obtain the posterior mean and variance at any arbitrary location based on the posterior Gaussian process model, serving as the surrogate model for the underlying function of the specific trading strategy.

Now let us look at the other critical component: the acquisition function.

Acquisition Function

The tools from Bayesian inference and the incorporation of the Gaussian process provide principled reasoning on the underlying distribution of the objective function. However, we would still need to incorporate such probabilistic information in our decision-making to search for the global maximum. We need to build a policy (by maximizing the acquisition function) that absorbs the most updated information on the objective function and recommends the following most promising sampling location in the face of uncertainties across the domain. The optimization policy guided by maximizing the acquisition function thus plays an essential role in connecting the Gaussian process to the eventual goal of Bayesian optimization. In particular, the posterior predictive distribution obtained from the updated Gaussian process provides an outlook on the objective value and the associated uncertainty for locations not explored yet, which could be used by the optimization policy to quantify the utility of any alternative location within the domain.

When converting the posterior knowledge about candidate locations, that is, posterior parameters such as the mean and the variance of the Gaussian distribution at each location, to a single scalar utility score, the acquisition function comes into play.

An acquisition function is a manually designed mechanism that evaluates the relative potential of each candidate location in the form of a scalar score, and the location with the maximum score will be used as the next sampling choice. It is a function that assesses how valuable a candidate's location is when we acquire/sample it.

The acquisition function takes into account both the expected value and the uncertainty (variance) of the function at unexplored locations, as provided by the Gaussian process posterior distribution. In this context, exploration means sampling in regions of high uncertainty, while exploitation involves sampling where the function value is expected to be high.

The acquisition function is also cheap to evaluate as a side computation since we need to evaluate it at every candidate location and then locate the maximum utility score, posing another (inner) optimization problem. Figure 9-9 provides a sample curve of the acquisition function.

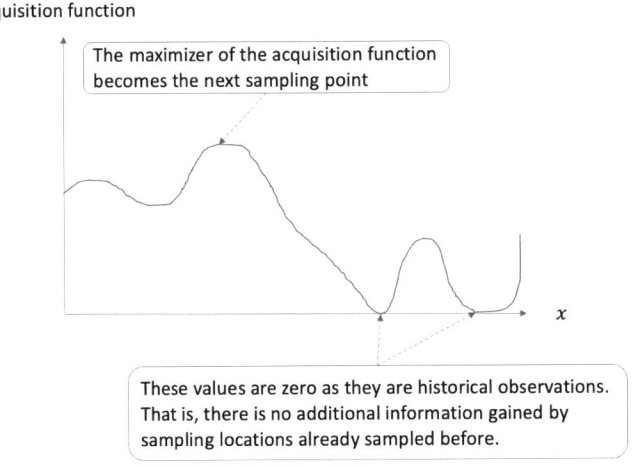

Figure 9-9.   *Illustrating a sample acquisition function curve. The location that corresponds to the highest value of the acquisition function is the next location (parameter value of a trading strategy) to sample. Since there is no value added if we were to sample those locations already sampled earlier, the acquisition function thus reports zero at these locations*

Many choices of acquisition functions have been proposed in the literature. Popular choices include the expected improvement (EI) and upper confidence bound (UCB). Still, it suffices, for now, to understand that it is a predesigned function that needs to balance two opposing forces: exploration and exploitation. Exploration encourages resolving the uncertainty across the domain by sampling at unfamiliar and distant locations, since these areas may bear a big surprise due to high certainty. Exploitation recommends a greedy move at promising regions where we expect the observation value to be high. The exploration-exploitation trade-off is a common topic in many optimization settings.

Another distinguishing feature is the short-term (myopic) and long-term (nonmyopic) trade-offs. A short-term acquisition function only focuses on one step ahead and assumes this is the last chance to sample from the environment; thus, the recommendation is to maximize the immediate utility. A long-term acquisition function employs a multistep lookahead approach by simulating potential evolutions/paths in the future and making a final recommendation by maximizing the long-run utility.

There are many other emerging variations in the design of the acquisition function, such as adding safety constraints to the system under study. In any case, we would judge the quality of the policy using a specific acquisition function based on how close we are to the location of the global maximum upon exhausting our budget. The distance between the current and optimal locations is often called instant regret or simple regret. Alternatively, the cumulative regret (cumulative distances between historical locations and the optimum location) incurred throughout the sampling process can also be used.

Let us dive more into two popular acquisition functions: expected improvement (EI) and upper confidence bound (UCB).

EI and UCB

Acquisition functions differ in multiple aspects, including the choice of the utility function, the number of lookahead steps, the level of risk aversion or preference, etc. Introducing risk appetite directly benefits from the posterior belief about the underlying objective function. In the case of GP regression as the surrogate model, the risk is quantified by the covariance function, with its credible interval expressing the uncertainty level about the objective's possible values.

Regarding the utility of the collected observations, the expected improvement chooses the historical maximum of the observed value as the benchmark for comparison upon selecting an additional sampling location. It also implicitly assumes that only one more additional sampling is left before the optimization process terminates. The expected marginal gain in utility (i.e., the acquisition function) becomes the expected improvement in the maximal observation, calculated as the expected difference between the observed maximum and the new observation after the additional sampling at an arbitrary sampling location.

Specifically, denote $y_{1:n} = \{y_1, ..., y_n\}$ as the set of collected observations at the corresponding locations $x_{1:n} = \{x_1, ..., x_n\}$. Assuming the noise-free setting, the actual observations would be exact, that is, $y_{1:n} = f_{1:n}$. Given the collected dataset $\mathcal{D}_n = \{x_{1:n}, y_{1:n}\}$, the corresponding utility is $u(\mathcal{D}_n) = \max\{f_{1:n}\} = f_n^*$, where f_n^* is the incumbent maximum observed so far. Similarly, assume we obtain another observation $y_{n+1} = f_{n+1}$ at a new location x_{n+1}, the resulting utility is $u(\mathcal{D}_{n+1}) = u(\mathcal{D}_n \cup \{x_{n+1}, f_{n+1}\}) = \max\{f_{n+1}, f_n^*\}$. Taking the difference between these two gives the increase in utility due to the addition of another observation:

$$u(\mathcal{D}_{n+1}) - u(\mathcal{D}_n) = \max\{f_{n+1}, f_n^*\} - f_n^* = \max\{f_{n+1} - f_n^*, 0\}$$

which returns the marginal increment in the incumbent if $f_{n+1} \geq f_n^*$ and zero otherwise, as a result of observing f_{n+1}. Readers familiar with the activation function in neural networks would instantly connect this form with the ReLU (rectified linear unit) function, which keeps the positive signal and silences the negative one.

Due to randomness in y_{n+1}, we can introduce the expectation operator to integrate it out, giving us the expected marginal gain in utility, that is, the expected improvement acquisition function:

$$\alpha_{EI}(x_{n+1}; \mathcal{D}_n) = \mathbb{E}\left[u(\mathcal{D}_{n+1}) - u(\mathcal{D}_n)|x_{n+1}, \mathcal{D}_n\right]$$
$$= \int \max\{f_{n+1} - f_n^*, 0\} p(f_{n+1}|x_{n+1}, \mathcal{D}_n) df_{n+1}$$

Under the framework of GP regression, we can obtain a closed-form expression of the expected improvement acquisition function as follows:

$$\alpha_{EI}(x_{n+1}; \mathcal{D}_n) = (\mu_{n+1} - f_n^*)\Phi\left(\frac{\mu_{n+1} - f_n^*}{\sigma_{n+1}}\right) + \sigma_{n+1}\phi\left(\frac{\mu_{n+1} - f_n^*}{\sigma_{n+1}}\right)$$

where f_n^* is the best-observed value so far, and ϕ and Φ denote the probability and cumulative density function of a standard normal distribution at the tentative point x_{n+1}, respectively. μ_{n+1} and σ_{n+1} denote the posterior mean and standard deviation at x_{n+1}.

The closed-form EI consists of two components: exploitation (the first term) and exploration (the second term). Exploitation means continuing sampling the neighborhood of the observed region with a high posterior mean, and exploration encourages sampling an unvisited area where the posterior uncertainty is high. The expected improvement acquisition function thus implicitly balances off these two opposing forces.

On the other hand, the UCB acquisition function, as defined in the following, encodes such a trade-off explicitly:

$$\alpha_{\text{UCB}}\left(x_{n+1};\mathcal{D}_n\right) = \mu_{n+1} + \beta_{n+1}\sigma_{n+1}$$

where β_{n+1} is a user-defined stagewise hyperparameter that controls the trade-off between the posterior mean and standard deviation. A low value of β_{n+1} encourages exploitation, and a high value of β_{n+1} leans more toward exploration.

Both acquisition functions will then be assessed globally in search of the maximizing location, which will serve as the next sampling choice. Let us summarize the full BO (Bayesian optimization) loop in the following section.

The Full BO Loop

Bayesian optimization is an iterative process between the (uncontrolled) environment and the (controlled) policy. The policy involves two components supporting the sequential decision-making: a Gaussian process as the surrogate model to approximate the true underlying function (i.e., the environment), and an acquisition function to recommend the best sampling location. The environment receives the probing request at a specific location and responds by revealing a new observation that follows a particular observation model. The Gaussian process surrogate model then uses the new observation to obtain a posterior process in support of follow-up decision-making by the preset acquisition function. This process continues until the stopping criterion, such as exhausting a given budget, is met. Figure 9-10 illustrates this process.

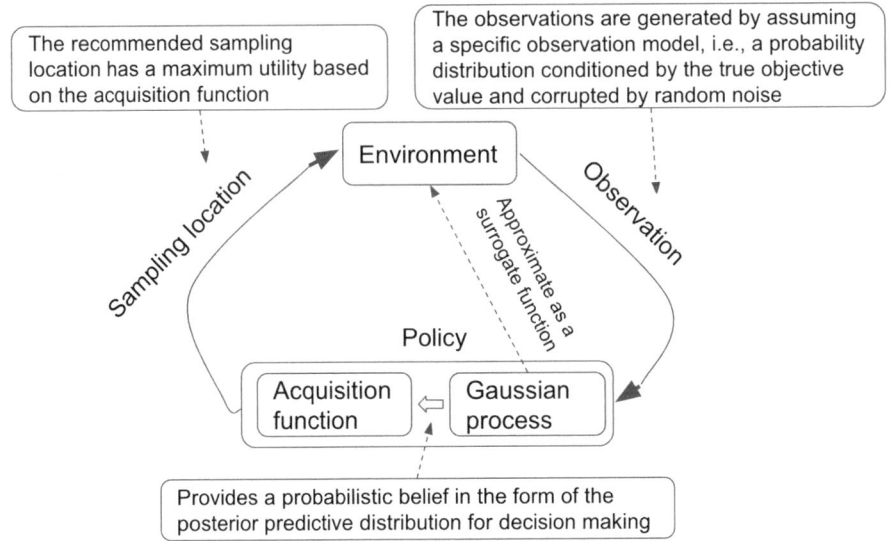

Figure 9-10. *The full Bayesian optimization loop featuring an iterative interaction between the unknown (black-box) environment and the decision-making policy that consists of a Gaussian process for probabilistic evaluation and acquisition function for utility assessment of candidate locations in the environment*

With the basic BO framework in mind, let us test it out by optimizing the window lengths of the pairs trading strategy.

Optimizing the Pairs Trading Strategy

As introduced earlier, the pairs trading strategy characterizes two input arguments: the entry and exit thresholds. More specifically, we would like to apply the BO technique to search for the optimal entry and exit thresholds such that the black-box function reaches a maximum value. For simplicity, we only perform the Sharpe ratio calculation once over one backtesting period. A more robust approach to minimize the observation noise is to test it over multiple representative backtesting periods and report the average Sharpe ratio as a fair indication of the goodness of the given input parameters.

To begin with, we will first install two packages: the botorch package that performs BO based on PyTorch and the yfinance package to facilitate data downloading.

```
!pip install botorch
!pip install yfinance
```

We also import a few supporting packages in the following, along with setting the random seed for reproducibility:

```
import os
import math
import torch
import random
import numpy as np
from matplotlib import pyplot as plt
import torch.nn as nn
import yfinance as yf
import pandas as pd
from statsmodels.tsa.stattools import adfuller
from statsmodels.regression.linear_model import OLS
import statsmodels.api as sm
%matplotlib inline

SEED = 1
random.seed(SEED)
np.random.seed(SEED)
torch.manual_seed(SEED)
```

The next section touches upon the performance of the pairs trading strategy as the black-box function.

Trading Strategy Performance As the Black-Box Function

The trend-following strategy will govern the output of the black-box function. Previously, we have illustrated how to calculate the Sharpe ratio given a specific set of entry and exit parameters. Assuming the Sharpe ratio calculated over one backtesting period is sufficiently representative, we would like to modularize the whole process of mapping a set of input parameters to the output performance metric. In other words, we need to code a function (or a class) that spits out the Sharpe ratio for a given set of entry and exit thresholds.

To start with, we define a class called QTS_OPTIMIZER that inherits the nn.Module class. This will serve as the main horsepower for generating observations given any query points. In the __init__() method, we require three compulsory arguments: the ticker pairs in `ticker_pair`, the starting date of the stock price in `start_date`, and the end date in `end_date`. We also set an optional argument `riskfree_rate` to control the risk-free interest rate used for Sharpe ratio calculation. This is shown in Listing 9-1.

Listing 9-1. Defining the black-box function for Bayesian optimization

```python
class QTS_OPTIMIZER(nn.Module):
    def __init__(self, ticker_pair, start_date, end_date, riskfree_
    rate=0.04):
        super(QTS_OPTIMIZER, self).__init__()
        self.ticker_pair = ticker_pair
        self.start_date = start_date
        self.end_date = end_date
        self.riskfree_rate = riskfree_rate
        self.stock = self.get_stock_data()
```

Upon instantiating this class, the __init__() function will get triggered, which also includes downloading the stock data for the selected ticker and date range. Listing 9-2 has the definition of the get_stock_data() method, where we use the usual download() function to download the data and extract the adjusted closing price that considers dividends and splits.

Listing 9-2. Defining the method to retrieve stock data

```python
def get_stock_data(self):
        print("===== DOWNLOADING STOCK DATA =====")
        df = yf.download(['GOOG'], start=self.start_date, end=self.end_
        date)['Adj Close']
        print("===== DOWNLOAD COMPLETE =====")

        return pd.DataFrame(df)
```

Next, we introduce the forward() method, which gets triggered automatically upon calling the class object itself. This is where we implement the mechanism of the black-box function, which takes two parameters as the input and outputs the corresponding Sharpe ratio over the prespecified stock data and backtesting period. As shown in Listing 9-3, upon passing the entry and exit thresholds entry_threshold and exit_threshold, we estimate the linear regression coefficients, calculate the residuals, and obtain the z-scores.

We then create the position columns to represent the trading position determined by the daily entry and exit signals. Based on the daily returns, we could then calculate the joint returns and the resulting annualized return and volatility, followed by the Sharpe ratio as the final return of the forward() function.

Listing 9-3. Defining the method to calculate the Sharpe ratio

```python
def forward(self, entry_threshold, exit_threshold, window_size=10):
    # add sma columns
    stock_df = self.stock.copy()
    # calculate the spread for GOOG and MSFT
    Y = stock_df[self.ticker_pair[0]]
    X = stock_df[self.ticker_pair[1]]
    # estimate linear regression coefficients
    X_with_constant = sm.add_constant(X)
    model = OLS(Y, X_with_constant).fit()
    # obtain the spread as the residuals
    spread = Y - model.predict()
    # calculate rolling mean and sd
    spread_mean = spread.rolling(window=window_size).mean()
    spread_std = spread.rolling(window=window_size).std()
    zscore = (spread - spread_mean) / spread_std
    # remove initial days with NA
    first_valid_idx = zscore.first_valid_index()
    zscore = zscore[first_valid_idx:]
    # initialize the daily positions to be zeros
    stock1_position = pd.Series(data=0, index=zscore.index)
    stock2_position = pd.Series(data=0, index=zscore.index)
    # generate daily entry and exit signals for each stock
    for i in range(1, len(zscore)):
        # zscore<-entry_threshold and no existing long position
        for stock 1
        if zscore[i] < -entry_threshold and stock1_position[i-1] == 0:
            stock1_position[i] = 1 # long stock 1
            stock2_position[i] = -1 # short stock 2
```

```python
        # zscore>entry_threshold and no existing short position
        for stock 2
        elif zscore[i] > entry_threshold and stock2_position[i-1] == 0:
            stock1_position[i] = -1 # short stock 1
            stock2_position[i] = 1 # long stock 2
        # -exit_threshold<zscore<exit_threshold
        elif abs(zscore[i]) < exit_threshold:
            stock1_position[i] = 0 # exit existing position
            stock2_position[i] = 0
        # -entry_threshold<zscore<-exit_threshold or exit_
        threshold<zscore<entry_threshold
        else:
            stock1_position[i] = stock1_position[i-1] # maintain
            existing position
            stock2_position[i] = stock2_position[i-1]
    # Calculate the returns of each stock
    stock1_returns = (Y[first_valid_idx:].pct_change() * stock1_
    position.shift(1)).fillna(0)
    stock2_returns = (X[first_valid_idx:].pct_change() * stock2_
    position.shift(1)).fillna(0)
    # calculate the total returns of the strategy
    total_returns = stock1_returns + stock2_returns
    # calculate annualized return
    annualized_return = (1 + total_returns).prod()**(252/Y[first_valid_
    idx:].shape[0])-1
    # calculate annualized volatility
    annualized_vol = total_returns.std()*(252**0.5)
    if annualized_vol==0:
        annualized_vol = 100
    # calculate Sharpe ratio
    sharpe_ratio = (annualized_return - self.riskfree_rate) /
    annualized_vol

    return sharpe_ratio
```

Let us test the class out. The following code instantiates the class into the `qts` variable by passing the ticker symbol of Google and Microsoft with a date range of the start and end dates of 2022. Note the printed message after running this line, showing that the `get_stock_data()` function gets triggered during the process. Note that there is no mention of entry and exit signals at this stage; the initialization stage is meant to handle all preparatory work before the actual scoring in the `forward()` function.

```
>>> qts = QTS_OPTIMIZER(ticker_pair=["GOOG","MSFT"], start_
date="2022-01-01", end_date="2023-01-01")
===== DOWNLOADING STOCK DATA =====
[********************100%**********************]  1 of 1 completed
===== DOWNLOAD COMPLETE =====
```

We can also print the first few rows of the object's stock attribute as a sanity check:

```
>>> qts.stock.head()
            GOOG        MSFT
Date
2022-01-03  145.074493  330.813873
2022-01-04  144.416504  325.141388
2022-01-05  137.653503  312.659851
2022-01-06  137.550995  310.189270
2022-01-07  137.004501  310.347412
```

Let us test out the scoring function. In the following code snippet, we pass in different values of entry and exit thresholds and obtain the corresponding Sharpe ratio for the whole year of 2022:

```
>>> qts(entry_threshold=2, exit_threshold=1)
1.690533096171306
>>> qts(entry_threshold=1.5, exit_threshold=0.5)
1.8278364562046485
```

We see that different values of the thresholds correspond to different Sharpe ratios. Our task is to find the optimal set of entry and exit thresholds that correspond to the highest Sharpe ratio, as fast as possible. This is where Bayesian optimization comes in.

Generating Training Set for Bayesian Optimization

Most machine learning models require a training set to start with. The training set provides the correct input-output mapping relationship for the model to fine-tune its weights and, therefore, learn such a mapping relationship. This is the same for the Bayesian optimization model. Specifically, the training set helps update the prior distribution used by the Gaussian process, so that its governing hyperparameters get updated, which would then be used to obtain a more representative posterior distribution.

The following code snippet creates a few preparatory variables for later use, where `device` denotes the computing device (CPU or GPU) to run the calculations later, `dtype` specifies the data type of the PyTorch tensor, and `x1_bound` and `x2_bound` contain the lower and upper bounds for the short and long windows, respectively. Here, we specify the short window to vary from 1 to 10 and the long window from 11 to 20:

```
# generate initial training dataset for optimization
device = torch.device("cuda" if torch.cuda.is_available() else "cpu")
dtype = torch.double
x1_bound = [1,3]
x2_bound = [0,1]
```

Next, we define a function named `generate_initial_data()` to get a set of training data. As shown in Listing 9-4, this function takes a single input n to specify the number of observations in the training set. Inside the function, we first generate a set of random values using the `torch.rand()` function from Torch. After combining the set of entry and exit thresholds into a single variable `train_x`, we iterate through each row to apply the black-box scoring function `qts()` and obtain the corresponding Sharpe ratio, collectively stored in `train_y`. Besides returning `train_x` and `train_y`, we also report the highest score in `best_observed_value`, as we will maintain a list of cumulative maximum values to indicate the search quality. The current best value observed so far also represents the utility of the dataset collected till now, that is, the utility value of the dataset in helping us locate the optimum window lengths.

Listing 9-4. Generating initial training data

```
def generate_initial_data(n=10):
    # generate random initial locations
    train_x1 = x1_bound[0] + (x1_bound[1] - x1_bound[0]) * torch.
    rand(size=(n,1), device=device, dtype=dtype)
    train_x2 = torch.rand(size=(n,1), device=device, dtype=dtype)
    train_x = torch.cat((train_x1, train_x2), 1)
    # obtain the exact value of the objective function and add output
    dimension
    train_y = []
    for i in range(len(train_x)):
        train_y.append(qts(entry_threshold=train_x1[i], exit_
        threshold=train_x2[i]))
    train_y = torch.Tensor(train_y, device=device).to(dtype).unsqueeze(-1)
    # get the current best observed value, i.e., utility of the
    available dataset
    best_observed_value = train_y.max().item()
    return train_x, train_y, best_observed_value
```

Let us generate three samples in the training set as follows:

```
train_x, train_y, best_observed_value = generate_initial_data(n=3)
>>> print(train_x)
>>> print(train_y)
>>> print(best_observed_value)
tensor([[1.1221, 0.1771],
        [1.4491, 0.5561],
        [1.4685, 0.1094]], dtype=torch.float64)
tensor([[0.0550],
        [2.2504],
        [1.0004]], dtype=torch.float64)
2.250356674194336
```

Next, we implement the first component in BO: the Gaussian process model.

Implementing the Gaussian Process Model

As mentioned earlier, we can use this training set to optimize the hyperparameters of the Gaussian process (GP) model so that it's more fine-tuned toward the data at hand. This is because a GP model is also governed by its own hyperparameters upon initialization, such as the length scale. Different GP models have different hyperparameters, and we will go with the default choice provided by BoTorch.

In Listing 9-5, we create a function called `initialize_model()` to initialize the GP model. We use the `SingleTaskGP()` class from `botorch.models` to instantiate a GP model based on the previous training data and then use the `ExactMarginalLogLikelihood()` function to obtain the exact marginal log-likelihood of the GP model.

Listing 9-5. Initializing the GP model

```
# initialize GP model
from botorch.models import SingleTaskGP
from gpytorch.mlls import ExactMarginalLogLikelihood

def initialize_model(train_x, train_y):
    # create a single-task exact GP model instance
    # use a GP prior with Matern kernel and constant mean function
      by default
    model = SingleTaskGP(train_X=train_x, train_Y=train_y)
    mll = ExactMarginalLogLikelihood(model.likelihood, model)

    return mll, model
```

Let us print out the values of the hyperparameters (including kernel parameters and noise variance) of the GP model before optimization:

```
mll, model = initialize_model(train_x, train_y)
>>> list(model.named_hyperparameters())
[('likelihood.noise_covar.raw_noise', Parameter containing:
  tensor([2.0000], dtype=torch.float64, requires_grad=True)),
 ('mean_module.raw_constant', Parameter containing:
  tensor(0., dtype=torch.float64, requires_grad=True)),
 ('covar_module.raw_outputscale', Parameter containing:
  tensor(0., dtype=torch.float64, requires_grad=True)),
```

```
('covar_module.base_kernel.raw_lengthscale', Parameter containing:
 tensor([[0., 0.]], dtype=torch.float64, requires_grad=True))]
```

Optimizing the GP hyperparameters can be done by following the maximum log-likelihood (MLL) approach, which is implemented in the `fit_gpytorch_mll()` function from `botorch.fit`. Listing 9-6 fits the GP hyperparameters and prints out their values.

Listing 9-6. Optimizing GP hyperparameters

```
# optimize GP hyperparameters
from botorch.fit import fit_gpytorch_mll
# fit hyperparameters (kernel parameters and noise variance) of a
GPyTorch model
fit_gpytorch_mll(mll.cpu());
mll = mll.to(train_x)
model = model.to(train_x)
>>> list(model.named_hyperparameters())
[('likelihood.noise_covar.raw_noise', Parameter containing:
  tensor([0.2238], dtype=torch.float64, requires_grad=True)),
 ('mean_module.raw_constant', Parameter containing:
  tensor(1.1789, dtype=torch.float64, requires_grad=True)),
 ('covar_module.raw_outputscale', Parameter containing:
  tensor(1.8917, dtype=torch.float64, requires_grad=True)),
 ('covar_module.base_kernel.raw_lengthscale', Parameter containing:
  tensor([[-0.8823, -0.9687]], dtype=torch.float64, requires_grad=True))]
```

The result shows a different set of hyperparameters after optimization. Note that we need to move the `mll` object to GPU to perform the optimization, after which it can be moved back to GPU (if available).

The optimized GP model can then be incorporated into the acquisition function to guide the following search process, as detailed in the next section.

Guiding the Sequential Search by Maximizing the Acquisition Function

We will use a few popular acquisition functions, including the expected improvement (EI), upper confidence bound (UCB), parallel expected improvement (qEI), and the parallel knowledge gradient (qKG). Instead of focusing on the derivation and reasoning of each choice, we will jump straight into their implementation and usage. Readers interested in a more in-depth discussion on different acquisition functions can refer to the book *Bayesian Optimization: Theory and Practice Using Python*.

To start with, we instantiate both acquisition functions via `ExpectedImprovement()`, `qExpectedImprovement()`, `UpperConfidenceBound()`, and `qKnowledgeGradient()` from `botorch.acquisition`. Note that different acquisition functions expect different input arguments. For example, other than the GP model instance from the previous section, EI requires the best-observed value so far, while UCB expects a beta parameter that adjusts the trade-off between exploitation and exploration. Such adjustment is implicitly handled in EI. This is shown in Listing 9-7.

Listing 9-7. Defining and initializing the acquisition functions

```
# define acquisition function
from botorch.acquisition import ExpectedImprovement
from botorch.acquisition import qExpectedImprovement
from botorch.acquisition import UpperConfidenceBound
from botorch.acquisition.knowledge_gradient import qKnowledgeGradient

# call helper functions to generate initial training data and
initialize model
train_x, train_y, best_observed_value = generate_initial_data(n=3)
train_x_ei = train_x
train_x_qei = train_x
train_x_ucb = train_x
train_x_qkg = train_x
train_y_ei = train_y
train_y_qei = train_y
train_y_ucb = train_y
train_y_qkg = train_y
```

```
mll_ei, model_ei = initialize_model(train_x_ei, train_y_ei)
mll_qei, model_qei = initialize_model(train_x_qei, train_y_qei)
mll_ucb, model_ucb = initialize_model(train_x_ucb, train_y_ucb)
mll_qkg, model_qkg = initialize_model(train_x_qkg, train_y_qkg)

EI = ExpectedImprovement(model=model_ei, best_f=best_observed_value)
qEI = qExpectedImprovement(model=model_qei, best_f=best_observed_value)
beta = 0.8
UCB = UpperConfidenceBound(model=model_ucb, beta=beta)
num_fantasies = 64
qKG = qKnowledgeGradient(
    model=model_qkg,
    num_fantasies=num_fantasies,
    X_baseline=train_x,
    q=1
)
```

The acquisition function is used to generate the next parameter value to be sampled, which is located by maximizing the acquisition function at hand. The process of searching for the maximum value of the acquisition function within the search domain is handled by the `optimize_acqf()` function, which is provided by the `botorch.optim` module. The new parameter value, along with the corresponding score from the unknown objective function, will be used as an additional training data point to support an updated version of the GP model and acquisition function in the next round.

Listing 9-8 provides the detailed implementation of passing an acquisition function and obtaining the next sampling decision and functional observation. Note the additional parameters required by the optimization procedure `optimize_acqf()`: bounds to define the search domain of each parameter, `BATCH_SIZE` to specify the number of samples to probe at each round (probing multiple points in parallel is possible), `NUM_RESTARTS` to control the number of initial conditions when optimization starts, and `RAW_SAMPLES` to indicate the number of initial samples to support heuristic-based optimization over the acquisition function.

Listing 9-8. Obtaining a new proposal by optimizing the acquisition function

```python
# optimize and get new observation
from botorch.optim import optimize_acqf

# get search bounds
bounds = torch.tensor([[x1_bound[0], x2_bound[0]], [x1_bound[1], x2_
bound[1]]], device=device, dtype=dtype)
# parallel candidate locations generated in each iteration
BATCH_SIZE = 1
# number of starting points for multistart optimization
NUM_RESTARTS = 10
# number of samples for initialization
RAW_SAMPLES = 1024

def optimize_acqf_and_get_observation(acq_func):
    """Optimizes the acquisition function, and returns a new candidate and
    a noisy observation."""
    # optimize
    candidates, value = optimize_acqf(
        acq_function=acq_func,
        bounds=bounds,
        q=BATCH_SIZE,
        num_restarts=NUM_RESTARTS,
        raw_samples=RAW_SAMPLES,  # used for intialization heuristic
    )
    # observe new values
    new_x = candidates.detach()
    # sample output value
    new_y = qts(entry_threshold=new_x.squeeze()[0].item(), exit_
    threshold=new_x.squeeze()[1].item())
    # add output dimension
    new_y = torch.Tensor([new_y], device=device).to(dtype).unsqueeze(-1)
    # print("new fn value:", new_y)

    return new_x, new_y
```

Let us test out this function with the qKG acquisition function:

```
>>> optimize_acqf_and_get_observation(qKG)
(tensor([[1.5470, 0.6003]], dtype=torch.float64),
 tensor([[2.2481]], dtype=torch.float64))
```

Before scaling up to multiple iterations, we will also test out the random search strategy, which selects a random window length for each moving series at each round. This serves as the baseline for comparison, since manual selection often amounts to a random search strategy in the initial phase. In the function update_random_observations() shown in Listing 9-9, we pass a running list of best-observed function values, perform a random selection, observe the corresponding functional evaluation, compare it with the current running maximum, and then return the list of running maxima with the current maximum appended.

Listing 9-9. Defining the random search strategy

```
def update_random_observations(best_random):
    """Simulates a random policy by drawing a new random points,
        observing their values, and updating the current best candidate to
        the running list.
    """

    new_x1 = x1_bound[0] + (x1_bound[1] - x1_bound[0]) * torch.
    rand(size=(1,1), device=device, dtype=dtype)
    new_x2 = torch.rand(size=(1,1), device=device, dtype=dtype)
    new_x = torch.cat((new_x1, new_x2), 1)

    new_y = qts(entry_threshold=new_x[0,0].item(), exit_
    threshold=new_x[0,1].item())
    best_random.append(max(best_random[-1], new_y))
    return best_random
```

Now we perform the sequential search based on the aforementioned acquisition functions, along with the random search strategy.

Performing Sequential Search

These three search strategies have different search qualities in terms of the maximum Sharpe ratio found within the same sampling budget. To measure the effectiveness of the search strategy at each round, we use the cumulative maximum value returned by the black-box function, which is a nondecreasing function by design. A more effective search strategy would be able to identify a higher Sharpe ratio faster than alternative strategies under the same environment setting.

Listing 9-10 creates a few lists (best_observed_ei, best_observed_ucb, best_observed_qei, best_observed_qkg, and best_random) to store the best-observed Sharpe ratios at each round. The same training set consisting of three samples is used to initialize the GP model (if any) of each search strategy using the initialize_model() function, with the resulting GP model instances stored in model_ei, model_qkg, model_qei, and model_ucb, respectively. For the random search strategy, we can simply simulate a random selection and update its running max without any explicit learning process.

Listing 9-10. Performing the sequential search

```
# single trial
import time
N_ROUND = 20
verbose = True
beta = 0.8

best_random, best_observed_ei, best_observed_qei, best_observed_ucb, best_
observed_qkg  = [], [], [], [], []

best_random.append(best_observed_value)
best_observed_ei.append(best_observed_value)
best_observed_qei.append(best_observed_value)
best_observed_ucb.append(best_observed_value)
best_observed_qkg.append(best_observed_value)

# run N_ROUND rounds of BayesOpt after the initial random batch
for iteration in range(1, N_ROUND + 1):
    t0 = time.monotonic()
    # fit the models
```

```
fit_gpytorch_mll(mll_ei)
fit_gpytorch_mll(mll_qei)
fit_gpytorch_mll(mll_ucb)
fit_gpytorch_mll(mll_qkg)

# for best_f, we use the best observed exact values
EI = ExpectedImprovement(model=model_ei, best_f=train_y_ei.max())
qEI = qExpectedImprovement(model=model_qei,
                           best_f=train_y_ei.max(),
                           num_samples=1024
                           )
UCB = UpperConfidenceBound(model=model_ucb, beta=beta)
qKG = qKnowledgeGradient(
    model=model_qkg,
    num_fantasies=64,
    objective=None,
    X_baseline=train_x_qkg,
)

# optimize and get new observation
new_x_ei, new_y_ei = optimize_acqf_and_get_observation(EI)
new_x_qei, new_y_qei = optimize_acqf_and_get_observation(qEI)
new_x_ucb, new_y_ucb = optimize_acqf_and_get_observation(UCB)
new_x_qkg, new_y_qkg = optimize_acqf_and_get_observation(qKG)

# update training points
train_x_ei = torch.cat([train_x_ei, new_x_ei], dim=0)
train_x_qei = torch.cat([train_x_qei, new_x_qei], dim=0)
train_x_ucb = torch.cat([train_x_ucb, new_x_ucb], dim=0)
train_x_qkg = torch.cat([train_x_qkg, new_x_qkg], dim=0)
train_y_ei = torch.cat([train_y_ei, new_y_ei], dim=0)
train_y_qei = torch.cat([train_y_qei, new_y_qei], dim=0)
train_y_ucb = torch.cat([train_y_ucb, new_y_ucb], dim=0)
train_y_qkg = torch.cat([train_y_qkg, new_y_qkg], dim=0)
```

```
# update progress
best_random = update_random_observations(best_random)
best_value_ei = max(best_observed_ei[-1], new_y_ei.item())
best_value_qei = max(best_observed_qei[-1], new_y_qei.item())
best_value_ucb = max(best_observed_ucb[-1], new_y_ucb.item())
best_value_qkg = max(best_observed_qkg[-1], new_y_qkg.item())

best_observed_ei.append(best_value_ei)
best_observed_qei.append(best_value_qei)
best_observed_ucb.append(best_value_ucb)
best_observed_qkg.append(best_value_qkg)

# reinitialize the models so they are ready for fitting on next
  iteration
mll_ei, model_ei = initialize_model(
    train_x_ei,
    train_y_ei
)
mll_qei, model_qei = initialize_model(
    train_x_qei,
    train_y_qei
)
mll_ucb, model_ucb = initialize_model(
    train_x_ucb,
    train_y_ucb
)
mll_qkg, model_qkg = initialize_model(
    train_x_qkg,
    train_y_qkg
)

t1 = time.monotonic()
```

Let us plot the search progress so far via the following code snippet:

```
iters = np.arange(N_ROUND + 1) * BATCH_SIZE
plt.plot(iters, best_random, label='random')
plt.plot(iters, best_observed_ei, label='EI')
```

```python
plt.plot(iters, best_observed_qei, label='qEI')
plt.plot(iters, best_observed_ucb, label='UCB')
plt.plot(iters, best_observed_qkg, label='qKG')
plt.legend()
plt.xlabel("Sampling iteration")
plt.ylabel("Sharpe ratio")
plt.show()
```

For each iteration, we fit the GP model to optimize its hyperparameters for each strategy, instantiate the acquisition function based on the updated GP model instance, optimize over the acquisition function, propose the next sampling point, obtain the corresponding function evaluation, append the new observation (parameter value and Sharpe ratio) to the training set, update the search progress by appending to running maximum Sharpe ratio, and finally reinitialize the GP for the next iteration.

Running the code generates Figure 9-11. The comparison demonstrates the benefits of adopting a principled model-based search strategy over random selections. UCB performs the best across all iterations, showing the advantage of a higher focus on early exploration embedded in this acquisition function. Other strategies pick up later and stay flat afterward. Both model-based strategies perform better than the random strategy.

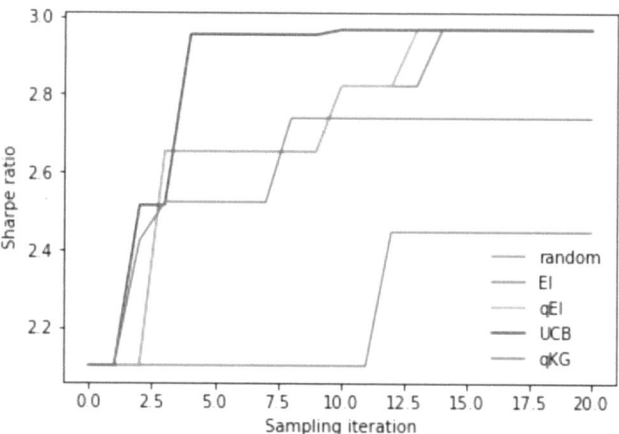

Figure 9-11. *Cumulative maximum Sharpe ratio of all search strategies. The UCB policy performs the best as it is able to identify the highest Sharpe ratio in just one iteration. Other policies pick up later but lack exploration toward the later iterations. The random strategy performs the worst, showing the advantage of a principled search policy over random selection*

Let us repeat the experiments a number of times to assess the stability of the results, as shown in Listing 9-11.

Listing 9-11. Assessing the stability of the results via repeated experiments

```
# multiple trials
# number of runs to assess std of different BO loops
N_TRIALS = 4
# indicator to print diagnostics
verbose = True
# number of steps in the outer BO loop
N_ROUND = 20
best_random_all, best_observed_ei_all, best_observed_qei_all, best_
observed_ucb_all, best_observed_qkg_all = [], [], [], [], []

# average over multiple trials
for trial in range(1, N_TRIALS + 1):

    best_random, best_observed_ei, best_observed_qei, best_observed_ucb,
    best_observed_qkg  = [], [], [], [], []

    # call helper functions to generate initial training data and
    initialize model
    train_x, train_y, best_observed_value = generate_initial_data(n=3)
    train_x_ei = train_x
    train_x_qei = train_x
    train_x_ucb = train_x
    train_x_qkg = train_x
    train_y_ei = train_y
    train_y_qei = train_y
    train_y_ucb = train_y
    train_y_qkg = train_y

    mll_ei, model_ei = initialize_model(train_x_ei, train_y_ei)
    mll_qei, model_qei = initialize_model(train_x_qei, train_y_qei)
    mll_ucb, model_ucb = initialize_model(train_x_ucb, train_y_ucb)
    mll_qkg, model_qkg = initialize_model(train_x_qkg, train_y_qkg)

    best_random.append(best_observed_value)
```

```python
best_observed_ei.append(best_observed_value)
best_observed_qei.append(best_observed_value)
best_observed_ucb.append(best_observed_value)
best_observed_qkg.append(best_observed_value)

# run N_ROUND rounds of BayesOpt after the initial random batch
for iteration in range(1, N_ROUND + 1):
    t0 = time.monotonic()
    # fit the models
    fit_gpytorch_mll(mll_ei)
    fit_gpytorch_mll(mll_qei)
    fit_gpytorch_mll(mll_ucb)
    fit_gpytorch_mll(mll_qkg)

    # for best_f, we use the best observed exact values
    EI = ExpectedImprovement(model=model_ei, best_f=train_y_ei.max())
    qEI = qExpectedImprovement(model=model_qei,
                               best_f=train_y_ei.max(),
                               num_samples=1024
                               )
    UCB = UpperConfidenceBound(model=model_ucb, beta=beta)
    qKG = qKnowledgeGradient(
        model=model_qkg,
        num_fantasies=64,
        objective=None,
        X_baseline=train_x_qkg,
    )

    # optimize and get new observation
    new_x_ei, new_y_ei = optimize_acqf_and_get_observation(EI)
    new_x_qei, new_y_qei = optimize_acqf_and_get_observation(qEI)
    new_x_ucb, new_y_ucb = optimize_acqf_and_get_observation(UCB)
    new_x_qkg, new_y_qkg = optimize_acqf_and_get_observation(qKG)

    # update training points
    train_x_ei = torch.cat([train_x_ei, new_x_ei], dim=0)
    train_x_qei = torch.cat([train_x_qei, new_x_qei], dim=0)
    train_x_ucb = torch.cat([train_x_ucb, new_x_ucb], dim=0)
```

```python
train_x_qkg = torch.cat([train_x_qkg, new_x_qkg], dim=0)
train_y_ei = torch.cat([train_y_ei, new_y_ei], dim=0)
train_y_qei = torch.cat([train_y_qei, new_y_qei], dim=0)
train_y_ucb = torch.cat([train_y_ucb, new_y_ucb], dim=0)
train_y_qkg = torch.cat([train_y_qkg, new_y_qkg], dim=0)

# update progress
best_random = update_random_observations(best_random)
best_value_ei = max(best_observed_ei[-1], new_y_ei.item())
best_value_qei = max(best_observed_qei[-1], new_y_qei.item())
best_value_ucb = max(best_observed_ucb[-1], new_y_ucb.item())
best_value_qkg = max(best_observed_qkg[-1], new_y_qkg.item())

best_observed_ei.append(best_value_ei)
best_observed_qei.append(best_value_qei)
best_observed_ucb.append(best_value_ucb)
best_observed_qkg.append(best_value_qkg)

# reinitialize the models so they are ready for fitting on next
iteration
mll_ei, model_ei = initialize_model(
    train_x_ei,
    train_y_ei
)
mll_qei, model_qei = initialize_model(
    train_x_qei,
    train_y_qei
)
mll_ucb, model_ucb = initialize_model(
    train_x_ucb,
    train_y_ucb
)
mll_qkg, model_qkg = initialize_model(
    train_x_qkg,
    train_y_qkg
)
```

```
    t1 = time.monotonic()
```

```
  best_observed_ei_all.append(best_observed_ei)
  best_observed_qei_all.append(best_observed_qei)
  best_observed_ucb_all.append(best_observed_ucb)
  best_observed_qkg_all.append(best_observed_qkg)
  best_random_all.append(best_random)
```

Running the code generates Figure 9-12, suggesting that BO-based search strategies consistently outperform the random search strategy.

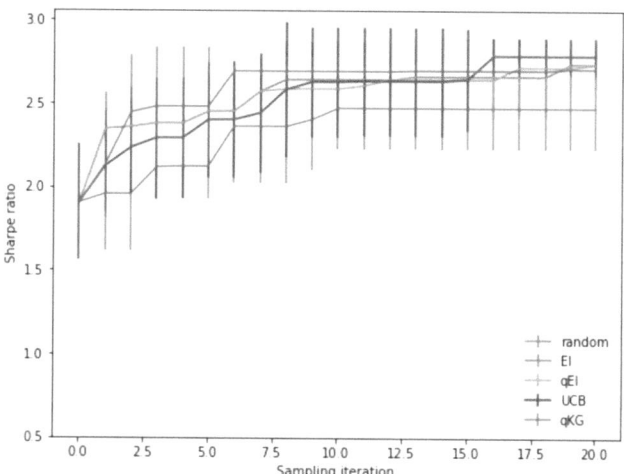

Figure 9-12. *Assessing the stability of the results via repeated experiments*

Finally, let us extract the mean and standard deviation of all experiments, as shown in Listing 9-12.

Listing 9-12. Extracting the mean and standard deviation for all experiments

```
def extract_last_entry(x):
    tmp = []
    for i in range(4):
        tmp.append(x[i][-1])
    return tmp
```

```
rst_df = pd.DataFrame({
    "EI": [np.mean(extract_last_entry(best_observed_ei_all)),
    np.std(extract_last_entry(best_observed_ei_all))],
    "qEI": [np.mean(extract_last_entry(best_observed_qei_all)),
    np.std(extract_last_entry(best_observed_qei_all))],
    "UCB": [np.mean(extract_last_entry(best_observed_ucb_all)),
    np.std(extract_last_entry(best_observed_ucb_all))],
    "qKG": [np.mean(extract_last_entry(best_observed_qkg_all)),
    np.std(extract_last_entry(best_observed_qkg_all))],
    "random": [np.mean(extract_last_entry(best_random_all)),
    np.std(extract_last_entry(best_random_all))],
}, index=["mean", "std"])
>>> rst_df
          EI       qEI      UCB      qKG    random
mean 2.736916 2.734416 2.786065 2.706545 2.470426
std  0.116130 0.146371 0.106940 0.041464 0.247212
```

Since there are multiple choices of acquisition functions available in the BO community, we expect this approach to be enjoying greater popularity down the road. However, it should be noted that the superior performance in our running example may be a result of overfitting. Instead of selecting only one backtesting period, scoring a set of parameters over multiple representative backtesting periods is recommended in order to get a fairer assessment of the functional evaluation at the specific sampling location. In other words, we need to have a more robust observation model for the black-box function to minimize the risk of overfitting the current training dataset.

Summary

In this chapter, we introduced the use of Bayesian optimization techniques to search for optimal parameters of a trading strategy. We started by illustrating the concept of optimizing trading strategies by tuning the corresponding governing parameters, a nontrivial task. By treating the performance measure as a black-box function of the tuning parameters, we introduced the Bayesian optimization framework, which uses Gaussian processes and acquisition functions (such as EI and UCB) to support the search of optimal parameters in a sample-efficient manner. With the full BO loop in perspective, we went through a case study that optimizes the entry and exit thresholds of a pairs trading strategy to obtain an optimal Sharpe ratio.

In the final chapter, we will look at the use of machine learning models in the pairs trading strategy.

Exercises

- How does Bayesian optimization approach the problem of hyperparameter tuning in trading strategies? What makes this approach particularly suitable for this task?

- Change the objective function to search for the parameters that minimize the maximum drawdown of the trend-following strategy.

- Bayesian optimization is based on a probabilistic model of the objective function, typically a Gaussian process (GP). How does this model assist in identifying areas of the search space to explore or exploit?

- Can you describe a scenario where a long-term (nonmyopic) acquisition function would be beneficial in the context of optimizing trading strategies? What about a scenario where a short-term (myopic) function might be preferable?

- Can you discuss how the incorporation of prior knowledge can be leveraged in the Bayesian optimization process for parameter tuning in trading strategies?

- How can Bayesian optimization handle noisy evaluations, a common occurrence in financial markets, during the optimization process of a trading strategy's parameters?

## CHAPTER 10

Pairs Trading Using Machine Learning

Machine learning can be used in pairs trading in several ways to improve the effectiveness of trading strategies. Examples include pair selection, feature engineering, spread prediction, etc. In this final chapter, we are going to focus on spread prediction using different machine learning algorithms in order to generate trading signals.

Machine Learning in Pairs Trading

As discussed in the previous chapter, pairs trading is a type of quantitative trading strategy that involves transacting two highly correlated/cointegrated assets at the same time and in the opposite direction. The financial instruments could be two stocks or two indices, based on which the relative price difference is used to derive the spread series and generate trading signals. The primary assumption behind pairs trading is that the price spread between two highly correlated or cointegrated assets should exhibit a mean reversion behavior over time. During this period, traders can profit by buying the underperforming asset and short-selling the overperforming asset in case of market mispricing due to temporary fluctuations. In other words, the two assets identified by the strategy should bear a long-term equilibrium relationship and move in tandem, while any deviation from this pattern is likely to be temporary and will eventually revert back to the mean.

In pairs trading, we start by identifying two assets that are highly correlated/ cointegrated and share a similar risk exposure. After taking a long position in one asset and a short position in the other when the z-score exceeds a predefined threshold, we would then hope to profit from the convergence of their spread. Specifically, as the spread between the two assets widens, we sell the overpriced asset and buy the underpriced asset. Similarly, as the spread narrows and the z-score drops below another predefined threshold, we will exit the positions and lock in the profits.

© Peng Liu 2023
P. Liu, *Quantitative Trading Strategies Using Python*, https://doi.org/10.1007/978-1-4842-9675-2_10

Being a market-neutral strategy, pairs trading can be profitable in either bull, bear, or sideways markets. The success of the strategy depends on two factors: whether the pair of correlated/cointegrated assets with a similar risk profile can be identified and whether the spread between the two assets can be accurately predicted. For example, we used a moving average in the previous chapter to standardize the daily spread into a z-score. Such a moving average acts as the predicted spread, which is then used to compare with the actual spread of the day and derive the unit of deviation in terms of the standard deviation.

In addition, we also need to have proper risk management in place. When the spread continues to widen and moves in an adverse direction due to unexpected market events, the larger spread can lead to a significant loss. A stop-loss order is thus often placed to limit the potential loss of the strategy.

Figure 10-1 summarizes the three critical components of a pairs trading strategy. The second component will be the focus of the following sections, where we illustrate the use of machine learning techniques to predict the spread series.

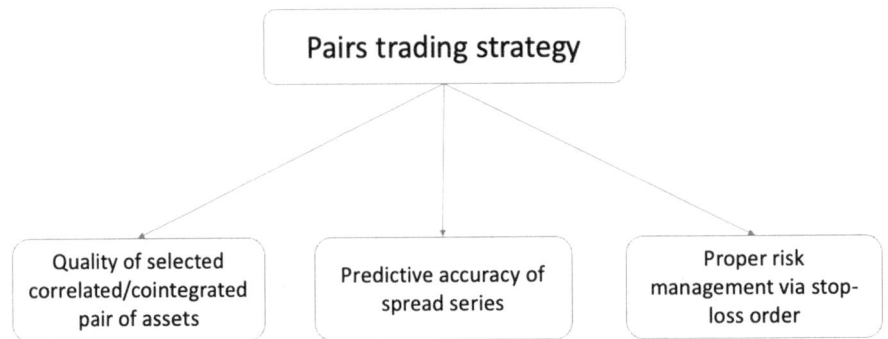

Figure 10-1. *Summarizing the three components that determine the success of a pairs trading strategy*

Machine Learning Workflow

Machine learning models are predictive functions that generate predictions given a specific set of inputs. In this case, we intend to use a machine learning model in pairs trading to predict the spread between the two assets, which will then be used to identify profitable trading signals. Since the spread is a continuous quantity, we will explore regression models in this chapter, including support vector machine (SVM), random forest (RF), and neural network models. We will also augment the feature space, that is, historical spread series, with additional features such as technical indicators. Once the spread is predicted, we can generate trading signals by taking a long position in the underperforming asset and a short position in the overperforming asset.

A machine learning model is a mathematical algorithm or a function that is trained on a training dataset and used to make predictions for the future unseen test dataset. Depending on the specific model class, the function can learn the underlying patterns and relationships from the given data, usually in the form of input-output pairs in the context of supervised learning. This process is called interpolation, where the model is expected to interpolate through the given data, subject to a certain degree of robustness against random noise in the dataset, as indicated by a relatively low training error.

Next, the trained model will be assessed using a new set of test data, a process called extrapolation, where the test data may be somewhat different from the training data. A model is expected to do well on the test set so that it gives confidence when we apply it to practical applications. The test set performance is also called the generalization performance, an indicator of how well the model generalizes to the test set data.

A typical machine learning model consists of two components: the parameters (or weights) serve as the building blocks of the model, and the model architecture specifies how the input data interact with the parameters to generate the output. Model training refers to the process of tuning these parameters such that the model produces a good performance on the test set and often a relatively good performance on the training set. During the training process, the machine learning algorithm adjusts the parameters of the model based on the input data to improve the accuracy of its predictions on the training data. Once the model is trained, it can be used to make predictions for the new data, which may not have been seen before.

If the model performs too well on the training set but not so well on the test set, then the model is considered as overfitting the training data. Since modern models are typically complex in architecture and large in the number of model parameters, overfitting is a common phenomenon in many training situations. Proper regularization techniques can be adopted to reduce the chance of overfitting.

Let us recall the graph on the overall model training process workflow displayed in Chapter 1, also shown in Figure 10-2 for ease of reference. We can apply regularization techniques to achieve a better generalization performance from these four components: the training data, the model, the cost measure, and the optimization procedure. Each component has a specific extent of regularization effect and can be combined together to achieve a good generalization performance for the specific training situation.

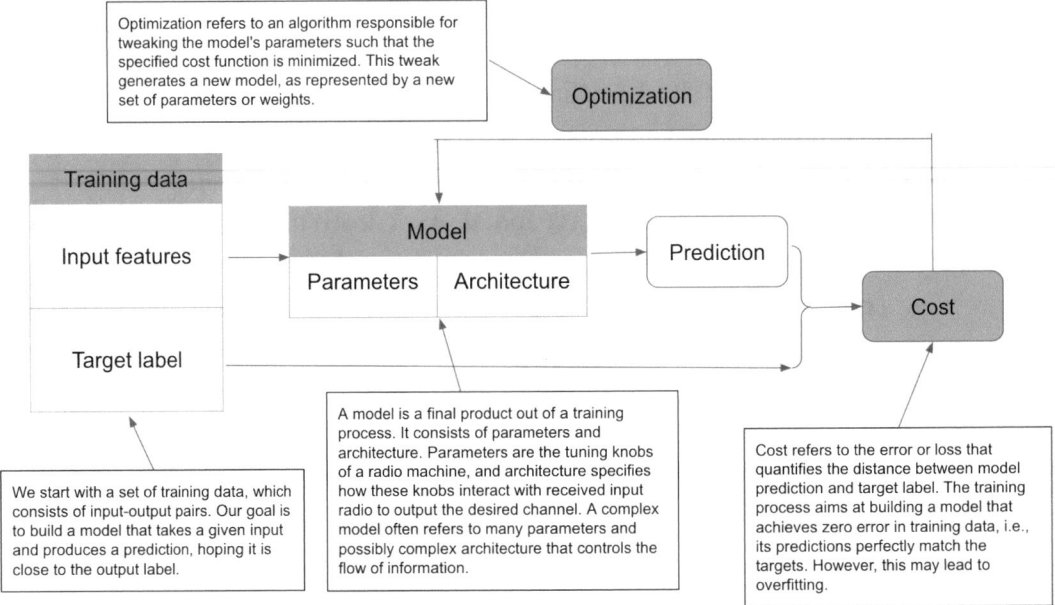

Figure 10-2. *Example of a typical model training process. The workflow starts with the available training data and gradually tunes a model. The tuning process requires matching the model prediction to the target output, where the gap is measured by a particular cost measure and used as feedback for the next round of tuning. Each tuning produces a new model, and we want to look for one that minimizes the cost*

In the following section, we will introduce the high-level principles of three different types of machine learning algorithms: support vector machine, random forest, and neural network.

Support Vector Machine

Support vector machine (SVM) is a popular supervised learning algorithm, especially in the Kaggle community, for both classification and regression. In the context of classification, SVM works by mapping the input data from its original feature space into a high-dimensional feature space using a kernel function, and then finding the hyperplane that best separates the different classes of data. The hyperplane is chosen in order to maximize the margin between the classes. Seeking a boundary based on the principle of maximal margin often leads to a better generalization performance, thus reducing the risk of overfitting.

Since we are interested in predicting the spread as a continuous outcome, making it a regression task, SVM instead finds the hyperplane that best separates the input data while minimizing the margin violations. In this case, our goal in the regression task is to fit a hyperplane as closely as possible to the actual data points by minimizing the sum of the squared errors (SSE) as the cost measure between the predicted output and the actual target values. Since minimizing SSE toward zero would easily lead to an overfitting model, the SVM model used in regression often assumes an ϵ-insensitive loss function, which allows the model to tolerate some error in its predictions, up to a certain threshold ϵ.

There are multiple technical terms here that serve more explanation. Let us start with the concept of the *hyperplane*. A hyperplane is a decision line used to predict the continuous output in the case of regression. The data points on either side of the hyperplane within a certain distance (specifically, within ϵ) are called *support vectors*. We can also use these support vectors to draw two *decision boundaries* around the hyperplane at a distance of ϵ.

Moving on, a *kernel* is a set of mathematical functions that take data as input and transform it into the required form, possibly in a different dimension. These are generally used for finding a hyperplane in the higher-dimensional space, which is considered easier to achieve linear separation than finding the same separating hyperplane in the original feature space. Using kernels in SVM provides a powerful and flexible tool for classification and regression tasks, allowing SVM to handle complex and even nonlinearly separable datasets.

Figure 10-3 helps illustrate these concepts. Given a set of training observations in the form of input-output pairs, the support vector regression model will build a hyperplane as the regression line to predict future test data. The hyperplane is surrounded by two decision boundaries, determined by a user-specified hyperparameter ϵ. Here, ϵ specifies the width of the ϵ-insensitive zone (or tolerance zone) around the regression line, where errors are not penalized. Not all the points are within the decision boundaries, and SVM is designed to minimize such margin violations by maximizing the number of points within the decision boundary upon estimating the hyperplane.

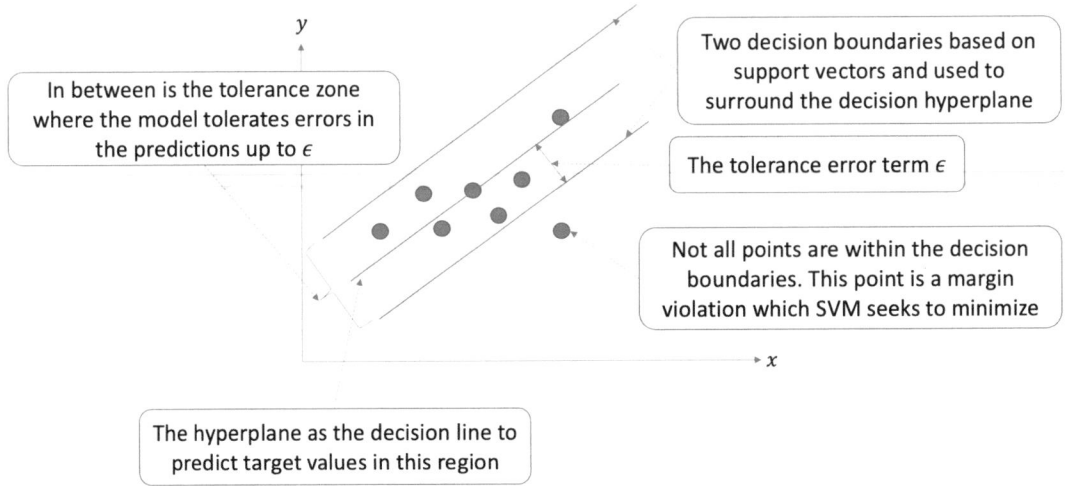

Figure 10-3. *Illustrating the training mechanism of the support vector regression model*

Note that ϵ controls the tolerance of the margin violation. It determines the trade-off between the model complexity and the predictive accuracy. A small value of ϵ will result in a complex model that closely fits the training data, but risks overfitting the training set and therefore generalizing poorly to the new data. On the other hand, a large value of ϵ will result in a simpler model with larger errors but potentially a better generalization performance.

As a user-specified hyperparameter, the choice of ϵ can be highly sensitive to the resulting predictive performance. A common approach is cross-validation, which involves partitioning the raw data into training and validation sets several times, each starting with a different random seed. The best ϵ is the one that reports the highest predictive performance on average.

We introduce the random forest model in the following section.

Random Forest

Random forest is a type of ensemble model, which includes multiple simple models combined together to make the final prediction. It is a powerful and flexible model that can be used for both regression and classification tasks. As the name suggests, the algorithm constructs multiple decision trees and combines all trees in the forest to make a final prediction.

The main differentiating factor about random forest compared with other models is how the raw training dataset is divided to support the training of each tree. Specifically, each tree is trained on a different subset of the data and a different subset of the features, a process known as *bagging* or *bootstrap aggregation.* By using random subsets of the data and features, the algorithm creates multiple independent submodels that have a low bias and high variance. The final prediction is then produced by taking the average of the predictions of all the individual trees, similar to collecting the views from multiple independent consultants and taking the average recommendation as the final decision.

Note that at each node of the tree, a random subset of features is considered to determine the best split, instead of considering all features. This process is called feature bagging. The randomness in feature selection ensures that the trees are decorrelated and reduces the chance of overfitting.

Random forests are widely used for their simplicity, versatility, and robustness. They can handle a mix of numerical and categorical features, require very little preprocessing of the data, and provide a built-in method for handling missing values. Furthermore, they offer measures of feature importance, which can provide insights into the underlying structure of the data.

Figure 10-4 illustrates the overall training process of the random forest model. We start by sampling from the original training set to obtain a total of B subsets. Each sampling randomly selects both observations and features, so that the resulting subsets appear to be independent of each other and uncorrelated in the feature space. We will then train a decision tree model for each subset, leading to B submodels. Upon assessing a new test data point, these B predictions will be aggregated together and averaged to produce the final prediction.

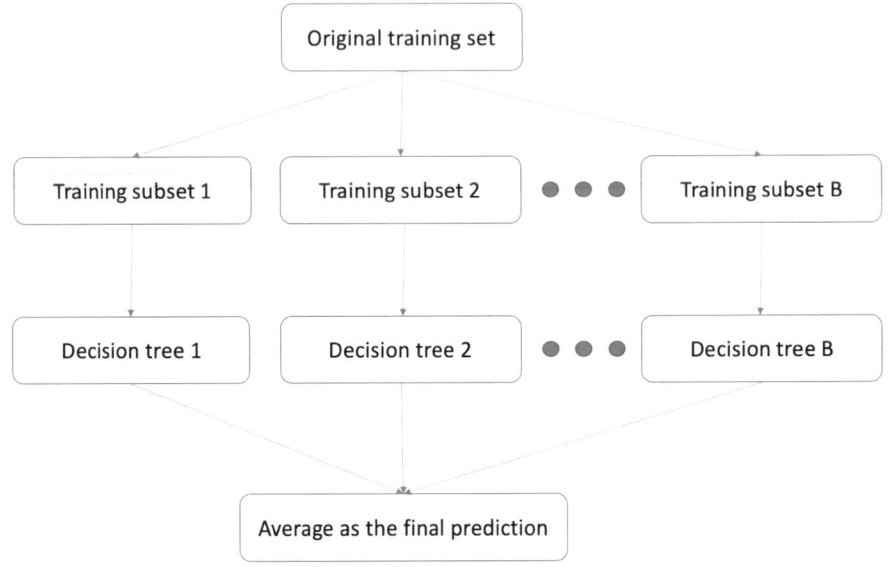

Figure 10-4. *Illustrating the training mechanism of the random forest model*

In the next section, we introduce the basic feed-forward neural network.

Neural Network

A neural network consists of multiple interconnected nodes, also called neurons, stacked together in layers. Each neuron serves as a function that receives input from the neurons in the preceding layer, performs a nonlinear transformation on that input, and sends an output to the neurons in the next layer. In between these neurons are the weights, also called parameters of the neural network. Learning a neural network model essentially means tuning the weights so that the final prediction is accurate, and the model generalizes well to the test set.

A typical neural network consists of an input layer representing the input data and an output layer generating the output. It can also include any number of layers in between (called hidden layers). Each layer contains at least one neuron, interpreted as an extracted hidden feature. When it comes to the number of layers of a neural network, it refers to the hidden layer plus the output layer. For example, a perceptron is a single-layer neural network, meaning it has only input and output layers and does not have any hidden layer in between.

Being the fundamental constituent of a neural network, a perceptron is a single neuron that completes two steps of mathematical operations: the weighted sum and the nonlinear transformation. For a single observation with p dimensions $\mathbf{x} \in \mathbb{R}^p$, the perceptron first calculates the weighted sum $\sum_{i=1}^{p} w_i x_i$ between $\mathbf{x}$ and its corresponding weight vector $\mathbf{w} \in \mathbb{R}^p$, which is (and should be) also p-dimensional. The weighted sum is often accompanied by one more term called *intercept* or *bias*, which acts as an additional parameter to exercise a global level shift to the weighted sum to fit the data better.

After adding an intercept/bias term b, the sum passes through an *activation function* which introduces a nonlinear transformation to the weighted sum. Note that the bias term is added by inserting a column of ones in the input data, which is the same bias trick as linear regression. Such nonlinear transformation, together with the number and width of layers, determines neural networks' flexibility, expressivity, and approximating power. Figure 10-5 summarizes the process flow of a perceptron.

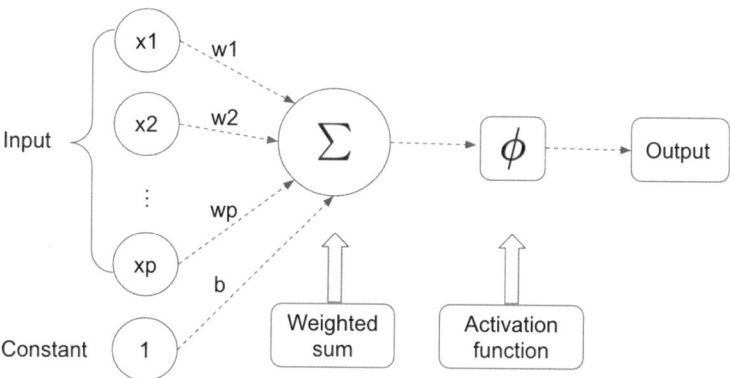

Figure 10-5. *The process flowchart of a perceptron, which consists of a weighted sum operation followed by an activation function. A column of ones is automatically added to correspond to the bias term in the weight vector*

The most popular choice of activation function is the *rectified linear unit* (ReLU), which acts as an on/off switch that fires the input signal as it is if its value is above a specific threshold and mutes it by outputting zero if it is below the threshold. In other words, the ReLU operation is an identity function if the input is positive; otherwise, the output is set as zero. Without such nonlinear activation, a multilayer neural network would simply become a series of linear functions stacked on top of each other, resulting in a linear model.

Figure 10-6 visualizes the ReLU function's shape and summarizes the characteristics of the perceptron operation discussed so far. Other than the architectural flexibility of a neural network model in terms of the number and width of its layers, another main added flexibility lies in the nonlinear operation. In fact, many exciting and meaningful hidden features could be automatically extracted using ReLU as an activation function. For example, when training an image classifier using a special architecture called convolutional neural networks, low-level features in the initial hidden layers tend to resemble fundamental structural components such as lines or edges, while high-level features at later hidden layers start to learn structural patterns such as squares, circles, or even complex shapes like the wheels of a car. This is not possible if we are limited to the linear transformation of features and is considered an extremely difficult task if we were to engineer such informative features manually.

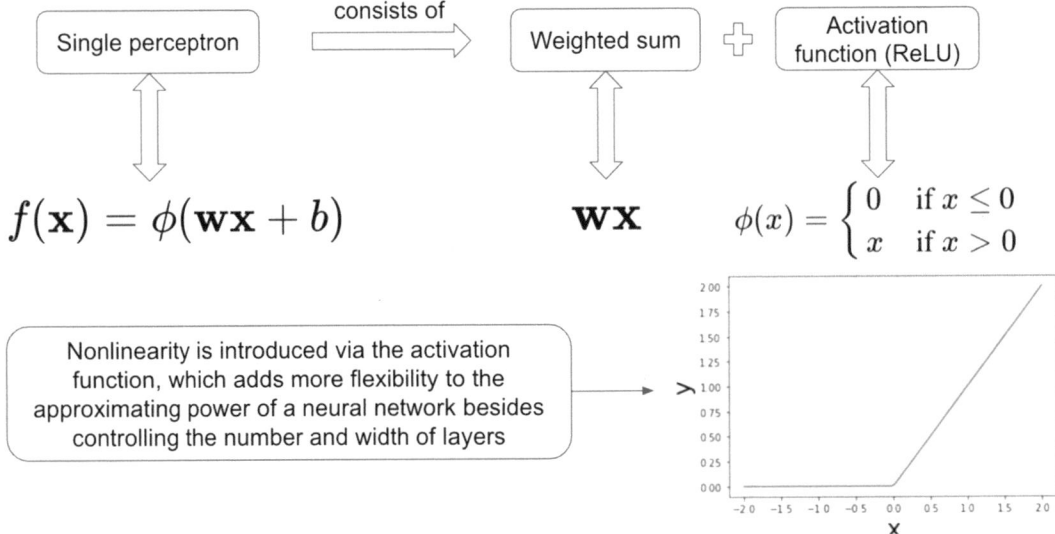

Figure 10-6. *Decomposing a single perceptron into a weighted sum and an activation function which is often ReLU. The ReLU operation passes through a signal if it is positive and mutes it if it is negative. Such nonlinearity also introduces great approximating power to the neural networks in addition to the flexibility in designing the number and width of layers*

One of the reasons why ReLU (and its variants) remains the most popular activation function is its fast gradient computation. When the input is less than or equal to zero, the gradient (of a constant number) becomes zero, thus saving the need for backpropagation and parameter update. When the input is positive, the gradient (of the original input variable) is simply one, which gets backpropagated as it is.

Having reviewed these three model classes, let us switch to the implementation of pairs trading and compare their performances after using machine learning models to predict the daily spread.

Implementing the Pairs Trading Strategy Using Machine Learning

In this section, we will follow a similar recipe to develop a pairs trading strategy as in the previous chapter, with the only change being the calculation of the predicted spread. The previous chapter used a rolling window to derive the mean and standard deviation of the daily spread. In other words, the predicted spread is the average of a collection of historical spreads in the moving window, whose volatility is also used to standardize the difference between the actual spread and the predicted spread.

Let us start by importing the necessary packages. As shown in Listing 10-1, we will focus on the same pair of stocks (Google and Microsoft) and trading horizon (the full year of 2022).

Listing 10-1. Downloading the stock data

```
import os
import random
import numpy as np
import yfinance as yf
import pandas as pd
from statsmodels.tsa.stattools import adfuller
from statsmodels.regression.linear_model import OLS
import statsmodels.api as sm
from matplotlib import pyplot as plt
%matplotlib inline

SEED = 8
random.seed(SEED)
np.random.seed(SEED)

# download data from yfinance
stocks = ['GOOG','MSFT']
start_date  = "2022-01-01"
end_date  = "2022-12-31"
df = yf.download(stocks, start=start_date, end=end_date)['Adj Close']
df.head()
          GOOG          MSFT
```

```
Date
2022-01-03  145.074493  330.813873
2022-01-04  144.416504  325.141327
2022-01-05  137.653503  312.659882
2022-01-06  137.550995  310.189270
2022-01-07  137.004501  310.347412
```

For simplicity, we will define spread as the difference in the log price of the two stocks, which is calculated and visualized in Listing 10-2.

Listing 10-2. Calculating the spread

```python
# Calculate the spread between the two assets
spread = np.log(df[stocks[0]]) - np.log(df[stocks[1]])

plt.plot(spread, label='Spread using difference of log price')
plt.legend()
plt.show()
```

Running this code generates Figure 10-7.

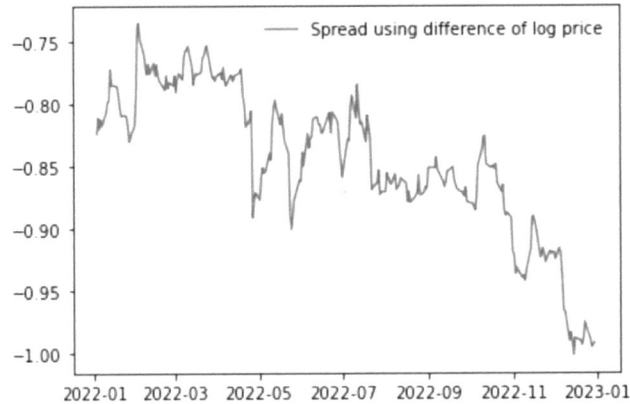

Figure 10-7. *Visualizing the daily spread defined as the difference in the log price of both stocks*

Next, we will perform feature engineering to boost the feature space.

Feature Engineering

Feature engineering is the process of selecting, transforming, and extracting relevant features from the raw data in order to boost the performance of a machine learning model. The quality and sometimes the quantity of the features are critical factors that influence the performance of a machine learning model. These additional engineered features may not necessarily make sense from an interpretability perspective, yet they will likely improve the predictive performance of the machine learning algorithm by offering a new knob for the model to tune with.

We have already encountered feature engineering in previous discussions, with the moving average being the most notable example. In this exercise, we will use five features to predict the spread series, including the daily returns for both stocks, the five-day moving average of the spread series, and the 20-day moving standard deviation of daily returns. These are created in Listing 10-3.

Listing 10-3. Generating additional features

```
# Define additional features
asset1_returns = np.log(df[stocks[0]]).diff()
asset2_returns = np.log(df[stocks[1]]).diff()
spread_ma5 = spread.rolling(5).mean()
asset1_volatility = asset1_returns.rolling(20).std()
asset2_volatility = asset2_returns.rolling(20).std()
```

Note that this is just one way to create additional features. In practice, we would create many more features to support algorithms such as SVM and random forest if the goal is to maximize the predictive accuracy. For neural networks, however, such feature engineering is helpful but not essential. Neural networks are powerful function approximators in that they can learn the correct feature extraction given a sufficiently complex architecture and enough training time.

We will then aggregate these features into a single DataFrame X, followed by filling NA values with zero. We also assign the spread series to y:

```
# Combine the features into a single DataFrame
X = pd.DataFrame({'Asset1Returns': asset1_returns,
                  'Asset2Returns': asset2_returns,
                  'SpreadMA5': spread_ma5,
```

```
                    'Asset1Volatility': asset1_volatility,
                    'Asset2Volatility': asset2_volatility})
X = X.fillna(0)
y = spread
```

Let us also split the data into a training and a test set. We will adopt the common 80-20 rule; that is, 80% of the data goes to the training set, and 20% goes to the test set. We will also observe the sequence of time, so the 80% training set does not peak in the future, as shown in Listing 10-4.

Listing 10-4. Performing train-test split

```
# Split the data into training and test sets
train_size = int(len(spread) * 0.8)
train_X = X[:train_size]
test_X = X[train_size:]
train_y = y[:train_size]
test_y = y[train_size:]
```

With the training and test data ready, we can now move into the model training part, starting with SVM.

Pairs Trading Using SVM

Since this is a regression task, we will use the SVR class from sklearn, specifying a linear kernel. After instantiating the model class, we use the fit() method to fit the model parameters to the training data and the predict() method to generate predictions for the test data. We will also check the root mean squared error (RMSE) for both training and test sets. Listing 10-5 completes the training and testing operations.

Listing 10-5. Model training and testing using SVM

```
from sklearn.svm import SVR
from sklearn.metrics import mean_squared_error

svm_model = SVR(kernel='linear')
svm_model.fit(train_X, train_y)
train_pred = svm_model.predict(train_X)
```

```
>>> print("training rmse: ", np.sqrt(mean_squared_error(train_y,
train_pred)))
test_pred = svm_model.predict(test_X)
>>> print("test rmse: ", np.sqrt(mean_squared_error(test_y, test_pred)))
training rmse:   0.039616044798431914
test rmse:   0.12296547390274865
```

The RMSE measures the model's predictive performance. However, we still need
to plug the model into the trading strategy and evaluate the ultimate profitability in
the pairs trading strategy. As the only change is on the predicted spread based on the
specific machine learning model, we can define a function to score the model as an
input parameter and output the terminal profit. The score_fn() function in Listing 10-6
completes the scoring operation.

Listing 10-6. Calculating cumulative return using pairs trading under a given
predictive model

```python
import torch

def score_fn(model, type="non_neural_net"):
    # Generate predicted spread using the SVM model
    if type == "non_neural_net":
        test_pred = model.predict(test_X)
    else:
        test_pred = model(torch.Tensor(test_X.values)).detach().numpy()
    # Calculate z-score of the actual and predicted spread
    zscore = (spread - test_pred.mean()) / test_pred.std()
    # set the threshold values for entry and exit signals
    entry_threshold = 2.0
    exit_threshold = 1.0
    # initialize the daily positions to be zeros
    stock1_position = pd.Series(data=0, index=zscore.index)
    stock2_position = pd.Series(data=0, index=zscore.index)
    # generate daily entry and exit signals for each stock
    for i in range(1, len(zscore)):
        # zscore<-2 and no existing long position for stock 1
        if zscore[i] < -entry_threshold and stock1_position[i-1] == 0:
```

```
            stock1_position[i] = 1 # long stock 1
            stock2_position[i] = -1 # short stock 2
        # zscore>2 and no existing short position for stock 2
        elif zscore[i] > entry_threshold and stock2_position[i-1] == 0:
            stock1_position[i] = -1 # short stock 1
            stock2_position[i] = 1 # long stock 2
        # -1<zscore<1
        elif abs(zscore[i]) < exit_threshold:
            stock1_position[i] = 0 # exit existing position
            stock2_position[i] = 0
        # -2<zscore<-1 or 1<zscore<2
        else:
            stock1_position[i] = stock1_position[i-1] # maintain existing
position
            stock2_position[i] = stock2_position[i-1]

    # Calculate the returns of each stock
    stock1_returns = (np.exp(test_X['Asset1Returns']) * stock1_position.
    shift(1)).fillna(0)
    stock2_returns = (np.exp(test_X['Asset2Returns']) * stock2_position.
    shift(1)).fillna(0)
    # calculate the total returns of the strategy
    total_returns = stock1_returns + stock2_returns
    cumulative_returns = (1 + total_returns).cumprod()
    return cumulative_returns[-1]
```

In this function, we add another input parameter to control if the model belongs to a neural network. This control is placed here to determine the specific prediction method to use. For standard `sklearn` algorithms such as SVM and random forest, we can call the `predict()` method of the model object to generate predictions for the given input data. However, when the model is a neural network trained using PyTorch, we need to first convert the input to a tensor object using `torch.Tensor()`, generate predictions by calling the model object itself (underlying, the forward() function within the model class is called), extracting the outputs without gradient information using the `detach()` method, and converting to a NumPy object using `numpy()`.

Next, we calculate the z-score using the mean and the standard deviation of the predicted spread series. We then use an entry threshold of two and an exit threshold of one to generate the trading signals based on the standardized z-scores. The rest of the calculations follow the same approach as in the previous chapter.

We can now use this function to obtain the terminal return for the pairs trading strategy using the SVM model:

```
>>> score_fn(svm_model)
1.143746922303926
```

Similarly, we can obtain the same measure using the random forest regressor.

Pairs Trading Using Random Forest

To build a random forest model for regression, we can use the RandomForestRegressor class and specify two main parameters: n_estimators as the number of trees to be built in the random forest and random_state as the random seed for reproducibility. Listing 10-7 trains the random forest model and evaluates its performance in the training and test sets using RMSE.

Listing 10-7. Model training and testing using random forest

```
# random forest
from sklearn.ensemble import RandomForestRegressor

# Create random forest regressor
rf_model = RandomForestRegressor(n_estimators=100, random_state=42)

# Train the model on the training and test set
rf_model.fit(train_X, train_y)
train_pred = rf_model.predict(train_X)
>>> print("training rmse: ", np.sqrt(mean_squared_error(train_y,
train_pred)))
test_pred = rf_model.predict(test_X)
>>> print("test rmse: ", np.sqrt(mean_squared_error(test_y, test_pred)))
training rmse:  0.005741011378501151
test rmse:  0.07322761976891506
```

The result shows that random forest can better fit the data with a lower training and test set RMSE compared with SVM.

We also calculate the terminal return as follows:

```
>>> score_fn(svm_model)
0.9489411965252148
```

The result reports a lower terminal return, despite a better predictive performance. This is also overfitting, in the sense that a more predictive model at the stage-one prediction task leads to a lower terminal return at the stage-two trading task. Combining these two tasks in a single stage is an interesting and active area of research.

We move to neural networks in the next section.

Pairs Trading Using Neural Networks

Training a deep neural network requires specifying the four major components: input data, model architecture, objective function, and optimizer. We start with the input data by converting them into tensor objects using the `torch.Tensor()` function as follows:

```
# Convert data to PyTorch tensors
train_X_ts = torch.Tensor(train_X.values)
train_y_ts = torch.Tensor(train_y).view(-1, 1)
test_X_ts = torch.Tensor(test_X.values)
test_y_ts = torch.Tensor(test_y).view(-1, 1)
```

Note that we use the `.values` attribute to access the values from the DataFrame and the `view()` function to reshape the target into a column.

Next, we define the neural network model in Listing 10-8. Here, we slot the attributes to the initialization function, including one input linear layer, one hidden linear layer, and one output linear layer. The number of incoming neurons in the input layer (i.e., `train_X.shape[1]`) and the number of outgoing neurons in the output layer (i.e., 1) are determined by the specific problem at hand. The number of neurons in the middle layers is user defined and directly determines the model complexity. All these layers are chained together with a ReLU activation function in the middle via the `forward()` function. Also, note that it is unnecessary to apply ReLU to the last layer since the output will be a scalar value representing the predicted spread.

Listing 10-8. Defining the network architecture

```
# Define the neural network model
class Net(nn.Module):
    def __init__(self):
        super(Net, self).__init__()
        self.fc1 = nn.Linear(train_X.shape[1], 64)
        self.fc2 = nn.Linear(64, 32)
        self.fc3 = nn.Linear(32, 1)
        self.relu = nn.ReLU()

    def forward(self, x):
        x = self.fc1(x)
        x = self.relu(x)
        x = self.fc2(x)
        x = self.relu(x)
        x = self.fc3(x)
        return x
```

Now we instantiate a neural network model in nn_model and inspect the architectural information of the model using the summary() function, as shown in Listing 10-9.

Listing 10-9. Checking network model summary

```
from torchsummary import summary

# Create an instance of the neural network model
nn_model = Net()
# print the summary of the customized neural network
>>> summary(nn_model, input_size=(1, train_X.shape[1]))
```

```
----------------------------------------------------------------
        Layer (type)               Output Shape         Param #
================================================================
            Linear-1                 [-1, 1, 64]             384
              ReLU-2                 [-1, 1, 64]               0
            Linear-3                 [-1, 1, 32]           2,080
              ReLU-4                 [-1, 1, 32]               0
```

```
                Linear-5                      [-1, 1, 1]                    33
================================================================
Total params: 2,497
Trainable params: 2,497
Non-trainable params: 0
----------------------------------------------------------------
Input size (MB): 0.00
Forward/backward pass size (MB): 0.00
Params size (MB): 0.01
Estimated Total Size (MB): 0.01
----------------------------------------------------------------
```

The result shows that the neural network contains a total of 2497 parameters over three linear layers. Note that the ReLU layer does not have any associated parameters as it involves deterministic mapping only.

Next, we define the loss function as the mean square error using MSELoss() and choose Adam as the optimizer over the network weights, with an initial learning rate of 0.001:

```
# Define the loss function and optimizer
criterion = nn.MSELoss()
optimizer = torch.optim.Adam(nn_model.parameters(), lr=0.001)
```

We now enter the iterative training loop to update the weights by minimizing the specified loss function, as shown in Listing 10-10.

Listing 10-10. The full model training procedure

```
# Train the model
for epoch in range(100):
    optimizer.zero_grad()
    outputs = nn_model(train_X_ts)
    loss = criterion(outputs, train_y_ts)
    loss.backward()
    optimizer.step()

    # Print the loss for every 10 epochs
    if epoch % 10 == 0:
        print("Epoch {}, Loss: {:.4f}".format(epoch, loss.item()))
```

Here, we iterate over the training set for a total of 100 epochs. In each epoch, we first clear the existing gradients in memory using the zero_grad() function of the optimizer. Next, we score the training set to obtain predicted targets in outputs, calculate the corresponding MSE loss, perform backward propagation to calculate the gradients using autograd functionality via the backward() method, and finally perform gradient descent update using the step() function.

Running the code generates the following results, where we see that the training loss continues to decrease as iteration proceeds:

```
Epoch 0, Loss: 0.4154
Epoch 10, Loss: 0.2246
Epoch 20, Loss: 0.0850
Epoch 30, Loss: 0.0093
Epoch 40, Loss: 0.0043
Epoch 50, Loss: 0.0051
Epoch 60, Loss: 0.0013
Epoch 70, Loss: 0.0016
Epoch 80, Loss: 0.0013
Epoch 90, Loss: 0.0012
```

We can also check the in-sample and out-of-sample RMSE as follows:

```
# evaluate the model on the training and testing set
train_pred = nn_model(train_X_ts).detach().numpy()
>>> print("training rmse: ", np.sqrt(mean_squared_error(train_y_ts,
train_pred)))
test_pred = nn_model(test_X_ts).detach().numpy()
>>> print("test rmse: ", np.sqrt(mean_squared_error(test_y_ts, test_pred)))
training rmse:   0.033806544
test rmse:   0.08466047
```

The result shows that the neural network is less overfitting than the random forest model.

Now we obtain the terminal return of the pairs trading strategy based on the neural network model:

```
>>> score_fn(nn_model, type="nn")
0.8999874304248494
```

Again, this result shows that an accurate machine learning model may not necessarily lead to a higher terminal return in the pairs trading strategy. Even if the machine learning model is predictive of future spreads, another layer of assumption imposed by the pairs trading strategy is that the temporary market fluctuations will ease down, and the two assets will revert back to the long-term equilibrium relationship. Such an assumption may not necessarily stand, along with the many unpredictable factors in the market.

Summary

In this chapter, we introduced different machine learning algorithms used in predicting the spread, a key component when employing the pairs trading strategy. We started by introducing the overall framework when training any machine learning algorithm and then elaborated on three specific algorithms: support vector machine, random forest, and neural network. Lastly, we plugged these models into the strategy and found that a higher predictive performance by the machine learning model, a sign of overfitting, may lead to a lower performance score in terms of cumulative return. It is thus important not to overfit the machine learning models at the prediction stage and instead focus more on the final performance of the trading strategy at the decision stage, where the actual trading action is made.

Exercises

- How does the SVM model determine the optimal hyperplane for predicting the spread in a pairs trading strategy? What are the key parameters that need to be adjusted in an SVM?

- How does a random forest algorithm handle feature selection when predicting the spread in a pairs trading strategy? What are the implications of feature importance in this context?

- Explain how SVM, random forest, and neural networks approach the problem of overfitting in the context of predicting the spread in a pairs trading strategy.

- How can you handle nonlinear relationships between features in SVM, random forest, and neural networks when predicting the spread in a pairs trading strategy?

- How can the layers in a neural network be optimized to improve the prediction of the spread in a pairs trading strategy?

Index

S

Printed in the United States
by Baker & Taylor Publisher Services